HEIRLOOM
CROCHET
TREASURES™

PUBLISHER
Donna Robertson

DESIGN DIRECTOR
Fran Rohus

PRODUCTION DIRECTOR
Ange Workman

EDITORIAL
SENIOR EDITOR: Jennifer A. Simcik
EDITOR: Sharon Lothrop
COPY EDITOR: Marianne Telesca

PHOTOGRAPHY
PHOTOGRAPHERS:
Tammy Cromer-Campbell, Mary Craft
PHOTO STYLIST/COORDINATOR: Ruth Whitaker

PRODUCTION ARTIST/MANAGER
Betty Gibbs Radla

GRAPHIC ARTIST
Debby Keel

BOOK DESIGN
Klaus Rothe
Sullivan Rothe Design

PRODUCT DESIGN
DESIGN COORDINATOR: Brenda Wendling

BUSINESS
CEO: John Robinson
VICE PRESIDENT/CUSTOMER SERVICE: Karen Pierce
VICE PRESIDENT/MARKETING: Greg Deily
VICE PRESIDENT/M.I.S.: John Trotter

Credits: Sincerest thanks to all the designers, manufacturers and other professionals whose dedication has made this book possible.
Special thanks to David Norris of Quebecor Printing Book Group, Kingsport, TN.

Library of Congress Cataloging-in-Publication Data ISBN: 0-9638031-7-4
Library of Congress Catalog Card Number: 95-69229 First Printing: 1995
Published and Distributed by *The Needlecraft Shop, LLC*.
Printed in the United States of America.

*D*ear Friends:

If you love old-fashioned thread crochet, then this book is for you. Filled with beautiful keepsake-quality home decor, gift and wearable ideas, it is truly a magnificent collection. Whether you've crocheted for years, or you've just learned, you'll be captivated by the exquisite array of fine designs featured in these pages. Take a look inside this exclusive treasury and let your imagination take flight — back to an age of innocence and elegance, when homes and garments decorated with lavish amounts of lace were the norm and not the exception.

During the Victorian Era, when thread crochet reached the pinnacle of its glory, a home was simply not a home without a full complement of fine needlework, and women wore lace like a badge of honor. Learning the patience and skill required to produce complex needlecraft designs was considered just as important as acquiring the social graces. Women even wore their tools, such as needles, scissors and thimbles, as fashion accessories.

With its ability to mimic some of the most intricate needle lace patterns in a fraction of the time, thread crochet became a prized art form. Quick and easily adaptable, it suited the needs of homemakers of all classes, granting both rich and poor alike the privilege of possessing its lasting beauty. Almost every family has at least a few precious heirlooms that have been lovingly passed from generation to generation, and many more are being made each day.

Through the years, thread has maintained its position as one of the most beautiful mediums to which crochet has been applied. For those who appreciate the ambiance of a home warmed by the inviting richness and charm of lace, the exhilarating designs showcased here are sure to become a constant source of inspiration. You'll find page after page of refreshing ideas, just waiting to come alive at the gentle coaxing of your hand and hook — waiting to become a part of your most cherished possessions.

Happy Crocheting,

Jennifer

CONTENTS

FILET ARTISTRY

SPRINGTIME SERENADE

ANTIQUE LACE

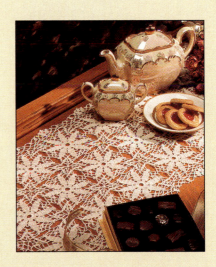

GIFTS TO TREASURE

ENGLISH MEADOW

*Envision yourself adrift in an
endless sea of delicate blossoms that beckon
invitingly — relax and enjoy. Blossoming with charm and
grace, these perennial beauties will add refined elegance to
their surroundings. Bring the distinctive spirit of a lush,
ever-blooming garden to your home with touchable
floral delights recreated in thread.*

Designed by Kathy Wigington

PINEAPPLE RUFFLES

ESSENTIALS

SIZE: 9½" tall including handle.

MATERIALS: Size 10 bedspread cotton — 500 yds. white; 2½ yds. satin ⅜" ribbon; fabric stiffener; two large plastic whipped topping containers measuring 5" across bottom; 8 flat craft sticks; craft glue or hot glue gun; No. 7 steel crochet hook or size needed to obtain gauge.

GAUGE: Rnds 1-2 = 1⅞" across.

INSTRUCTIONS

BASKET

Rnd 1: Ch 5, sl st in first ch to form ring, ch 4, 19 tr in ring, join with sl st in top of ch-4 (20 tr).

Rnd 2: Ch 4, tr in same st, 2 tr in each st around, join as before (40).

Rnd 3: Ch 4, 2 tr in next st, (tr in next st, 2 tr in next st) around, join (60).

Rnd 4: Ch 4, tr in next st, 2 tr in next st, (tr in each of next 2 sts, 2 tr in next st) around, join (80).

Rnd 5: Ch 4, tr in each of next 2 sts, 2 tr in next st, (tr in each of next 3 sts, 2 tr in next st) around, join (100).

Rnd 6: Ch 1, sc in first 4 sts, 2 sc in next st, (sc in next 4 sts, 2 sc in next st) around, join with sl st in first sc (120 sc).

Rnd 7: Ch 1, sc in first 5 sts, 2 sc in next st, (sc in next 5 sts, 2 sc in next st) around, join as before (140).

Rnd 8: Ch 1, sc in first 6 sts, 2 sc in next st, (sc in next 6 sts, 2 sc in next st) around, join (160).

Rnd 9: Working this rnd in **back lps,** ch 4, tr in each st around, join with sl st in top of ch-4.

Rnd 10: Ch 5, skip next st, (tr in next st, ch 1, skip next st) around, join with sl st in 4th ch of ch-5 (80 tr, 80 ch-1 sps).

Rnds 11-12: Sl st in first ch-1 sp, ch 5, skip next st, (tr in next ch-1 sp, ch 1, skip next st) around, join as before.

Rnd 13: Sl st in first ch-1 sp, ch 7, skip next 2 tr, (tr in next ch-1 sp, ch 3, skip next 2 tr) around, join (40 tr, 40 ch-3 sps).

Rnd 14: Sl st in first 2 chs, ch 5, dc in next ch sp, ch 2; *[for **shell,** (3 dc, ch 2, 3 dc) in next ch sp; ch 2, 6 dc in next ch sp, ch 2, shell in next ch sp, ch 2],

(dc in next ch sp, ch 2) 2 times; repeat from * 6 more times; repeat between [ ], join with sl st in 3rd ch of ch-5 (16 shells, 64 dc).

NOTE: Skip dc sts of shells unless otherwise stated.

Rnd 15: Ch 4, dc in same st, *[ch 2; for **V-st,** (dc, ch 1, dc) in next st; ch 2, shell in next shell, ch 2, dc in next st, (ch 1, dc in next st) 5 times, ch 2, shell in next shell, ch 2], V-st; repeat from * 6 more times; repeat between [ ], join with sl st in 3rd ch of ch-4 (16 shells, 48 dc, 16 V-sts).

Rnd 16: Sl st in first ch-1 sp, *[ch 4, sl st in ch-1 sp of next V-st, ch 4, shell in next shell, ch 2, sl st in next ch-1 sp, (ch 4, sl st in next ch-1 sp) 4 times, ch 2, shell in next shell, ch 4], sl st in ch-1 sp of next V-st; repeat from * 6 more times; repeat between [ ], join with sl st in first sl st.

Rnd 17: Sl st in first 2 chs, ch 4, sl st in next ch-4 sp, ch 4, *[shell in next shell, ch 2, skip next ch-2 sp, sl st in next ch-4 lp, (ch 4, sl st in next ch-4 lp) 3 times, ch 2, shell in next shell, ch 4], (sl st in next ch-4 sp, ch 4) 3 times; repeat from * 6 more times; repeat between [ ], sl st in next ch-4 sp, ch 4, join as before.

Rnd 18: Sl st in first 2 chs, ch 4, sl st in next ch-4 sp, ch 4, *[shell in next shell, ch 2, sl st in next ch-4 lp, (ch 4, sl st in next ch-4 lp) 2 times, ch 2, shell in next shell, ch 4], (sl st in next ch-4 sp, ch 4) 4 times; repeat from * 6 more times; repeat between [ ], (sl st in next ch-4 sp, ch 4) 2 times, join.

Rnd 19: Sl st in first 2 chs, ch 4, sl st in next ch-4 sp, ch 4, *[shell in next shell, ch 2, sl st in next ch-4 lp, ch 4, sl st in next ch-4 lp, ch 2, shell in next shell, ch 4], (sl st in next ch-4 sp, ch 4) 5 times; repeat from * 6 more times; repeat between [ ], (sl st in next ch-4 sp, ch 4) 3 times, join.

Rnd 20: Sl st in first 2 chs, ch 4, sl st in next ch-4 sp, ch 4, *[shell in next shell, ch 2, sl st in next ch-4 lp, ch 2, shell in next shell, ch 4], (sl st in next ch-4 sp, ch 4) 6 times; repeat from * 6 more times; repeat between [ ], (sl st in next ch-4 sp, ch 4) 4 times, join.

Rnd 21: Sl st in first 2 chs, ch 4, sl st in next ch-4 sp, ch 4, *[3 dc in next shell, ch 2, 3 dc in next shell, (ch 4, sl st in next ch-4 sp) 2 times, ch 2, shell in next ch-4 sp, ch 2, 6 dc in next ch-4 sp, ch 2, shell in next ch-4 sp, ch 2], (sl st in next ch-4 sp, ch 4) 2

Continued on next page

PINEAPPLE RUFFLES

Continued from page 9

times; repeat from * 6 more times; repeat between [ ], join (16 shells, 96 dc).

Rnd 22: Sl st in first 2 chs, ch 4, sl st in next ch-4 sp, ch 4, *[3 dc in next ch-2 sp, (ch 4, sl st in next ch-4 sp) 2 times, ch 4, sl st in next ch-2 sp, ch 2, shell in next shell, ch 2, dc in next dc, (ch 1, dc in next dc) 5 times, ch 2, shell in next shell, ch 2, sl st in next ch-2 sp, ch 4], (sl st in next ch-4 sp, ch 4) 2 times; repeat from * 6 more times; repeat between [ ], join.

Rnd 23: Sl st in first 2 chs, ch 4, sl st in next ch-4 sp, ch 4, *[skip next dc, sl st in next dc, (ch 4, sl st in next ch-4 sp) 3 times, ch 4, sl st in next ch-2 sp, ch 2, shell in next shell, ch 2, sl st in next ch-1 sp, (ch 4, sl st in next ch-1 sp) 4 times, ch 2, shell in next shell, ch 2, sl st in next ch-2 sp, ch 4], (sl st in next ch-4 sp, ch 4) 3 times; repeat from * 6 more times; repeat between [ ], sl st in next ch-4 sp, ch 4, join.

Rnd 24: Sl st in first 2 chs, (ch 4, sl st in next ch-4 sp) 5 times, ch 4, sl st in next ch-2 sp, ch 2, *[shell in next shell, ch 2, sl st in next ch-4 lp, (ch 4, sl st in next ch-4 lp) 3 times, ch 2, shell in next shell, ch 2, sl st in next ch-2 sp], (ch 4, sl st in next ch-4 sp) 8 times, ch 4, sl st in next ch-2 sp, ch 2; repeat from * 6 more times; repeat between [ ], (ch 4, sl st in next ch-4 sp) 2 times, ch 4, join (16 shells, 96 ch-4 sps, 32 ch-2 sps).

Rnd 25: Sl st in first 2 chs, (ch 4, sl st in next ch-4 sp) 5 times, ch 4, sl st in next ch-2 sp, ch 2, *[shell in next shell, ch 2, sl st in next ch-4 lp, (ch 4, sl st in next ch-4 lp) 2 times, ch 2, shell in next shell, ch 2, sl st in next ch-2 sp], (ch 4, sl st in next ch-4 sp) 9 times, ch 4, sl st in next ch-2 sp, ch 2; repeat from * 6 more times; repeat between [ ], (ch 4, sl st in next ch-4 sp) 3 times, ch 4, join.

Rnd 26: Sl st in first 2 chs, (ch 4, sl st in next ch-4 sp) 5 times, ch 4, sl st in next ch-2 sp, ch 2, *[shell in next shell, ch 2, sl st in next ch-4 lp, ch 4, sl st in next ch-4 lp, ch 2, shell in next shell, ch 2, sl st in next ch-2 sp], (ch 4, sl st in next ch-4 sp) 10 times, ch 4, sl st in next ch-2 sp, ch 2; repeat from * 6 more times; repeat between [ ], (ch 4, sl st in next ch-4 sp) 4 times, ch 4, join.

Rnd 27: Sl st in first 2 chs, (ch 4, sl st in next ch-4 sp) 5 times, ch 4, sl st in next ch-2 sp, ch 2, *[shell in next shell, ch 2, sl st in next ch-4 lp, ch 2, shell in next shell, ch 2, sl st in next ch-2 sp], (ch 4, sl st in next ch-4 sp) 11 times, ch 4, sl st in next ch-2 sp, ch 2; repeat from * 6 more times; repeat between [ ], (ch 4, sl st in next ch-4 sp) 5 times, ch 4, join.

Rnd 28: Sl st in first 2 chs, (ch 4, sl st in next ch-4 sp) 5 times, *[ch 4, sl st in next ch-2 sp, ch 2, 3 dc in next shell, ch 2, 3 dc in next shell, ch 2, sl st in next ch-2 sp], (ch 4, sl st in next ch-4 sp) 12 times; repeat from * 6 more times; repeat between [ ], (ch 4, sl st in next ch-4 sp) 6 times, ch 4, join.

Rnd 29: Sl st in first 2 chs, (ch 4, sl st in next ch-4 sp) 5 times, *[ch 4, sl st in next ch-2 sp, ch 2, 3 dc in next ch-2 sp, ch 2, sl st in next ch-2 sp], (ch 4, sl st in next ch-4 sp) 13 times; repeat from * 6 more times; repeat between [ ], (ch 4, sl st in next ch-4 sp) 7 times, ch 4, join.

Rnd 30: Sl st in first 2 chs, ch 4, (sl st in next ch sp, ch 4) 6 times, *[skip next dc, sl st in next dc, ch 4], (sl st in next ch sp, ch 4) 16 times; repeat from * 6 more times; repeat between [ ], (sl st in next ch-4 sp, ch 4) 9 times, join (136 ch-4 sps).

Rnd 31: Sl st in first ch-4 sp, ch 1, (sc, hdc, 3 dc, hdc, sc) in each ch-4 sp around, join with sl st in first sc, fasten off.

HANDLE

Ch 218, dc in 14th ch from hook, (ch 5, skip next 5 chs, dc in next ch) across, **do not turn,** (sc, hdc, 2 dc, hdc, sc) over dc just made, *(sc, hdc, 2 dc, hdc, sc) in next 35 ch-5 sps*, (sc, hdc, 2 dc, hdc, sc) over turning ch; repeat between **, join with sl st in first sc, fasten off.

FINISHING

1: Apply fabric stiffener to Basket and Handle according to manufacturer's instructions.

2: Place crocheted Basket into one plastic container, place second container into Basket, pushing down securely. Insert craft sticks evenly spaced around between Basket and outer container; shape ruffles over craft sticks while drying. Allow Handle to dry flat, shape when dry.

3: Weave ribbon through ch-1 sps on rnd 10 of Basket and ch-3 sps on rnd 13, secure ends. Weave ribbon through ch-5 sps of Handle, secure ends. Glue Handle inside Basket.❖

HEIRLOOM CROCHET TREASURES

FLOWER GARDEN DOILY

ESSENTIALS

SIZE: 8½" x 15".

MATERIALS: *Size 20 crochet cotton — 125 yds. green and 75 yds. each pink variegated and white; No. 9 steel crochet hook or size needed to obtain gauge.

GAUGE: One shell (see Note below) = ½" across; 4 shell rnds = 1". Rnd 1 of Motif = ¾" across.

INSTRUCTIONS

MOTIF NO. 1

NOTES: For **shell,** (3 dc, ch 3, 3 dc) in next ch sp.

For **2-tr cluster (2-tr cl),** *yo 2 times, insert hook in sp, yo, draw lp through, (yo, draw through 2 lps on hook) 2 times; repeat from * one more time in same sp, yo, draw through all 3 lps on hook.

Rnd 1: With pink variegated, ch 5, sl st in first ch to form ring, ch 1, sc in ring, ch 3, 2-tr cl in ring, ch 3, *sc in ring, ch 3, 2-tr cl in ring, ch 3; repeat from *

Continued on page 21

Designed by Carol Smith

ENGLISH MEADOW

SIZE: 17" across after blocking.
GAUGE: Rnd 1 = 1" across.
MATERIALS: Size 10 bedspread cotton — 400 yds. green variegated; 100 yds. white; small amount yellow variegated; tapestry needle; No. 7 steel crochet hook or size needed to obtain gauge.
NOTE: Doily may ruffle slightly until blocked.

INSTRUCTIONS

DOILY

Rnd 1: With green variegated, ch 4, sl st in first ch to form ring, ch 6, (tr, ch 2) 7 times in ring, join with sl st in 4th ch of ch-6 (8 tr, 8 ch sps).

Rnd 2: Sl st into first ch sp, ch 4, tr in same sp, ch 1, 6 tr in next ch sp, ch 1, (2 tr in next ch sp, ch 1, 6 tr in next ch sp, ch 1) around, join with sl st in top of ch-4 (32 tr, 8 ch-1 sps).

Rnd 3: Ch 4, tr in next st, (ch 2, skip next ch sp, 2 tr in next st, tr in each of next 2 sts, ch 2, tr in each of next 2 sts, 2 tr in next st, ch 2, skip next ch sp), *tr in each of next 2 sts; repeat between ( )*; repeat between ** around, join (40 tr, 12 ch-2 sps).

Rnd 4: (Ch 4, tr, ch 1, tr) in same st, (tr, ch 1, 2 tr) in next st, *ch 2, skip next ch sp, 2 tr in next st, tr in each of next 3 sts, ch 2, skip next ch sp, tr in each of next 3 sts, 2 tr in next st, ch 2, skip next ch sp*, [(2 tr, ch 1, tr) in next st, (tr, ch 1, 2 tr) in next st; repeat between **]; repeat between [ ] around, join (64 tr, 12 ch-2 sps, 8 ch-1 sps).

Rnd 5: Ch 4, 2 tr in same st, 3 tr in next st, (ch 1, skip next ch-1 sp, tr in each of next 2 sts, ch 1, skip next ch-1 sp, 3 tr in each of next 2 sts, ch 2, skip next ch-2 sp, tr next 2 sts tog, tr in each of next 3 sts, ch 2, skip next ch-2 sp, tr in each of next 3 sts, tr next 2 sts tog, ch 2, skip next ch-2 sp), *3 tr in each of next 2 sts; repeat between ( )*; repeat between ** around, join (88 tr, 12 ch-2 sps, 8 ch-1 sps).

Rnd 6: Ch 4, tr in same st, *(tr in each of next 2 sts, ch 2, tr in each of next 2 sts, 2 tr in next st), ch 1, skip next ch-1 sp, tr in each of next 2 sts, ch 1, skip next ch-1 sp, 2 tr in next st; repeat between ( ), ch 2, skip next ch-2 sp, tr next 2 sts tog, tr in each of next 2 sts, skip next ch-2 sp, tr in each of next 2 sts, tr next 2 sts tog, ch 2, skip next ch-2 sp*, [2 tr in next st; repeat between **]; repeat between [ ] around, join (96 tr, 16 ch-2 sps, 8 ch-1 sps).

Rnd 7: Ch 4, tr in same st, *(tr in each of next 3 sts, ch 2, skip next ch-2 sp, tr in each of next 3 sts, 2 tr in next st), ch 2, skip next ch-1 sp, tr in each of next 2 sts, ch 2, skip next ch-1 sp, 2 tr in next st; repeat between ( ), ch 2, skip next ch-2 sp, tr next 2 sts tog, tr in each of next 2 sts, tr next 2 sts tog, ch 2, skip next ch-2 sp*, [2 tr in next st; repeat between **]; repeat between [ ] around, join (104 tr, 24 ch-2 sps).

NOTE: Ch-3 is not used or counted as a stitch.

Rnd 8: Ch 3, tr in next 4 sts, *(ch 2, skip next ch sp, tr in each of next 3 sts, tr next 2 sts tog), ch 2, skip next ch sp, tr in each of next 2 sts, ch 2, skip next ch sp, tr next 2 sts tog, tr in each of next 3 sts; repeat between ( ), ch 4, sc in next ch sp, ch 4, tr next 4 sts tog, ch 4, sc in next ch sp, ch 4*, [tr next 2 sts tog, tr in each of next 3 sts; repeat between **]; repeat between [ ] around, join (76 tr, 16 ch-4 sps, 16 ch-2 sps).

Rnd 9: Ch 3, tr in each of next 3 sts, *skip next ch-2 sp, tr in each of next 2 sts, tr next 2 sts tog, (ch 4, sc in next ch-2 sp, ch 4, tr next 2 sts tog) 2 times, tr in each of next 2 sts, skip next ch-2 sp, tr in each of next 2 sts, tr next 2 sts tog, ch 4, (sc in next ch-4 sp, ch 4) 2 times, sc in next st, ch 4, (sc in next ch-4 sp, ch 4) 2 times*, [tr next 2 sts tog, tr in each of next 2 sts; repeat between **]; repeat between [ ] around, join (52 tr, 40 ch-4 sps).

Rnd 10: Ch 3, tr in each of next 3 sts, *tr next 2 sts tog, ch 4, (sc in next ch sp, ch 4) 4 times, tr next 2 sts tog, tr in each of next 2 sts, tr next 2 sts tog, ch 4, (sc in next ch sp, ch 4) 6 times*, [tr next 2 sts tog, tr in each of next 2 sts; repeat between **]; repeat between [ ] around, join (48 ch-4 sps, 32 tr).

Rnd 11: Ch 3, tr next 3 sts tog, *ch 4, (sc in next ch sp, ch 4) 2 times, (sc, ch 4, sc) in next ch sp, ch 4, (sc in next ch sp, ch 4) 2 times, tr next 4 sts tog, ch 4, (sc in next ch sp, ch 4) 3 times, (sc,

Continued on page 24

SHASTA DAISIES

SIZE: Lady's small (bust 32"-34"), medium (36"-38"), large (44"-46"), or extra-large (48"-50").

GAUGE: With No. 8 hook, each motif is 2¾" across. With No. 6 hook, each motif is 3" across.

MATERIALS: White size 10 bedspread cotton — 2,400 yds. for small, 2,750 yds. for medium, 3,050 yds. for large, or 3,750 yds. for extra-large; No. 8 or No. 6 steel crochet hook or size needed to obtain gauge.

NOTES: This sweater is designed to be 3"-4½" larger than actual bust measurement. Size is changed by adding motifs and by using different hook sizes.

Use No. 8 hook for small or large sizes or No. 6 hook for medium and extra-large sizes.

FIRST BLOUSE SIDE
Motif A

Rnd 1: Ch 8, sl st in first ch to form ring, ch 5, (dc, ch 2) 11 times in ring, join with sl st in 3rd ch of ch-5 (12 dc, 12 ch sps).

NOTES: For **beginning treble cluster (beg tr cl),** ch 3, *yo 2 times, insert hook in same sp, yo, draw lp through, (yo, draw through 2 lps on hook) 2 times; repeat from * one more time, yo, draw through all 3 lps on hook.

For **treble cluster (tr cl),** *yo 2 times, insert hook in next sp, yo, draw lp through, (yo, draw through 2 lps on hook) 2 times; repeat from * 2 more times in same sp, yo, draw through all 4 lps on hook.

Rnd 2: Sl st into first ch sp, beg tr cl, ch 5, (tr cl, ch 5) around, join with sl st in top of beg tr cl (12 tr cls, 12 ch sps).

Rnd 3: Sl st in first 2 chs, ch 1, sc in same sp, ch 9, (sc in next ch sp, ch 7) 2 times, [sc in next ch sp, ch 9, (sc in next ch sp, ch 7) 2 times]; repeat between [ ] around, join with sl st in first sc (12 sc, 8 ch-7 lps, 4 ch-9 lps).

Rnd 4: Sl st into first ch-9 lp, ch 1, (5 sc, ch 7, 5 sc) in each ch-9 lp and (4 sc, ch 3, 4 sc) in each ch-7 lp around, join, fasten off.

Motif B

Rnds 1-3: Repeat same rnds of Motif A.

NOTES: For **joining ch-3 sp,** ch 1, sc in next ch-3

sp on previous motif, ch 1 (see Assembly Diagram B on page 23).

For **joining ch-7 lp,** ch 3, sc in next ch-7 lp on previous motif, ch 3 (see Diagram B).

Rnd 4: Holding Motif B to Motif A according to Assembly Diagram A-1 or A-2, repeat same rnd of Motif A, using joining ch-3 sps and joining ch-7 lps as needed to join Motifs according to Assembly Diagram B.

For **remaining Motifs,** following Assembly Diagram A for your size, join motifs according to Assembly Diagram B on page 23, using joining ch-3 sp and joining ch-7 lps where needed to join.

Motif C

NOTE: See Diagram A-1 or A-2 for number of Motifs needed.

Rnd 1: Repeat same rnd of Motif A.

Rnd 2: Sl st into first ch sp, beg tr cl in same sp, ch 5, (tr cl in next ch sp, ch 5) 7 times, (dc, hdc, sc) in next ch sp, 2 sc in each of next 2 ch sps, (sc, hdc, dc) in next ch sp, ch 5, join with sl st in top of beg tr cl (8 tr cls, 9 ch sps, 10 sts).

Rnd 3: Sl st in first 2 chs, ch 1, sc in same sp, ch 9, sc in next ch sp, *(ch 7, sc in next ch sp) 2 times, ch 9*, sc in next ch sp; repeat between **, 3 sc in next ch sp, sc in next 10 sts, 3 sc in next ch sp, ch 7, join with sl st in first sc (5 ch-7 lps, 3 ch-9 lps, 23 sc).

Rnd 4: To join to B Motifs (see Diagram A-1 or A-2), ch 1, (5 sc, joining ch-7 lp, 5 sc) in each ch-9 lp and (4 sc, joining ch-3 sp, 4 sc) in each ch-7 lp around to first 3-sc group, sc in each of next 3 sts, ch 3, sc in next 10 sts, ch 3, sc in each of next 3 sts, (4 sc, ch 3, 4 sc) in last ch-7 lp, join as before, fasten off.

Motif D

Row 1: Ch 5, sl st in first ch to form ring, ch 5, dc in ring, (ch 2, dc) 5 times in ring, turn (7 dc, 6 ch sps).

Row 2: Ch 6, tr cl in first ch sp, (ch 5, tr cl in next ch sp) 5 times, ch 2, tr in 3rd ch of ch-5, turn (6 tr cls, 5 ch-5 sps, 2 ch-2 sps, 2 tr).

Row 3: Ch 9, sc in first ch-2 sp, *(ch 7, sc in next ch-5 sp) 2 times, ch 9*, sc in next ch-5 sp; repeat between **, sc in last ch-2 sp, turn (4 ch-7 lps, 3 ch-9 lps).

Row 4: Ch 1, (5 sc, joining ch-7 lp, 5 sc) in each ch-9 lp and (4 sc, joining ch-3 sp, 4 sc) in each ch-7 lp across; working in ends of rows, 4 sc in next row, 3 sc

Continued on page 23

HEIRLOOM CROCHET TREASURES

EMBROIDERED DRESSER SET

ESSENTIALS

DOILY

SIZE: 9" across.

MATERIALS: Size 10 bedspread cotton — 70 yds. white; embroidery floss — small amount each blue and green; embroidery needle; fabric stiffener; No. 6 steel crochet hook or size needed to obtain gauge.

GAUGE: Rnds 1-7 = 2½" across.

NOTE: Doily will ruffle until blocked.

INSTRUCTIONS

DOILY

Rnd 1: Ch 8, sl st in first ch to form ring, ch 1, sc in ring, (ch 6, sc in ring) 7 times; to **join,** ch 3, dc in first sc (8 ch-6 lps).

Rnd 2: Ch 1, 2 sc over joining dc just made, ch 1, (4 sc in next ch lp, ch 1) around to last ch lp, 2 sc in same sp as first 2 sc made, join with sl st in first sc (32 sc, 8 ch-1 sps).

Rnd 3: Ch 1, sc in each st around with 2 sc in each ch sp, join (48 sc).

Rnds 4-5: Ch 1, sc in each st around, join.

Rnd 6: Ch 1, (2 sc in next st, sc in next 5 sts) around, join (56).

Rnd 7: Repeat rnd 4.

Rnd 8: Ch 1, sc in same st, (ch 6, skip next 2 sts, sc in next st) around to last sc, join with ch 3, dc in first sc (19 ch-6 lps).

Rnd 9: Repeat rnd 2 (76 sc, 19 ch-1 sps).

Rnd 10: Ch 1, sc in each st and in each ch-1 sp around, join (95).

Rnds 11-14: Repeat rnd 4.

Rnd 15: Repeat rnd 8.

Rnd 16: Repeat rnd 2.

Rnds 17-21: Repeat rnds 10-14 (190 sts).

Rnd 22: Repeat rnd 8 (63 ch-6 lps).

Rnds 23-24: Ch 1, sc over joining dc just made, (ch 6, sc in next ch sp) around, join as before. Fasten off at end of last rnd.

FINISHING

1: For **motifs** (see Large and Small Motif Diagrams below), separate floss into 2 strands; using Outline Stitch and Lazy Daisy Stitch, embroider as shown in photo.

2: Apply fabric stiffener to Doily according to manufacturer's instructions. Shape; let dry.

BOX

SIZE: 1⅝" x 3⅜".

MATERIALS: Size 10 bedspread cotton — 40 yds. white; 12" blue ¼" satin picot ribbon; 1½" x 3" round foam cylinder for form; fabric stiffener; embroidery floss — small amount each blue and green; embroidery needle; No. 9 steel crochet hook or size needed to obtain gauge.

GAUGE: 9 sc rnds = 1".

BOTTOM

Rnds 1-2: Repeat same rnds of Doily.

Rnd 3: Ch 1, sc in each st and in each ch-1 sp around, join (40 sc).

Rnd 4: Ch 1, sc in each of first 2 sts, 2 sc in next st, (sc in next 4 sts, 2 sc in next st) around with sc in each of last 2 sts, join (48).

Rnds 5-6: Ch 1, sc in each st around, join.

Rnd 7: Ch 1, sc in each of first 3 sts, 2 sc in next st, (sc in next 5 sts, 2 sc in next st) around with sc in each of last 2 sts, join (56).

Rnd 8: Repeat rnd 5.

Rnd 9: Ch 1, sc in first 4 sts, 2 sc in next st, (sc in next 6 sts, 2 sc in next st) around with sc in each of last 2 sts, join (64).

Rnd 10: Repeat rnd 5.

Rnd 11: Repeat rnd 8 of Doily (21 ch-6 lps).

Rnd 12: Ch 1, 2 sc over joining dc just made, ch 1, (2 sc in next ch lp, ch 1) around, join (42 sc, 21 ch-1 sps).

Rnd 13: Repeat rnd 3 (63).

Rnds 14-17: Repeat rnd 5.

Rnds 18-20: Repeat rnds 11-13. Fasten off at end of last rnd.

LID

Rnds 1-3: Repeat same rnds of Doily.

Rnd 4: Ch 1, sc in each st around, join.

Rnd 5: Repeat rnd 4 of Bottom (48).

Rnds 6-7: Repeat rnd 4.

Rnds 8-10: Repeat same rnds of Doily. Fasten off at end of last rnd.

FINISHING

1: Work same step of Doily Finishing.

2: Apply fabric stiffener to pieces according to manufacturer's instructions. Shape Bottom around foam cylinder; shape Lid flat. Allow to dry.

3: Weave ribbon through last ch-6 rnds of Bottom and Lid, tie in bow on top of Box.⚜

SMALL MOTIF

LARGE MOTIF

= Lazy Daisy Stitch   = Outline Stitch

HEIRLOOM CROCHET TREASURES

SUNBURST DOILY

ESSENTIALS

SIZE: 13" across, after blocking.

MATERIALS: Size 10 bedspread cotton — 85 yds. yellow variegated, 54 yds. white; tapestry needle; No. 7 steel crochet hook or size needed to obtain gauge.

GAUGE: Rnds 1-2 = 1¾" across.

NOTE: This doily will ruffle until blocked.

INSTRUCTIONS

DOILY

Rnd 1: With yellow variegated, ch 4, sl st in first ch to form ring, ch 4, 19 tr in ring, join with sl st in top of ch-4 (20 tr).

NOTES: For **treble crochet front post (tr fp, see Stitch Guide),** yo 2 times, insert hook around post of st, complete as tr.

For **double crochet front post (dc fp, see Stitch Guide),** yo, insert hook around post of st, complete as dc.

When working fp, skip next st on the row you are working.

Rnd 2: Ch 5, tr in same st, tr fp around next st, *(tr, ch 1, tr) in next st, tr fp around next st; repeat from * around, join with sl st in 4th ch of ch-5 (20 tr, 10 tr fp).

NOTE: Joining (ch 1, dc) counts as ch-4 sp.

Rnd 3: Sl st in first ch sp, ch 5, skip next st, dc fp around next fp, *ch 4, sc in next ch sp, ch 4, skip next st, dc fp around next fp; repeat from * around; to **join,** ch 1, dc in first ch of ch-5 (20 ch sps).

Rnd 4: Ch 4, sc in next ch sp, ch 4, dc fp around next fp, *ch 4, (sc in next ch-4 sp, ch 4) 2 times, dc fp around next fp; repeat from * around, ch 1, dc in top of joining dc (30 ch sps).

Rnd 5: Ch 4, (sc in next ch sp, ch 4) 2 times, dc fp around next fp, *ch 4, (sc in next ch sp, ch 4) 3 times, dc fp around next fp; repeat from * around, join as before (40 ch sps).

Rnd 6: Ch 4, (sc in next ch sp, ch 4) 3 times, dc fp around next fp, *ch 4, (sc in next ch sp, ch 4) 4 times, dc fp around next fp; repeat from * around, join (50 ch sps).

NOTE: For **cluster (cl),** (yo, insert hook in sp, yo, draw lp through, yo, draw through 2 lps on hook) 3 times in next ch lp, yo, draw through all 4 lps on hook.

Rnd 7: Ch 4, sc in first ch sp, ch 4, cl, ch 4, (sc in next ch sp, ch 4) 2 times, dc fp around next fp, *ch 4, (sc in next ch sp, ch 4) 2 times, cl, ch 4, (sc in next ch sp, ch 4) 2 times, dc fp around next fp; repeat from * around, join (60 ch sps).

Rnd 8: Ch 4, (sc in next ch sp, ch 4) 5 times, dc fp around next fp, *ch 4, (sc in next ch sp, ch 4) 6 times, dc fp around next fp; repeat from * around, join (70 ch sps). Fasten off.

Rnd 9: Join white with sl st around joining dc, ch 3, 2 dc in same sp, 3 dc in each ch sp around with dc fp around each fp, join with sl st in top of ch-3.

Rnd 10: Sl st in next 2 sts, sl st in next sp between 3-dc groups, ch 1, sc in same sp, ch 4, skip next 3 sts, (sc in next sp between 3-dc groups, ch 4, skip next 3 sts) 5 times, dc fp around next fp, *ch 4; repeat between ( ) 6 times, dc fp around next fp; repeat from * around; to **join,** ch 2, dc in first sc.

Rnd 11: Ch 3, 3 dc in each ch sp and dc fp around each fp around, ending with 2 dc in joining ch-2 sp, join with sl st in top of ch-3. Fasten off.

Rnd 12: Join yellow variegated with sc in next sp between 3-dc groups, ch 4, (sc in next sp, ch 4) 5 times, dc fp around next fp, *ch 4, (sc in next sp, ch 4) 6 times, dc fp around next fp; repeat from * around; to **join,** ch 2, dc in first sc.

Rnd 13: Ch 4, (sc in next ch sp, ch 4) 6 times, dc fp around next fp, *ch 4, (sc in next ch sp, ch 4) 7 times, dc fp around next fp; repeat from * around; to **join,** ch 2, dc in first dc (80 ch sps).

Rnd 14: Ch 4, (sc in next ch sp, ch 4) 7 times, dc fp around next fp, *ch 4, (sc in next ch sp, ch 4) 8 times, dc fp around next fp; repeat from * around, join as before (90 ch sps).

Row 15: For **first point,** working in rows, (ch 4, sc in next ch sp) 7 times, ch 2, dc in next ch sp, turn leaving remaining sts and ch sps unworked (8 ch sps).

Rows 16-21: (Ch 4, sc in next ch sp) across to last ch sp, ch 2, dc in last ch sp, turn, ending with 2 ch sps in last row.

Row 22: Ch 4, sc in last ch sp. Fasten off.

For **remaining nine points,** join yellow variegated with sl st in first ch sp after next fp on rnd 14, repeat rows 15-22.

Continued on page 25

HEIRLOOM CROCHET TREASURES

WINDOW ORNAMENT

SIZE: 10" across.

MATERIALS: Size 20 crochet cotton — 200 yds. ecru; 10" steel ring; No. 7 steel crochet hook or size needed to obtain gauge.

GAUGE: 11 dc sts = 1"; 5 dc rnds = 1".

INSTRUCTIONS

DOILY

Rnd 1: Ch 7, sl st in first ch to form ring, ch 1, 9 sc in ring, join with sl st in first sc (9 sc).

Rnd 2: Ch 5, (dc in next st, ch 2) around, join with sl st in 3rd ch of ch-5 (9 dc).

Rnd 3: Sl st in first ch sp, ch 3, 2 dc in same sp, ch 2, (3 dc in next ch sp, ch 2) around, join with sl st in top of ch-3 (27 dc, 9 ch sps).

Rnd 4: Ch 3, dc in same st, dc in each of next 2 sts, *(dc, ch 2, dc) in next ch sp, dc in each of next 3 sts; repeat from * around to last ch sp, (dc, ch 2) in last ch sp, join (45 dc, 9 ch sps).

Rnds 5-6: Ch 3, dc in same st, dc in each st around with (dc, ch 2, dc) in each ch sp, ending with (dc, ch

2) in last ch sp, join (63 dc, 9 ch sps; 81 dc, 9 ch sps).

Rnd 7: Sl st in next st, ch 3, dc in next 6 sts, *ch 4, skip next st, sc in next ch sp, ch 4*, [skip next st, dc in next 7 sts; repeat between **]; repeat between [ ] around, join (63 dc, 18 ch-4 sps).

Rnd 8: Sl st in next st, ch 3, dc in next 4 sts, *ch 4, skip next st, (sc in next ch-4 sp, ch 4) 2 times*, [skip next st, dc in next 5 sts; repeat between **]; repeat between [ ] around, join (45 dc, 27 ch-4 sps).

NOTE: Joining (ch 2, dc) counts as ch-5 sp.

Rnd 9: Sl st in next st, ch 3, dc in each of next 2 sts, *ch 5, skip next st, (sc in next ch-4 sp, ch 5) 3 times, skip next st, dc in each of next 3 sts; repeat from * 7 more times, ch 5, skip next st, sc in next ch-4 sp, (ch 5, sc in next ch-4 sp) 2 times; to **join,** ch 2, dc in top of ch-3 (36 ch-5 sps, 27 dc).

Rnd 10: Ch 1, sc over joining dc just made, *ch 6, sc in next ch-5 sp, ch 4*, [sc in next ch-5 sp; repeat between **]; repeat between [ ] around, join (18 ch-4 sps, 18 ch-6 lps).

Rnd 11: Sl st in next ch-6 lp, ch 3, 2 dc in same lp, *ch 7, 9 sc in next ch-6 lp, ch 7*, [3 dc in next ch-6 lp; repeat between **]; repeat between [ ] around, join (81 sc, 27 dc).

Rnd 12: Ch 3, dc in each of next 2 dc, *3 dc in next ch-7 lp, ch 7, skip next sc, sc in next 7 sc, ch 7, skip next sc, 3 dc in next ch-7 lp*, [dc in each of next 3 dc; repeat between **]; repeat between [ ] around, join (81 dc, 63 sc).

Rnd 13: Sl st in first 5 dc, ch 3, *3 dc in next ch-7 lp, ch 7, skip next sc, sc in next 5 sc, ch 7, skip next sc, 3 dc in next ch-7 lp, dc in next dc, ch 7, skip next 7 dc*, [dc in next dc; repeat between **]; repeat between [ ] around, join (72 dc, 45 sc).

Rnd 14: Sl st in next 3 dc, ch 3, *3 dc in next ch-7 lp, ch 7, skip next sc, sc in each of next 3 sc, ch 7, skip next sc, 3 dc in next ch-7 lp, dc in next dc, ch 4, skip next 3 dc, (dc, ch 4) 2 times in next ch-7 lp, skip next 3 dc*, [dc in next dc; repeat between **]; repeat between [ ] around, join (90 dc, 27 sc).

Rnd 15: Sl st in next 3 dc, ch 3, *3 dc in next ch-7 lp, ch 7, skip next sc, sc in next sc, ch 7, skip next sc, 3 dc in next ch-7 lp, dc in next dc, ch 4, dc in next ch-4 sp, ch 4, (dc, ch 4) 2 times in next ch-4 sp, dc in next ch-4 sp, ch 4, skip next 3 dc*, [dc in next dc; repeat between **]; repeat between [ ] around, join (108 dc, 9 sc).

Rnd 16: Sl st in next 3 dc, ch 3, *2 dc in next ch-7 lp, skip next sc, 2 dc in next ch-7 lp, dc in next dc, ch 4, skip next 3 dc, (dc in next ch-4 sp, ch 4) 2 times, (dc, ch 4) 2 times in next ch-4 sp, (dc in next ch-4 sp, ch 4) 2 times, skip next 3 dc*, [dc in next dc; repeat between **]; repeat between [ ] around, join (108 dc, 63 ch-4 sps).

NOTES: For **picot,** ch 3, sc in top of last dc made.

For **picot shell,** (2 dc, picot, 2 dc) in next ch-4 sp.

Rnd 17: Sl st in next 2 dc, ch 1, *sc in space between 3-dc groups, ch 2, picot shell in each of next 3 ch-4 sps, picot, picot shell in next ch-4 sp, picot, picot shell in each of next 3 ch-4 sps, ch 2*, [skip next 3 dc; repeat between **]; repeat between [ ] around, join with sl st in first sc. Fasten off.

To **join Doily to ring;** working over ring (see ill.), join with sc over ring and through picot at one point at same time, work approximately 60 sc over ring to next point, covering ring completely, *sc over ring and through picot on next point at same time, work approximately 60 sc over ring to next point; repeat from * around, join with sl st in first sc; for **hanger,** make a chain desired length, ch 10 more, sl st in 10th ch from hook, fasten off. ⚜

SC AROUND RING ILLUSTRATION

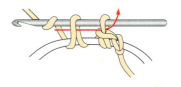

FLOWER GARDEN DOILY

Continued from page 11

2 more times, join with sl st in first sc, fasten off (8 ch-3 sps, 4 cls).

Rnd 2: Join green with sc in any sc, ch 3, shell in top of next cl, ch 3, *sc in next sc, ch 3, shell in top of next cl, ch 3; repeat from * around, join, fasten off (8 ch-3 sps, 4 shells).

MOTIFS NO. 2-4

Rnd 1: Repeat same rnd of Motif No. 1.

NOTE: For **joining shell,** 3 dc in top of next cl, ch 1, sc in ch-3 sp of shell on other Motif (see Joining Diagram on next page), ch 1, 3 dc in same cl on this Motif.

Rnd 2: Join green with sc in any sc, ch 3, shell in top of next cl, (ch 3, sc in next sc, ch 3, joining shell, ch 3) 2 times, sc in next sc, ch 3, shell in top of next cl, ch 3, join, fasten off (8 ch-3 sps, 4 shells).

DOILY

NOTES: Doily may ruffle slightly until blocked.

For **beginning half shell, (beg half shell),** ch 3, 2

Continued on next page

FLOWER GARDEN DOILY

Continued from page 21

dc in same sp.

For **ending half shell (end half shell),** 3 dc in same sp as beg half shell.

Rnd 1: Join green with sl st in ch-3 sp of shell according to diagram, beg half shell, [ch 4, (sc in next ch-3 sp, ch 4) 2 times, *3 dc in ch-1 sp of next joining shell, ch 2, 3 dc in ch-1 sp of next joining shell, ch 4, (sc in next ch-3 sp, ch 4) 2 times; repeat from * 2 more times, shell in ch sp of next shell, ch 4, (sc in next ch-3 sp, ch 4) 2 times], shell in ch sp of next shell; repeat between [ ], end half shell; to **join,** ch 1, sc in top of ch-3 (30 ch-4 sps, 6 ch-2 sps, 4 shells).

Rnd 2: Beg half shell over joining sc just made, (ch 4, sc in next ch-4 sp, ch 4, skip next ch-4 sp, sc in next ch-4 sp, ch 4), *shell in next ch-2 sp or next shell; repeat between ( ); repeat from * around, end half shell, join as before (30 ch-4 sps, 10 shells).

Rnd 3: Beg half shell over joining sc just made, (ch 4, skip next ch sp, shell in next ch sp, ch 4, skip next ch sp), *shell in next shell; repeat between ( ); repeat from * around, end half shell, join (20 ch-4 sps, 20 shells).

Rnd 4: Beg half shell over joining sc, *(ch 4, skip next ch sp, shell in next shell) 8 times, ch 4, sc in next ch sp, ch 4, shell in next shell, ch 4, sc in next ch sp, ch 4*, shell in next shell; repeat between **, end half shell, join (24 ch-4 sps, 20 shells).

Rnd 5: Beg half shell over joining sc, *(ch 4, skip next ch sp, shell in next shell) 8 times, ch 4, (sc in next ch sp, ch 4) 2 times, shell in next shell, ch 4, (sc in next ch sp, ch 4) 2 times*, shell in next shell; repeat between **, end half shell, join (28 ch-4 sps, 20 shells).

Rnd 6: Beg half shell over joining sc, *(ch 4, skip next ch sp, shell in next shell) 8 times, ch 4, skip next ch sp, shell in next ch sp, ch 4, shell in next shell, ch 4, skip next ch sp, shell in next ch sp, ch 4*, shell in next shell; repeat between **, end half shell, join, fasten off (24 ch-4 sps, 24 shells).

Rnd 7: Join white with sc over joining sc, (ch 6, sc in next ch sp or next shell) around; to **join,** ch 3, dc in first sc (48 ch lps).

Rnd 8: Ch 1, sc over joining dc just made, (ch 6, sc in next ch lp) around, join as before.

Rnd 9: Ch 1, sc over joining dc just made, [ch 6, (sc, ch 6, sc) in next ch lp, *ch 6, sc in next ch lp, ch 6, (sc, ch 6, sc) in next ch lp*, ch 6, (sc in next ch lp, ch 6) 11 times, (sc, ch 6, sc) in next ch lp; repeat between ** 4 more times], ch 6, sc in next ch lp; repeat between [ ], join (62 ch lps).

Rnds 10-13: Ch 1, sc over joining dc, (ch 6, sc in next ch lp) around, join. Fasten off at end of last rnd.

Rnd 14: Join green with sl st in any ch lp; for **beginning shell (beg shell), (ch 3, 2 dc, ch 3, 3 dc) in same lp;** shell in each ch lp around, join with sl st in top of ch-3, fasten off.

NOTES: For **beginning 3-tr cluster (beg 3-tr cl),** ch 3, *yo 2 times, insert hook in same sp, yo, draw lp through, (yo, draw through 2 lps on hook) 2 times; repeat from * one more time, yo, draw through all 3 lps on hook.

For **3-tr cluster (3-tr cl),** *yo 2 times, insert hook in sp, yo, draw lp through, (yo, draw through 2 lps on hook) 2 times; repeat from * 2 more times in same sp, yo, draw through all 4 lps on hook.

Rnd 15: Join pink variegated with sl st in any shell, (beg 3-tr cl, ch 3, sc, ch 3, 3-tr cl) in same sp, (3-tr cl, ch 3, sc, ch 3, 3-tr cl) in each shell around, join with sl st in top of beg cl (124 3-tr cls).

Rnd 16: (Beg 3-tr cl, ch 3, sc, ch 3, 3-tr cl) in same st, skip next cl, *(3-tr cl, ch 3, sc, ch 3, 3-tr cl) in next cl, skip next cl; repeat from * around, join, fasten off.

Rnd 17: Join green with sc in any sc between cls, ch 4, skip next cl, shell in top of next cl, *ch 4, sc in next sc, ch 4, skip next cl, shell in top of next cl; repeat from * around; to join, ch 2, hdc in first sc.

Rnd 18: Ch 1, sc over joining hdc, ch 4, sc in next ch sp, ch 4, (sc, ch 4, sc) in next shell, ch 4, *(sc in next ch sp, ch 4) 2 times, (sc, ch 4, sc) in next shell, ch 4; repeat from * around, join with sl st in first sc, fasten off. ⚜

JOINING DIAGRAM

Left-handed crocheters join here for rnd 1 of Doily.

Right-handed crocheters join here for rnd 1 of Doily.

SHASTA DAISIES

Continued from page 15

in next row, 2 sc in ring, 3 sc in next row, 4 sc in next row, join with sl st in first sc, fasten off.

SLEEVE FILLER

Row 1: With wrong side of Motifs at bottom of sleeve facing you, join with sc in first ch-3 sp after corner ch-9 lp (see Assembly Diagram B), ch 7, sc in next ch-3 sp, ch 8, sc in next ch-7 lp, ch 8, sc in next ch-3 sp on Motif C, turn.

Row 2: Ch 1, (4 sc, ch 3, 4 sc) in each ch lp across, fasten off.

SECOND BLOUSE SIDE

Work same as First Blouse Side, using joining ch-7 lps and joining ch-3 sps to join Motifs at sides, shoulders, and along edges of sleeves. **(NOTE:** Work Sleeve Fillers where needed before joining bottom edges of sleeves.)

CUFFS

For **each cuff,** make three of Motif A, using joining ch-3 sps and joining ch-7 lps to join motifs together and to end of sleeve.

BOTTOM & SLEEVE EDGING

Rnd 1: Working around bottom edge of blouse, join with sl st in joining of any corner ch-7 lp, ch 5, *(dc in next sc, ch 2, skip next 2 sc) 3 times, sc in next ch-3 sp, ch 2, skip next 2 sc; repeat between ( ) 2 more times, sc in next ch-3 sp, ch 2, skip next 2 sc; repeat between ( ) 2 more times, dc in next sc, ch 2*, [dc in joining of next ch-7 lp; repeat between **]; repeat between [ ] around, join with sl st in 3rd ch of ch-5.

Rnd 2: Ch 3, 4 dc in same st; skipping ch sps, sc in next dc or sc, (5 dc in next dc or sc, sc in next dc or sc) around, join with sl st in top of ch-3, fasten off.

Repeat edging around end of each sleeve.

Repeat edging around neck opening, working in sts only along edge of each Motif D.

NECK EDGING

Rnd 1: Working around neck opening, join with sl st in joining of corner ch-7 lps at one shoulder seam, ch 5, *(dc in next st, ch 2, skip next 2 sts) 8 times, ch 2, dc in next joining ch-7 lp, ch 2*, [dc in next st on center Motif, (ch 2, skip next 2 sts, dc in next st) 2 times, ch 2, sc in next ch-3 sp, ch 2, skip next 2 sts, (dc in next st, ch 2, skip next 2 sts) 2 times, sc in next ch-3 sp, (ch 2, skip next 2 sts, dc in next st) 3 times, ch 2, dc in next joining ch-7 lp, ch 2]; repeat between ** 2 more times; repeat between [ ], (dc in next st, ch 2, skip next 2 sts) 8 times, ch 2, join with sl st in 3rd ch of ch-5.

Rnd 2: Repeat same rnd of Bottom & Sleeve Edging. ⚜

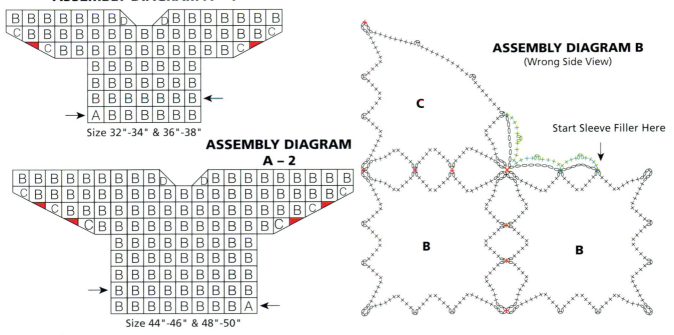

ASSEMBLY DIAGRAM A – 1

Size 32"-34" & 36"-38"

ASSEMBLY DIAGRAM A – 2

Size 44"-46" & 48"-50"

ASSEMBLY DIAGRAM B
(Wrong Side View)

C

Start Sleeve Filler Here

B

B

ENGLISH MEADOW

Continued from page 12

ch 4, sc) in next ch sp, ch 4, (sc in next ch sp, ch 4) 3 times*, [tr next 4 sts tog; repeat between **]; repeat between [ ] around, join (64 ch-4 sps, 8 tr).

Rnd 12: Ch 1, sc in same st, *ch 4, (sc in next ch sp, ch 4) 3 times, (sc, ch 4, sc) in next ch sp, ch 4, (sc in next ch sp, ch 4) 3 times, sc in next st, ch 4, (sc in next ch sp, ch 4) 4 times, (sc, ch 4, sc) in next ch sp, ch 4, (sc in next ch sp, ch 4) 4 times*, [sc in next st; repeat between **]; repeat between [ ] around, join with sl st in first sc (80 ch-4 sps).

Rnd 13: Sl st in first ch sp, ch 1, sc in same sp, *ch 4, (sc in next ch sp, ch 4) 3 times, (sc, ch 4, sc) in next ch sp, ch 4, (sc in next ch sp, ch 4) 9 times, (sc, ch 4, sc) in next ch sp, ch 4*, [(sc in next ch sp, ch 4) 5 times, sc in next ch sp; repeat between **]; repeat between [ ] 2 times, sc in next ch sp, (ch 4, sc in next ch sp) 4 times; to **join,** ch 1, dc in first sc (88 ch-4 sps).

Rnd 14: Ch 1, sc over joining dc just made, *ch 4, (sc in next ch sp, ch 4) 3 times, 2 tr in next ch sp, ch 2, 6 tr in next ch sp, ch 2, 2 tr in next ch sp, ch 4, (sc in next ch sp, ch 4) 3 times, (sc, ch 4, sc) in next ch sp, ch 4, (sc in next ch sp, ch 4) 5 times, (sc, ch 4, sc) in next ch sp, ch 4, (sc in next ch sp, ch 4) 5 times*, [(sc, ch 4, sc) in next ch sp; repeat between **]; repeat between [ ] 2 times, sc in last ch sp, join as before (92 ch-4 sps, 40 tr, 8 ch-2 sps).

Rnd 15: Ch 1, sc over joining dc just made, *ch 4, (sc in next ch-4 sp, ch 4) 3 times, skip next ch-4 sp, tr in each of next 2 sts, ch 2, skip next ch-2 sp, 2 tr in next st, tr in each of next 2 sts, ch 2, tr in each of next 2 sts, 2 tr in next st, ch 2, skip next ch-2 sp, tr in each of next 2 sts, ch 4, skip next ch-4 sp, (sc in next ch-4 sp, ch 4) 3 times, (sc, ch 4, sc) in next ch-4 sp, ch 4, (sc in next ch-4 sp, ch 4) 6 times, (sc, ch 4, sc) in next ch-4 sp, ch 4, (sc in next ch-4 sp, ch 4) 6 times*, [(sc, ch 4, sc) in next ch-4 sp; repeat between **]; repeat between [ ] 2 times, sc in last ch-4 sp, join (100 ch-4 sps, 12 ch-2 sps, 48 tr).

Rnd 16: Ch 1, sc over joining dc just made, *ch 4, (sc in next ch-4 sp, ch 4) 2 times, sc in next ch-4 sp, ch 2, skip next ch-4 sp, 3 tr in each of next 2 sts, ch 2, skip next ch-2 sp, 2 tr in next st, tr in each of next 3 sts, ch 2, skip next ch-2 sp, tr in each of next 3 sts, 2 tr in next st, ch 2, skip next ch-2 sp, 3 tr in each of next 2 sts, ch 2, skip next ch-4 sp, (sc in next ch-4 sp, ch 4) 3 times, (sc, ch 4, sc) in next ch-4 sp, ch 4, (sc in next ch-4 sp, ch 4) 6 times, 2 tr in next ch-4 sp, ch 2, 6 tr in next ch-4 sp, ch 2, 2 tr in next ch-4 sp, ch 4, (sc in next ch-4 sp, ch 4) 6 times*, [(sc, ch 4, sc) in next ch-4 sp; repeat between **]; repeat between [ ] 2 times, sc in last ch-4 sp, join (128 tr, 88 ch-4 sps, 28 ch-2 sps).

Rnd 17: Ch 1, sc over joining dc just made, *ch 4, sc in next ch-4 sp, ch 4, sc in next ch-4 sp, ch 2, skip next ch-4 sp, ◊skip next ch-2 sp, 2 tr in next st, tr in each of next 2 sts, ch 2, tr in each of next 2 sts, 2 tr in next st, ch 2, skip next ch-2 sp◊, tr next 2 sts tog, tr in each of next 3 sts, ch 2, skip next ch-2 sp, tr in each of next 3 sts, tr next 2 sts tog, ch 2; repeat between ◊◊ one time, skip next ch-4 sp, (sc in next ch-4 sp, ch 4) 2 times, (sc, ch 4, sc) in next ch-4 sp, ch 4, (sc in next ch-4 sp, ch 4) 6 times, skip next ch-4 sp, tr in each of next 2 sts, ch 2; repeat between ◊◊ one more time, tr in each of next 2 sts, ch 4, skip next ch-4 sp, (sc in next ch-4 sp, ch 4) 6 times*, [(sc, ch 4, sc) in next ch-4 sp; repeat between **]; repeat between [ ] 2 times, sc in last ch-4 sp, join (144 tr, 80 ch-4 sps, 40 ch-2 sps).

Rnd 18: Ch 1, sc over joining dc just made, *ch 4, sc in next ch-4 sp, ch 2, skip next ch-4 sp, ◊skip next ch-2 sp, 2 tr in next st, tr in each of next 3 sts, ch 2, skip next ch-2 sp, tr in each of next 3 sts, 2 tr in next st, ch 2, skip next ch-2 sp◊, tr next 2 sts tog, tr in each of next 2 sts, skip next ch-2 sp, tr in each of next 2 sts, tr next 2 sts tog, ch 2; repeat between ◊◊ one time, skip next ch-4 sp, sc in next ch-4 sp, ch 4, (sc, ch 4, sc) in next ch-4 sp, (ch 4, sc in next ch-4 sp) 6 times, ch 2, skip next ch-4 sp, 3 tr in each of next 2 sts, ch 2; repeat between ◊◊ one more time, 3 tr in each of next 2 sts, ch 2, skip next ch-4 sp, sc in next ch-4 sp, (ch 4, sc in next ch-4 sp) 5 times, ch 4*, [(sc, ch 4, sc) in next ch-4 sp; repeat between **]; repeat between [ ] 2 times, sc in last ch-4 sp, join (192 tr, 64 ch-4 sps, 44 ch-2 sps).

Row 19: For **first point,** ch 1, sc over joining dc just made, ch 4, skip next ch-4 sp, skip next ch-2 sp, (tr next 2 sts tog, tr in each of next 3 sts, ch 2, skip next ch-2 sp, tr in each of next 3 sts, tr next 2 sts tog), ch 4, sc in next ch-2 sp, ch 4, tr next 2 sts tog, tr in each of next 2 sts, tr next 2 sts tog, ch 4, sc in next ch-2 sp, ch 4; repeat between ( ), ch 2, skip next ch-2 sp, sc in next ch-4 sp, ch 1, dc in next ch-4 sp leaving remaining sts and ch sps unworked, turn (20 tr, 6 ch-4 sps, 4 ch-2 sps).

Row 20: Ch 1, sc over joining dc just made, ch 2, skip next ch-2 sp, *tr next 2 sts tog, tr in each of next 2 sts, skip next ch-2 sp, tr in each of next 2 sts, tr next 2 sts tog*, ch 4, (sc in next ch-4 sp, ch 4) 2 times, tr next 4 sts tog, ch 4, (sc in next ch-4 sp, ch 4) 2 more times; repeat between ** one time, ch 2, skip next ch-2 sp, sc in last ch-4 sp, turn (13 tr, 6 ch-4 sps, 2 ch-2 sps).

Row 21: Ch 4, skip next ch-2 sp, *tr next 2 sts tog,

tr in each of next 2 sts, tr next 2 sts tog*, ch 4, (sc in next ch-4 sp, ch 4) 3 times, sc in next st, ch 4, (sc in next ch-4 sp, ch 4) 3 more times; repeat between **, ch 1, skip next ch-2 sp, dc in last sc, turn (10 ch-4 sps, 8 tr).

Row 22: Ch 4, tr next 4 sts tog, ch 4, (sc in next ch sp, ch 4) 8 times, tr next 4 sts tog, ch 1, dc in last ch sp (11 ch-4 sps, 2 tr).

Row 23: Ch 1, sc in first ch sp, ch 4, sc in next st, ch 4, (sc in next ch sp, ch 4) 4 times, (sc, ch 4, sc) in next ch sp, ch 4, (sc in next ch sp, ch 4) 4 times, sc in next st, ch 1, dc in last ch sp, turn (13 ch sps).

Row 24: Ch 1, sc over joining dc just made, ch 4, (sc in next ch sp, ch 4) 5 times, (sc, ch 4, sc) in next ch sp, (ch 4, sc in next ch sp) 6 times, turn, fasten off (13 ch sps).

Row 19: For **second point,** join green variegated with sc in same ch-4 sp as last dc made on row 19 of previous point, (ch 4, sc in next ch-4 sp) 5 times, ch 2, skip next ch-4 sp, skip next ch-2 sp, *2 tr in next st, tr in each of next 2 sts, ch 2, tr in each of next 2 sts, 2 tr in next st, ch 2, skip next ch-2 sp*, tr next 2 sts tog, tr in each of next 3 sts, ch 2, skip next ch-2 sp, tr in each of next 3 sts, tr next 2 sts tog, ch 2, skip next ch-2 sp; repeat between **, skip next ch-4 sp, sc in next ch-4 sp; (ch 4, sc in next ch-4 sp) 4 times, ch 1, dc in next ch-4 sp leaving remaining sts and ch sps unworked, turn (24 tr, 10 ch-4 sps, 7 ch-2 sps).

Row 20: Ch 1, sc over joining dc just made, (ch 4, sc in next ch-4 sp) 3 times, ch 2, skip next ch-4 sp, skip next ch-2 sp, *2 tr in next st, tr in each of next 3 sts, ch 2, skip next ch-2 sp, tr in each of next 3 sts, 2 tr in next st, ch 2, skip next ch-2 sp*, tr next 2 sts tog, tr in each of next 2 sts, skip next ch-2 sp, tr in each of next 2 sts, tr next 2 sts tog, ch 2, skip next ch-2 sp; repeat between **, skip next ch-4 sp, sc in next ch-4 sp, (ch 4, sc in next ch-4 sp) 2 more times, ch 1, dc in last ch-4

sp, turn (26 tr, 6 ch-2 sps, 6 ch-4 sps).

Rows 21-26: Repeat rows 19-24 of first point.

Rows 19-24: For **third, fifth and seventh points,** join green variegated with sc in same ch-4 sp as last dc made on row 19 of previous point; complete same rows of **first point.**

Rows 19-24: For **fourth, sixth and eighth points,** join green variegated with sc in same ch-4 sp as last dc made on row 19 of previous point; complete same rows of **second point.**

Rnd 27: For **edging,** working around outer edge of doily, with right side of rnd 1 facing you, join green variegated with sc in last ch sp of row 24 on **first point,** ch 4, sc in same sp, ◊*ch 4, (sc in next ch sp, ch 4) 5 times, (sc, ch 4, sc) in next ch sp, ch 4; repeat from *, (sc in next ch sp, ch 4) 12 times◊, [(sc, ch 4, sc) in next ch sp; repeat between ◊◊]; repeat between [ ] around, join with sl st in first sc, fasten off.

FLOWER (make 11)

Row 1: With white, ch 6, sl st in first ch to form ring; for **first petal,** ch 4, 7 tr in ring, **turn** (8 tr).

Row 2: Ch 4, tr in same st, tr in each st across with 2 tr in last st, turn (10).

Row 3: Ch 1, sc in each st across; working in end of rows, 3 sc in end of next 2 rows, sl st into ring, **do not** turn.

Row 4: For **next petal,** ch 4, 7 tr in ring, turn (8).

Rows 5-6: Repeat rows 2 and 3.

Rows 7-12: Repeat rows 4-6 consecutively. Fasten off at end of last row.

Sew one Flower between each point. Sew last 3 Flowers to rnd 1 of Doily.

For **stigma** (make 11), with yellow variegated, ch 6, sl st in first ch to form ring, ch 2, 11 hdc in ring, join with sl st in top of ch-2, fasten off. Sew one stigma to center of each Flower. ⚜

SUNBURST DOILY

Continued from page 18

BORDER

Rnd 1: Working around outer edge of doily, join white with sl st in first ch sp after joining dc on rnd 14, ch 3, 2 dc in same sp, 3 dc in each of next 6 ch sps or around side of dc at end of row, *(3 dc, ch 1, 3 dc) in point, 3 dc in each of next 7 ch sps or around side of dc at end of row, skip next ch sp, dc fp around next fp*, [3 dc in each of next 7 ch sps or around side of dc at end of row; repeat between **]; repeat between [ ] around, join with sl st in top of ch-3.

Rnd 2: Sl st in next 2 sts, sl st in next sp between 3-dc groups, ch 1, sc in same sp; skipping each fp, ch 4, (sc in next sp between 3-dc groups, ch 4) around with (sc, ch 4) 2 times in each point, join with sl st in first sc. Fasten off. ⚜

VICTORIAN ELEGANCE

*Glowing with the characteristic
opulence of a lavish age gone by, this
exceptional assortment recalls the Victorian passion
for fine needlework. No surface in the well-dressed home of
that sophisticated era was left unadorned, and exquisite
crochet pieces were highly prized. Display your good
taste by adding these distinctive treasures
to your collection.*

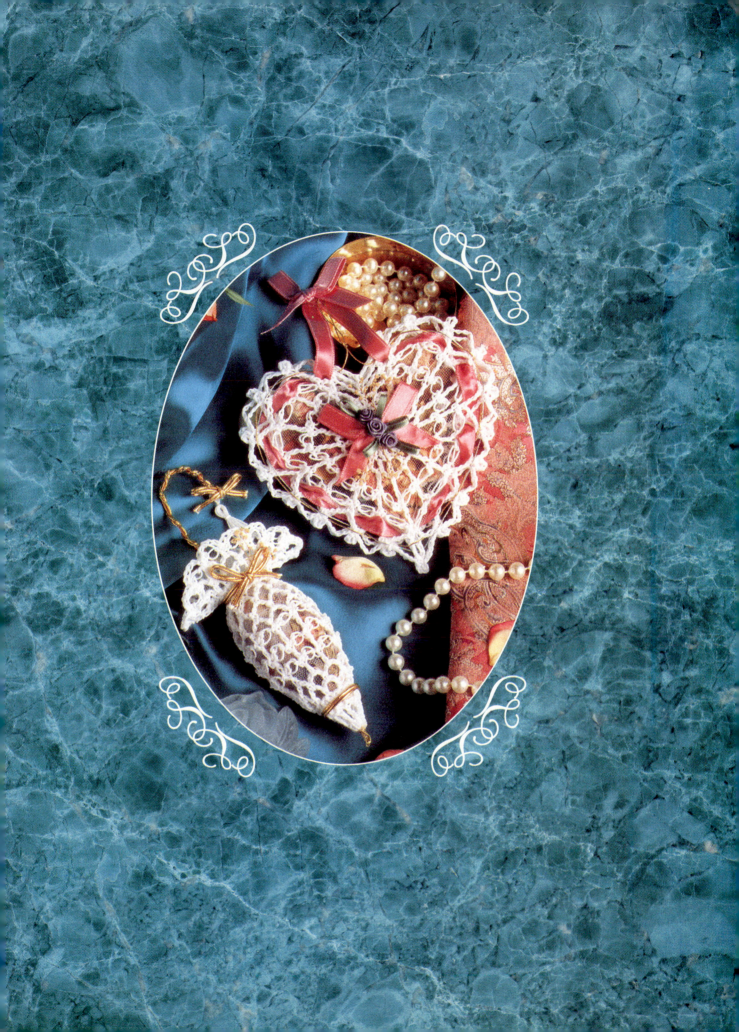

SUMMER COLORS

ESSENTIALS

SIZE: 15" across when blocked.

MATERIALS: Size 10 bedspread cotton — 150 yds. green, 35 yds. pink, 20 yds. blue and 15 yds. yellow; No. 9 steel crochet hook or size needed to obtain gauge.

GAUGE: Rnds 1-2 = 2" across.

INSTRUCTIONS

DOILY

Rnd 1: With green, ch 12, sl st in first ch to form ring, ch 1, 24 sc in ring, join with sl st in first sc (24 sc).

Rnd 2: Ch 3, dc in same st, 2 dc in each st around, join with sl st in top of ch-3 (48 dc).

Rnd 3: Ch 5, skip next st, (dc in next st, ch 2, skip next st) around, join with sl st in 3rd ch of ch-5 (24 dc, 24 ch-2 sps).

Rnd 4: Ch 6, (dc in next dc, ch 3) around, join with sl st in 3rd ch of ch-6.

Rnd 5: Ch 4, tr in same st, ch 4, (2 tr in next dc, ch 4) around, join with sl st in top of ch-4.

NOTES: For **beginning cluster (beg cl),** ch 4, *yo 2 times, insert hook in same sp, yo, draw lp through, (yo, draw through 2 lps on hook) 2 times; repeat from *, yo, draw through all 3 lps on hook.

For **cluster (cl),** *yo 2 times, insert hook in sp, yo, draw lp through, (yo, draw through 2 lps on hook) 2 times; repeat from * 2 times in same sp, yo, draw through all 4 lps on hook.

Rnd 6: Sl st in next st, sl st in first ch sp, beg cl, ch 5, cl in same sp, ch 7, skip next ch sp, *(cl, ch 5, cl) in next ch sp, ch 7, skip next ch sp; repeat from * around, join with sl st in top of beg cl (24 cls, 12 ch-7 sps, 12 ch-5 sps).

Rnd 7: Ch 1, sc in same st, *ch 11, sl st in 7th ch from hook, ch 4, sc in top of next cl, 7 sc in next ch-7 sp*, [sc in top of next cl; repeat between **]; repeat between [ ] around, join with sl st in first sc, fasten off.

Rnd 8: Join yellow with sl st in any ch-6 lp, beg cl, *(ch 3, cl) 5 times in same lp, skip next 4 sc, (dc, ch 3, dc) in next sc*, [cl in next ch-6 lp; repeat between **]; repeat between [ ] around, join with sl st in top of beg cl, fasten off (72 ch-3 sps).

Rnd 9: Join green with sc in any ch-3 sp between dc, 3 sc in same sp, 4 sc in each ch-3 sp around, join with sl st in first sc (288 sc).

Rnd 10: Ch 4, *skip next 2 sc, tr in next sc, ch 2, skip next 3 sc, sc in next sc, (ch 5, skip next 3 sc, sc in next sc) 3 times, ch 2, skip next 4 sc*, [tr in next sc; repeat between **]; repeat between [ ] around, join with sl st in top of ch-4 (36 ch-3 sps, 24 tr, 24 ch-2 sps).

NOTE: Joining hdc on next rnd counts as ch-2 sp.

Rnd 11: Ch 6, tr in next tr, ch 2, *skip next ch-2 sp, dc in 3rd ch of next ch-5 sp, (ch 3, dc in next sc, ch 3, dc in 3rd ch of next ch-5 sp) 2 times*, [ch 2, skip next ch-2 sp, (tr in next tr, ch 2) 2 times; repeat between **]; repeat between [ ] around to last ch-2 sp; to **join,** hdc in 4th ch of ch-5, **turn,** sl st in last dc made, **turn.**

Rnd 12: Ch 4, tr in same st, *ch 7, skip next 2 tr, (2 tr in next dc, ch 7, skip next dc) 2 times*, [2 tr in next dc; repeat between **]; repeat between [ ] around, join with sl st in top of ch-4 (36 ch-7 sps).

Rnd 13: Sl st in next tr, sl st in next ch sp, ch 1, (sc, 2 hdc, 2 dc, 2 hdc, sc) in each ch-7 sp around, join with sl st in first sc, fasten off.

NOTE: For **picot cluster (picot cl),** ch 4, sl st in 4th ch from hook, (ch 4, sl st in same ch) 2 times, *ch 6, sl st in 4th ch from hook, (ch 4, sl st in same ch) 2 times; repeat from *, sl st in same ch as first ch-4.

Rnd 14: Join blue with sl st in last st made on last rnd, ch 4, tr in next st, *(ch 4, skip next 2 sts, sc in each of next 2 sts, ch 4, skip next 2 sts), tr in next st, picot cl, tr in next st; repeat between ( ), tr in each of next 2 sts, ch 4, skip next 2 sts, sc in next st, picot cl, sc in next st, ch 4, skip next 2 sts*, [tr in each of next 2 sts; repeat between **]; repeat between [ ] around, join with sl st in top of ch-4, fasten off (24 picot cls).

Rnd 15: Join green with sc in center ch-4 lp of any picot cl, ch 15, (sc in center ch-4 lp of next picot cl, ch 15) around, join with sl st in first sc (24 ch-15 sps).

Rnd 16: Sl st in first ch, ch 4, tr in same ch, ch 3, tr in next ch, skip next 3 chs, (2 tr in next ch, ch 3, tr in next ch, skip next 3 chs) 2 times, skip next sc, *2 tr in next ch, ch 3, tr in next ch, skip next 3

Continued on page 46

Designed by Lucille LaFlamme

GALAXY TABLE TOPPER

E S S E N T I A L S

SIZE: 37" x 42" when blocked.

MATERIALS: Size 10 bedspread cotton — 2,000 yds. white; bobby pins for markers; No. 9 steel crochet hook or size needed to obtain gauge.

GAUGE: Rnds 1-3 of Motif No. 1 = 1" across.

I N S T R U C T I O N S

MOTIF NO. 1

Rnd 1: Ch 5, sl st in first ch to form ring, ch 1, 6 sc in ring, join with sl st in first sc (6 sc).

Rnd 2: Ch 7, (dc in next st, ch 4) around, join with sl st in 3rd ch of ch-7.

Rnd 3: Sl st in first ch sp, ch 1, 6 sc in each ch sp around, join with sl st in first sc (36 sc).

Rnd 4: Sl st in next st, ch 1, sc in same st, sc in next 4 sts, *ch 3, skip next st, sc in next 5 sts; repeat from * around; to **join,** ch 1, hdc in first sc.

Rnd 5: Ch 1, sc over joining hdc just made, ch 3, skip first sc of last rnd, sc in next 4 sts, *ch 3, sc in next ch-3 sp, ch 3, skip next st, sc in next 4 sts; repeat from * around, join as before.

Rnd 6: Ch 1, sc over joining hdc just made, ch 3, sc in next ch sp, ch 3, skip next st, sc in each of next 3 sts, *ch 3, (sc in next ch sp, ch 3) 2 times, skip next st, sc in each of next 3 sts; repeat from * around, join.

Rnd 7: Ch 1, sc over joining hdc just made, ch 3, (sc in next ch sp, ch 3) 2 times, skip next st, sc in each of next 2 sts, *ch 3, (sc in next ch sp, ch 3) 3 times, skip next st, sc in each of next 2 sts; repeat from * around, join.

Rnd 8: Ch 1, sc over joining hdc just made, ch 3, (sc in next ch sp, ch 3) 3 times, skip next st, sc in next st, *ch 3, (sc in next ch sp, ch 3) 4 times, skip next st, sc in next st; repeat from * around, join.

NOTE: For **double treble crochet (dtr),** yo 3 times, insert hook in st, yo, draw through st, (yo, draw through 2 lps on hook) 4 times.

Rnd 9: Ch 1, sc over joining hdc just made, (ch 3, sc in next ch sp) 4 times, *ch 11, sc in next ch sp, (ch 3, sc in next ch sp) 4 times; repeat from * around; to **join,** ch 6, dtr in first sc.

NOTE: Start marking last st of each rnd.

Rnd 10: Ch 6, dc over joining dtr just made, ch 3, (sc in next ch-3 sp, ch 3) 4 times, *dc in 3rd ch of next ch-11 lp, ch 3, (dc, ch 5, dc) in 6th ch of same lp, ch 3, dc in 9th ch of same lp, ch 3, (sc in next ch-3 sp, ch 3) 4 times; repeat from * around to last ch-6 sp, dc in 3rd ch of last ch-6 sp, ch 3, dc in top of joining dtr of last rnd; to **join,** ch 2, dc in 3rd ch of ch-6.

Rnd 11: Ch 6, dc in same ch as joining dc of last rnd, ch 3, dc in next dc, ch 3, *skip next ch-3 sp, (sc in next ch-3 sp, ch 3) 3 times, skip next ch-3 sp, (dc in next dc, ch 3) 2 times*, [(dc, ch 5, dc) in 3rd ch of next ch-5 sp, ch 3, (dc in next dc, ch 3) 2 times; repeat between **]; repeat between [ ] around, dc in top of joining dc on last rnd, ch 5, join with sl st in 3rd ch of ch-6.

Rnd 12: Ch 6, (dc in next dc, ch 3) 2 times, *skip next ch-3 sp, (sc in next ch-3 sp, ch 3) 2 times, (dc in next dc, ch 3) 3 times, (dc, ch 5, dc) in 3rd ch of next ch-5 sp, ch 3*, [(dc in next dc, ch 3) 3 times; repeat between **]; repeat between [ ] around, join.

Rnd 13: Ch 6, (dc in next dc, ch 3) 2 times, *skip next ch-3 sp, sc in next ch-3 sp, ch 3, (dc in next dc, ch 3) 4 times, (dc, ch 5, dc) in 3rd ch of next ch-5 sp, ch 3*, [(dc in next dc, ch 3) 4 times; repeat between **]; repeat between [ ] around to last dc, dc in last dc, ch 3, join.

Rnd 14: Ch 1, sc in same st, ch 3, (sc in next dc, ch 3) 2 times, *skip next 2 ch-3 sps, (sc in next dc, ch 3) 5 times, sc in 3rd ch of next ch-5 sp, ch 3*, [(sc in next dc, ch 3) 5 times; repeat between **]; repeat between [ ] around to last 2 dc, (sc in next dc, ch 3) 2 times, join with sl st in first sc.

Rnd 15: Ch 1, sc in same st, *ch 15, skip next 5 ch-3 sps, sc in next sc, (3 sc in next ch-3 sp, sc in next sc) 3 times, ch 5*, [(3 sc in next ch-3 sp, sc in next sc) 3 times; repeat between **]; repeat between [ ] around to last 3 ch-3 sps, 3 sc in next ch-3 sp, (sc in next st, 3 sc in next ch-3 sp) 2 times, join, fasten off.

MOTIFS NO. 2-37

NOTES: For **joining ch-15 lp,** ch 7, sc in ch-15 lp of next motif, ch 7.

Continued on page 47

HEIRLOOM CROCHET TREASURES

STARFLOWER DOILY

ESSENTIALS

SIZE: 12½" x 19" after blocking.

MATERIALS: Size 20 crochet cotton — 405 yds. blue; No. 11 crochet hook or size needed to obtain gauge.

GAUGE: Rnd 1 of Motif No. 1 = 1" across.

INSTRUCTIONS

MOTIF NO. 1

Rnd 1: Ch 9, sl st in first ch to form ring, ch 4, 3 tr in ring, ch 3, (4 tr in ring, ch 3) 7 times, join with sl st in top of ch-4 (32 tr, 8 ch-3 lps).

NOTES: For **beginning 4-tr cluster (beg 4-tr cl),** ch 4, *yo 2 times, insert hook in next st, yo, draw lp through, (yo, draw through 2 lps on hook) 2 times; repeat from * 2 times, yo, draw through all 4 lps on hook.

For **4-tr cluster (4-tr cl),** *yo 2 times, insert hook in next st, yo, draw lp through, (yo, draw through 2 lps on hook) 2 times; repeat from * 3 times, yo, draw through all 5 lps on hook.

Rnd 2: Beg 4-tr cl, ch 5, sc in next ch sp, ch 5, *4-tr cl, ch 5, sc in next ch sp, ch 5; repeat from * around, join with sl st in top of beg 4-tr cl (16 ch-5 lps, 8 cls, 8 sc).

Rnd 3: Sl st in first ch-5 lp, ch 1, (5 sc in each of next 2 ch-5 lps, ch 12) around, join with sl st in first sc (80 sc, 8 ch-12 lps).

NOTE: For **picot,** ch 5, sl st in 5th ch from hook.

Rnd 4: Sl st in next sc, ch 1, sc in same st, sc in each of next 2 sc, *make 3 picots, skip next 2 sc, sc in each of next 3 sc, ch 1, skip next sc, (7 sc, ch 5, 7 sc) in next ch-12 lp, ch 1, skip next sc*, [sc in each of next 3 sc; repeat between **]; repeat between [ ] around, join, fasten off (160 sc, 24 picots, 8 ch-5 lps).

MOTIFS NO. 2-3

Rnds 1-3: Repeat same rnds of Motif No 1.

NOTES: For **joining ch-5 lp,** ch 2, sl st in corresponding ch-5 lp on next Motif, ch 2.

Rnd 4: Repeat same rnd of Motif No. 1 using joining ch-5 lps to join Motifs according to Joining Diagram on page 48.

BORDER

Rnd 1: Working around outer edge of all Motifs, join with sc in ch-5 lp as incidated in Joining Diagram, *ch 11, sc in next ch-5 lp, ch 27, sc in next ch-5 lp, (ch 15, sc in next ch-5 lp) 5 times, ch 27*, sc in next ch-5 lp; repeat between **, join with sl st in first sc (16 sc, 10 ch-15 lps, 4 ch-27 lps, 2 ch-11 lps).

Rnd 2: Work in either sc sts or in chs for this rnd only as follows: ch 1, sc in same st, ch 3, skip next 2 sts, sc in next st, *ch 9, skip next 5 sts, sc in next st, ch 3, skip next 2 sts, sc in next st; repeat from * around to last 4 sts, ch 9, skip last 4 sts, join with sl st in first sc (33 ch-9 lps, 33 ch-3 lps).

NOTES: For **beginning 3-tr cluster (beg 3-tr cl),** ch 4, *yo 2 times, insert hook in same sp, yo, draw lp through, (yo, draw through 2 lps on hook) 2 times; repeat from *, yo, draw through all 3 lps on hook.

For **3-tr cluster (3-tr cl),** yo 2 times, insert hook in next lp, *yo, draw lp through, (yo, draw through 2 lps on hook) 2 times*, [yo 2 times, insert hook in same lp; repeat between **]; repeat between [ ] one time, yo, draw through all 4 lps on hook.

Rnd 3: Sl st in first ch-3 lp, beg 3-tr cl, ch 5, sc in next ch-9 lp, ch 5, *3-tr cl in next ch-3 lp, ch 5, sc in next ch-9 lp, ch 5; repeat from * around, join with sl st in top of beg 3-tr cl (66 ch-5 sps, 33 cls, 33 sc).

Rnd 4: Ch 9, tr in same st, *ch 6, skip next ch-5 sp, (sc, ch 4, sc) in next sc, ch 6, skip next ch-5 sp*, [(tr, ch 5, tr) in next 3-tr cl; repeat between **]; repeat between [ ] around, join with sl st in 4th ch of ch-9.

Rnd 5: Sl st in next 3 chs, ch 1, sc in same lp, (ch 11, skip next 2 ch-6 sps, sc in next ch-5 lp) 6 times, (ch 15, skip next 2 ch-6 sps, sc in next ch-5 lp) 6 times, (ch 11, skip next 2 ch-6 sps, sc in next ch-5 lp) 10 times, (ch 15, skip next 2 ch-6 sps, sc in next ch-5 lp) 6 times, (ch 11, skip next 2 ch-6 sps, sc in next ch-5 lp) 4 times, ch 11, skip last 2 ch-6 sps, join with sl st in first sc (21 ch-11 lps, 12 ch-15 lps).

Rnd 6: Sl st in next 6 chs, ch 1, sc in same lp, ch 11, (sc in next ch lp, ch 11) 4 times, (sc in next ch

Continued on page 48

H E I R L O O M   C R O C H E T   T R E A S U R E S

Needlework Tool Holders

ESSENTIALS	INSTRUCTIONS

SCISSORS CASES

SIZE: Small Case is 4" long. Large Case is 7" long.

MATERIALS FOR SMALL CASE: Size 10 bedspread cotton — 50 yds. white; 6" x 7" piece blue felt; 14" blue ⅛" satin ribbon; blue sewing thread; sewing and tapestry needles; No. 6 steel crochet hook or size needed to obtain gauge.

MATERIALS FOR LARGE CASE: Size 10 bedspread cotton — 95 yds. white; 9" x 10" piece red felt; ½ yd. red ¼" satin ribbon; red sewing thread; sewing and

tapestry needles; No. 6 steel crochet hook or size needed to obtain gauge.

GAUGE: Rnds 1-2 of Motif = 1" across.

NOTES: For **beginning cluster (beg cl),** ch 3, *yo, insert hook in same st or sp, yo, draw lp through, yo, draw through 2 lps on hook; repeat from * one more time, yo, draw through all 3 lps on hook.

For **cluster (cl),** (yo, insert hook, yo, draw lp through, yo, draw through 2 lps on hook) 3 times in next st or sp, yo, draw through all 4 lps on hook.

SMALL CASE
SIDE (make 2)
Motif No. 1
Rnd 1: Ch 2, 8 sc in 2nd ch from hook, join with sl st in first sc (8 sc).

Rnd 2: Beg cl, ch 4, (cl, ch 4) around, join with sl st in top of beg cl, fasten off (8 cls, 8 ch lps).

Motif No. 2
Rnd 1: Repeat same rnd of Motif No. 1.

Rnd 2: Beg cl; to join Motifs, holding Motifs with wrong sides tog, ch 2, sc in any ch-4 lp on Motif No. 1, ch 2, cl on this Motif, ch 2, sc in next ch-4 lp on Motif No. 1, ch 2, cl on this Motif, ch 4, (cl, ch 4) around, join with sl st in top of beg cl, fasten off.

Case
Row 1: Working in rows, join with sl st in 7th ch-4 lp on Motif No. 2, ch 6, cl in next ch-4 lp, ch 2, tr next 2 ch sps tog, ch 2, cl in next ch-4 lp, ch 2, tr in next ch-4 lp leaving remaining ch-4 lps unworked, turn (4 ch-2 sps, 3 tr, 2 cls).

Row 2: Ch 4, cl in next ch-2 sp, (ch 2, cl in next ch-2 sp) 3 times, ch 1, dc in 4th ch of last ch-6, turn (4 cls, 3 ch-2 sps, 2 dc, 2 ch-1 sps).

Row 3: Ch 5, skip next ch-1 sp, cl in next ch-2 sp, ch 2, skip next ch-2 sp, cl in next ch-2 sp, ch 2, dc in 3rd ch of ch-4, turn.

Row 4: Ch 6, skip next cl, cl in next ch-2 sp, ch 3, dc in 3rd ch of ch-5, turn.

Row 5: Ch 5, cl in first ch-3 sp, ch 2, cl in last ch-6 sp, ch 2, dc in 3rd ch of same ch-6, turn.

Row 6: Repeat row 4.

Row 7: Ch 5, cl in first ch-3 sp, ch 1, cl in last ch-6 sp, ch 2, dc in 3rd ch of same ch-6, turn.

Row 8: Ch 3; for **decrease,** (yo, insert hook, yo, draw lp through, yo, draw through 2 lps on hook) 3 times in first ch-2 sp leaving all lps on hook; repeat between ( ) 3 more times in last ch-5, yo, draw through all 7 lps on hook; dc in 3rd ch of same ch-5, turn.

Row 9: Working around outer edge, in sts and around post of each st at end of each row, ch 1, sc in same st, skip next dec, 3 sc around side of next ch-3, 4 sc in next row, 3 sc in each of next 6 rows; working in unworked ch-4 lps on Motifs, 2 sc in next ch sp, 4 sc in each of next 4 ch lps, 2 sc in next ch sp, sc in next joining, 2 sc in next ch sp, 4 sc in each of next 4 ch lps, 2 sc in next ch sp; 3 sc in each of next 6 rows, 4 sc in next row, 3 sc in next row, join with sl st in first sc, fasten off.

FINISHING
1: To **join,** with wrong sides held together, working through both thicknesses, sc Case Sides together leaving 28 sts across Motifs open, fasten off.

2: Working around opening, join with sc in first st, sc in each st around both Sides, join with sl st in first sc, fasten off.

3: Using Side as pattern, cut two pieces slightly smaller from felt; hand or machine sew together leaving top open same as crocheted Sides.

4: Place inside crocheted Case. Sew felt to crocheted piece on each Side around top opening.

5: Cut ribbon in half, sew one end inside Case on each Side. Tie into a bow.

LARGE CASE
FIRST SIDE
Motif No. 1
Rnds 1-2: Repeat same rnds of Small Case Motif No. 1, **do not** fasten off.

Rnd 3: Ch 1, sc in same st, ch 4, sc in next ch lp, (ch 4, sc in next cl, ch 4, sc in next ch lp) around, ch 4, join with sl st in first sc, fasten off (16 ch lps).

Motif No. 2
Rnds 1-2: Repeat same rnds of Small Case Motif No. 1, **do not** fasten off.

Rnd 3: Ch 1, sc in same st, (ch 4, sc in next ch lp or in next cl) 4 times; to join, holding Motifs wrong sides together, matching cls, ch 2, sc in corresponding ch lp on Motif No. 1, ch 2, sc in next ch sp on this Motif, ch 2, sc in next ch lp on Motif No. 1, ch 2, sc in next cl on this Motif, (ch 4, sc in next ch lp or in next cl) around; to join, ch 1, dc in first sc, **do not** fasten off.

Case
Row 1: Working in rows across Motifs, beg cl over dc just made, ch 2, sc in next ch-4 lp, (ch 4, sc in next ch-4 lp) 2 times, ch 2, cl in each of next 2 ch-4 lps skipping ch-2 sps, ch 2, sc in next ch-4 lp, (ch 4, sc in next ch-4 lp) 2 times, ch 2, cl in next ch-4 lp leaving remaining ch-4 lps unworked, turn (4 cls, 4 ch-2 sps, 4 ch-4 lps).

Row 2: Sl st in first ch-2 sp, ch 6, sc in next ch-4 lp, ch 4, sc in next ch-4 lp, ch 2, cl in next ch-2 sp, ch 1, skip next 2 cls, cl in next ch-2 sp, ch 2, sc in next ch-4 lp, ch 4, sc in next ch-4 lp, ch 3, dc in last ch-2 sp leaving last cl unworked, turn.

NOTE: For **treble cluster (tr cl),** yo 2 times, insert hook in next sp, *yo, draw lp through, (yo, draw through 2 lps on hook) 2 times*, [yo 2 times, insert hook in same sp; repeat between **]; repeat between [ ] one more time, yo, draw through all 4 lps on hook.

Row 3: Ch 5, cl in first ch-3 sp, ch 2, sc in next ch-4 lp, ch 4, skip next ch-2 sp, skip next cl, tr cl in next ch-1 sp, ch 4, skip next cl, skip next ch-2 sp, sc in next ch-4 lp, ch 2, cl in next ch-6 sp, ch 1, tr in 3rd ch of same ch-6, turn.

Row 4: Ch 6, skip next cl, sc in next ch-2 sp, ch 4, sc in next ch-4 sp, ch 4, skip next tr cl, sc in next ch-4 sp, ch 4, sc in next ch-2 sp, ch 3, skip next cl, dc in 4th ch of last ch-5, turn.

Row 5: Ch 5, cl in next ch-3 sp, ch 2, sc in next ch-4 lp, ch 4, tr cl in next ch-4 lp, ch 4, sc in next ch-4 lp, ch 2, cl in last ch-6 sp, ch 1, tr in 3rd ch of same ch-6, turn.

Continued on next page

NEEDLEWORK TOOL HOLDERS

Continued from page 35

Rows 6-8: Repeat rows 4 and 5 alternately, ending with row 4.

Row 9: Ch 5, cl in next ch-3 sp, ch 1, sc in next ch-4 lp, ch 4, tr cl in next ch-4 lp, ch 4, sc in next ch-4 lp, ch 1, cl in last ch-6 sp, ch 1, tr in 3rd ch of same ch-6, turn.

Row 10: Ch 6, skip next ch-1 sp, skip next cl, sc in next ch-1 sp, ch 3, sc in next ch-4 lp, ch 3, skip next tr cl, sc in next ch-4 lp, ch 3, sc in next ch-1 sp, ch 3, skip next cl, dc in 4th ch of ch-5, turn.

Row 11: Ch 5, cl in next ch-3 sp, ch 1, sc in next ch-3 sp, ch 4, tr cl in next ch-3 sp, ch 4, sc in next ch-3 sp, ch 1, cl in last ch-6 sp, ch 1, tr in 3rd ch of same ch-6, turn.

Rows 12-21: Repeat rows 10 and 11 alternately.

Row 22: Ch 5, skip next cl, skip next ch-1 sp, tr cl in next ch-4 lp, skip next tr cl, tr cl in next ch-4 lp, ch 5, skip next cl, sc in 4th ch of last ch-5, turn.

Rnd 23: Working around outer edge, in sts and in top of sts at end of rows, ch 1, sc in same st, ch 4, sc in next ch-5 lp, ch 4, sc in next sp between tr cls, ch 4, sc in next ch-5 lp, ch 4, sc in next row, (ch 3, sc in next row, ch 2, sc in next row) 10 times; working in unworked ch-4 lps around Motifs, ch 4, sc in first ch-4 lp, (ch 3, sc in next ch-4 lp) 8 times, ch 4, skip next joining, sc in next ch-4 lp on next Motif, (ch 3, sc in next ch-4 lp) 8 times; working across opposite side of Case, ch 4, (sc in next row, ch 2, sc in next row, ch 3) across, join with sl st in first sc, fasten off.

SECOND SIDE
Motif No. 1
Work same as Motif No. 1 of First Side on page 35.

Motif No. 2
Work same as Motif No. 2 of First Side.

Case
NOTES: For **joining ch-4 lp,** ch 2, sc in corresponding ch lp on First Side, ch 2.

For **joining ch-3 lp,** ch 1, sc in corresponding ch lp on First Side, ch 1.

Rows 1-22: Repeat same rows of Case on First Side.

Rnd 23: Working around outer edge, in sts and in tops of sts at ends of rows, ch 1, sc in same st, make joining ch-4 lp, sc in next ch-5 lp, make joining ch-4 lp, sc in next sp between tr cls, make joining ch-4 lp, sc in next ch-5 lp, make joining ch-4 lp, sc in next row, (make joining ch-3 lp, sc in next row, ch 2, sc in next row) 10 times, make joining ch-4 lp; working in unworked ch-4 lps around Motifs, sc in first ch-4 lp, (make joining ch-3 lp, sc in next ch-4 lp) 3 times, (ch 3, sc in next ch-4 lp) 5 times, ch 4, skip next joining, sc in next ch-4 lp on next Motif, (ch 3, sc in next ch-4 lp) 5 times, (make joining ch-3 lp, sc in next ch-4 lp) 3 times; working across opposite side of Case, make joining ch-4 lp, (sc in next row, ch 2, sc in next row, make joining ch-3 lp) across, join with sl st in first sc, fasten off.

Rnd 24: Join with sc in any ch-4 lp on top opening, 3 sc in same ch sp, 4 sc in each ch-4 lp around with 2 sc in ch sp of each joining, join, fasten off.

FINISHING
Repeat Finishing of Small Case on page 35.

HOOK CASE
SIZE: 6" x 8½" when open. Holds 21 crochet hooks.

MATERIALS: Size 10 bedspread cotton — 75 yds. white; embroidery floss — small amount each yellow, brown and green; 9" x 12" piece pink felt; 1 yd. pink ¼" satin ribbon; 24 white 3-mm pearl beads; pink sewing thread; sewing and tapestry needles; No. 6 steel crochet hook or size needed to obtain gauge.

GAUGE: 11 dc sts = 1"; 4 dc rows = 1".

NOTES: For **horizontal-cluster (h-cl),** ch 2, *yo, insert hook in top of dc or cl just made, yo, draw lp through, yo, draw through 2 lps on hook; repeat from * one more time in same dc, yo, draw through all 3 lps on hook.

For **cluster (cl),** (yo, insert hook, yo, draw lp through, yo, draw through 2 lps on hook) 3 times in next dc or next cl on last row, yo, draw through all 4 lps on hook.

CASE
Row 1: Ch 60, dc in 4th ch from hook, dc in each ch across, turn (58 dc).

Row 2: Ch 3, dc in each of next 3 sts, ch 2, skip next 2 sts, (dc in next st, ch 2, skip next 2 sts) across to last 4 sts, dc in last 4 sts, turn (24 dc, 17 ch-2 sps).

Row 3: Ch 3, dc in each of next 3 dc, ch 2, *dc in next dc, h-cl, cl, h-cl, dc in next dc, (ch 2, dc in next dc) 3 times, h-cl, cl, h-cl, dc in next dc, ch 2; repeat from *, dc in last 4 dc, turn (20 dc, 8 h-cls, 4 cls).

Row 4: Ch 3, dc in each of next 3 dc, ch 2, *dc in next dc, ch 2, skip next h-cl, cl, ch 2, skip next h-cl, (dc in next dc, ch 2) 4 times, skip next h-cl, cl, ch 2, skip next h-cl, dc in next dc*, 2 dc in next ch-2 sp; repeat between **, ch 2, dc in last 4 dc, turn (22 dc, 16 ch-2 sps, 4 cls).

Row 5: Ch 3, dc in each of next 3 dc, ch 2, (dc in next dc or in next cl, ch 2) 6 times, dc in next cl, 2 dc in next

Continued on page 48

Designed by Carol Smith

HEIRLOOM CROCHET TREASURES

PINEAPPLE SACHET

ESSENTIALS

SIZE: 5" x 7".

MATERIALS: Size 10 bedspread cotton — 150 yds. variegated blue; 1 yd. satin ⅜" ribbon and four small matching bows; two 5" round pieces netting material and matching sewing thread; 10 small white satin roses; potpourri; 30 small white single pearl-head stamens; twelve 4" lengths 2½-mm white strung pearl beads; 3" foam ball; fabric stiffener; craft glue; sewing and tapestry needles; No. 9 steel crochet hook.

INSTRUCTIONS

M O T I F (make 2)

Row 1: Ch 4, sl st in first ch to form ring, ch 3, dc in ring, (ch 1, 2 dc in ring) 3 times, turn (8 dc, 3 ch-1 sps).

NOTES: For **beginning shell (beg shell),** sl st in first 2 sts, sl st in first ch-1 sp, ch 3, (dc, ch 1, 2 dc) in same sp.

For **shell,** (2 dc, ch 1, 2 dc) in next ch-1 sp.

Row 2: Beg shell, shell in each of next 2 ch-1

Continued on page 39

H E I R L O O M   C R O C H E T   T R E A S U R E S

CUP & SAUCER

ESSENTIALS

SIZE: 2" tall.
MATERIALS: Size 10 bedspread cotton — 100 yds. white; ½ yd. gold metallic cord; eight beige ³⁄₈" ribbon roses with stems; 2" foam ball; plastic wrap; fabric stiffener; craft glue or hot glue gun; No. 5 steel crochet hook or size needed to obtain gauge.
GAUGE: 7 dc sts = 1"; 3 dc rnds = 1".

INSTRUCTIONS

CUP
Rnd 1: Starting at bottom, ch 4, sl st in first ch to form ring, ch 3, 17 dc in ring, join with sl st in top of ch-3 (18 dc).
Rnd 2: Working this rnd in **back lps,** ch 3, dc in same st, 2 dc in each st around, join (36).
Rnds 3-6: Ch 3, dc in same st, dc in each st around, join, ending with 40 sts in last rnd.
Rnd 7: Ch 2, hdc in each st around, join with sl st in top of ch-2, fasten off.

38

BASE

NOTE: For **picot,** ch 3, sl st in top of last sc made.

Rnd 1: With top of Cup facing you, working in **front lps** of rnd 1, join with sc in any st, ch 2, (skip next st, sc in next st, picot, ch 2, skip next st, sc in next st, ch 2) 4 times, sc in next st, picot, ch 2, join with sl st in first sc (10 sc, 10 ch sps, 5 picots).

NOTE: For **double love knot (d-lk,** see Stitch Guide), (draw up ⅜"-long lp on hook, yo, draw lp through, sc in back strand of long lp) 2 times.

Rnd 2: Ch 1, sc in first st, d-lk, skip next picot, (sc in next sc, d-lk, skip next picot) around, join with sl st in first sc, fasten off (5 sc, 5 d-lks).

For **handle,** ch 33, sl st in 2nd ch from hook, sl st in each ch across, fasten off.

SAUCER

Rnd 1: Starting at bottom, ch 4, sl st in first ch to form ring, ch 3, 17 dc in ring, join with sl st in top of ch-3 (18 dc).

Rnd 2: Ch 3, dc in same st, 2 dc in each st around, join (36).

Rnd 3: Ch 4, skip next st, (hdc in next st, ch 2, skip next st) around, join with sl st in 2nd ch of ch-4 (18 hdc, 18 ch sps).

Rnd 4: Ch 3, dc in same st, dc in next 5 sts and chs, (2 dc in next st or in next ch, dc in next 5 sts and chs) around, join with sl st in top of ch-3 (63).

Rnd 5: Ch 1, sc in same st, ch 2, sc in next st, picot, ch 2, skip next st, (sc in next st, ch 2, skip next st, sc in next st, picot, ch 2, skip next st) around, join with sl st in first sc (32 sc, 32 ch sps, 16 picots).

Rnd 6: Repeat rnd 2 of Base (16 sc, 16 d-lks).

FINISHING

1: Apply fabric stiffener to all pieces following manufacturer's instructions. Cover foam ball with plastic wrap; place inside Cup. Shape Handle as shown in photo. Let Saucer dry flat. Let all pieces dry completely, shaping Base with fingers while drying.

2: Cut cord to measure around Cup between rnds 4 and 5 and glue in place.

3: Cut cord to measure around rnd 4 of Saucer and glue in place.

4: Cut and glue cord to one side of Handle. Glue Handle to Cup as shown.

5: Cut stem from each rose. Shape each stem into figure eight. Starting 1½" from Handle, glue three stems at an angle on cord around Cup evenly spaced 1½" apart. Glue remainder of stems on cord around Saucer evenly spaced 1½" apart. Glue ribbon rose to center of each stem.

6: Glue d-lks of Base to rnd 2 of Saucer. ⚜

PINEAPPLE SACHET

Continued from page 37

sps, turn (3 shells).

Row 3: Beg shell, ch 3, (dc, ch 4, dc) in next shell, ch 3, shell in last shell, turn.

Row 4: Beg shell, ch 3, skip next ch-3 sp, 12 dc in next ch-4 sp, ch 3, shell in last shell, turn.

Row 5: Beg shell, ch 4, (dc in next dc, 2 dc in next dc) 3 times, dc in each of next 2 dc, (2 dc in next dc, dc in next dc) 2 times, ch 4, shell in last shell, turn (17 dc, 2 ch-4 sps).

Row 6: Beg shell, ch 4, dc in next dc, (ch 1, dc) in next 16 dc, ch 4, shell in last shell, turn.

Row 7: Beg shell, ch 4, (sc, ch 4) in next 16 ch-1 sps, shell in last shell, turn.

Rows 8-21: Beg shell, ch 4, skip next ch sp, (sc, ch 4) in each ch-4 lp across to last ch-4 sp, skip last ch sp, shell in last shell, turn. **(NOTE:** You will have one less ch-4 lp on each row.)

Row 22: Beg shell, ch 4, skip next ch sp, sc in next ch lp, ch 4, shell in last shell, turn.

Row 23: Beg shell, (dtr, ch 2, dtr) in next sc, shell in last shell, turn (2 shells, 2 dtr, 1 ch-2 sp).

Row 24: Beg shell, sc in next ch-2 sp, shell in last shell, turn.

Row 25: Sl st in first 2 sts, sl st in first ch-1 sp, ch 3, dc in same sp, ch 1, 2 dc in last shell, turn.

Row 26: Sl st in first 2 sts, sl st in next ch-1 sp, ch 3, (dc, ch 1, 2 dc) in same sp, fasten off.

FINISHING

1: Apply fabric stiffener to Motifs according to manufacturer's instructions. Cut foam ball in half, shape each Motif over half of ball. Allow to dry.

2: Sew two pieces of netting material together, leaving 2" unsewn. Stuff with potpourri, finish sewing.

3: Place potpourri "pillow" between Motifs. Glue or sew Motifs together.

4: Weave ribbon through ch-4 spaces along edge of Motifs, tie in bow at wide end of Motif.

5: Glue three roses, 9 pearl stamens and three 4" strings of pearls on top of each small bow. Glue two bows to each side of Motif. ⚜

Designed by Jo Ann Maxwell

SWEET SCENTS

PARASOL

SIZE: 7" long.
GAUGE: 1 tr rnd = ½" tall.
MATERIALS: Size 10 bedspread cotton — 75 yds. white; 8" circle white tulle; White sewing thread; 1 yd. gold metallic cord; 10" of 26-gauge copper wire; One twig of baby's breath; potpourri; fabric stiffener; craft glue or hot glue gun; polyester fiberfill; wire cutters; sewing and tapestry needles; No. 5 steel crochet hook or size needed to obtain gauge.

INSTRUCTIONS

PARASOL

Rnd 1: Ch 4, sl st in first ch to form ring, ch 5, (tr, ch 1) 9 times in ring, join with sl st in 4th ch of ch-5 (10 tr, 10 ch sps).

Rnd 2: Ch 3, dc in each st and in each ch sp around, join with sl st in top of ch-3 (20 dc).

Rnd 3: Ch 1, sc in same st, (ch 4, skip next st, sc in next st) around to last st; to **join,** ch 1, skip last st, dc in first sc (10 sc, 10 ch sps).

Rnd 4: Ch 1, sc over joining dc, **(**ch 4, sc in next ch sp**)** around; to **join,** ch 1, dc in first sc.

NOTE: For **¼"-love knot (¼"-lk,** see Stitch Guide), draw up ¼"-long lp on hook, yo, draw lp through, sc in back strand of long lp.

Rnd 5: Ch 3, ¼"-lk, (dc in next ch sp, ¼"-lk) around, join with sl st in top of ch-3 (10 dc, 10 lks).

Rnds 6-7: Ch 3, ¼"-lk, (dc in next dc, ¼"-lk) around, join with sl st in top of ch-3.

Rnd 8: Ch 1, sc in same st, (ch 4, sc in next dc) around; to **join,** ch 1, dc in first sc (10 sc, 10 ch lps).

Rnds 9-10: Ch 1, sc over joining dc, (ch 4, sc in next ch lp) around; to **join,** ch 1, dc in first sc.

Rnd 11: Ch 1, sc over joining dc, ch 2, (sc in next ch lp, ch 2) around, join with sl st in first sc.

Rnd 12: Ch 3, dc in each st and in each ch around, join with sl st in top of ch-3 (30 dc).

Rnd 13: Ch 1, sc in same st, (ch 4, skip next st, sc in next st) around to last st; to **join,** ch 1, skip last st, dc in first sc (15 sc, 15 ch lps).

Rnd 14: Ch 1, sc over joining dc, (ch 4, sc in next ch lp) around, join as before.

NOTE: For **⅜"-love knot (⅜"-lk),** draw up ⅜"-long lp on hook, yo, draw lp through, sc in back strand of long lp.

Rnd 15: Ch 1, sc over joining dc, ⅜"-lk, (sc in next ch lp, ⅜"-lk) around, join with sl st in first sc (15 sc, 15 lks).

Rnd 16: Ch 1, (sc in next sc, ch 5) around, join, fasten off.

FINISHING

1: Apply fabric stiffener to Parasol according to manufacturer's instructions. Wrap polyester fiberfill with plastic wrap, shape and place inside Parasol.

2: When dry, remove stuffing and plastic wrap. Place tulle inside Parasol; fill with potpourri. With sewing thread and needle, sew tulle closed.

3: For handle, cut wire in half, twist both pieces together. Place glue on one end. Insert inside Parasol. Bend other end as shown in photo. Wrap 18" of cord around handle and glue in place.

4: Wrap 4" of cord around rnd 12 of Parasol. Glue in place.

5: Make 1½" bow from cord. Glue to center front of Parasol over cord around rnd 12.

6: Make 1¼" bow from cord. Glue to handle according to photo.

7: Wrap 3" piece cord around rnd 2 of Parasol. Glue in place.

8: For tip of parsol, dip 1" piece of cord into glue. Let dry completely. Cut ¼" off each end and glue ½" piece to center of rnd 1.

9: For tassel, cut 10 strands white each 2" long. Tie separate strand tightly around center of all strands leaving ¼" ends. Wrap separate small piece ¼" from top of tassel. Secure. Trim ends. Glue ¼" ends to bow on handle.

HEART

SIZE: 4¾" x 5".
GAUGE: Rnds 1-2 = 1¾" across.
MATERIALS: Size 10 bedspread cotton — 150 yds.

Continued on page 42

SWEET SCENTS

Continued from page 40

white; 1 yd. each gold and silver metallic thread; white sewing thread; 5" x 10" piece white tulle; 1½ yds. rose ⅜" satin ribbon; 5" green ⅛" satin ribbon; 3 blue ⅜" ribbon roses; small amount baby's breath; potpourri; fabric stiffener; craft glue or hot glue gun; sewing and tapestry needle; No. 5 steel crochet hook or size needed to obtain gauge.

HEART SIDE (make 2)

NOTE: For **double treble crochet (dtr),** yo 3 times, insert hook in st, yo, draw lp through, (yo, draw through 2 lps on hook) 4 times.

Rnd 1: Ch 5, sl st in first ch to form ring, ch 4, (2 tr, 2 dc, 2 tr, 2 dtr, tr, dc, sc, dc, tr, 2 dtr, 2 tr, 2 dc, 2 tr) in ring, join with sl st in top of ch-4 (11 tr, 6 dc, 4 dtr, 1 sc).

Rnd 2: Ch 5, (dc in next st, ch 2) 9 times, sc in each of next 3 sts, ch 2; repeat between ( ) 9 more times, join with sl st in 3rd ch of ch-5 (20 ch sps, 19 dc, 3 sc).

NOTES: For ⅜"-love knot (⅜"-lk, see Stitch Guide), draw up ⅜"-long lp on hook, yo, draw lp through, sc in back strand of long lp.

For **½"-love knot (½"-lk),** draw up ½"-long lp on hook, yo, draw lp through, sc in back strand of long lp.

Rnd 3: Ch 3, ⅜"-lk, (dc in next st, ⅜"-lk) 4 times, (tr in next st, ⅜"-lk) 3 times, dc in next st, ch 3, sc in next st, ch 1, skip next sc, sc in next sc, ch 1, skip next sc, sc in next st, ch 3, dc in next st, ⅜"-lk, (tr in next st, ⅜"-lk) 3 times, (dc in next st, ⅜"-lk) 4 times, join with sl st in top of ch-4 (20 sts, 16 ⅜"-lks, 2 ch-3 sps, 2 ch-1 sps).

Rnd 4: Ch 4, ½"-lk, (dc in next st, ½"-lk) 4 times, (tr in next st, ½"-lk) 3 times, (hdc, ch 2, hdc) in next st, ch 4, skip next sc, sc in next sc, ch 4, skip next sc, (hdc, ch 2, hdc) in next st, ½"-lk, (tr in next st, ½"-lk) 3 times, (dc in next st, ½"-lk) 4 times, join (20 sts, 16 ½"-lks, 2 ch-4 sps, 2 ch-2 sps).

Rnd 5: Ch 1, (sc, ch 7, sc) in same st, ch 6, (sc in next st, ch 6) 7 times, hdc in next st, ch 2, hdc in next st, ch 4, skip next sc, sc in next sc, ch 4, skip next sc, hdc in next st, ch 2, hdc in next st, (ch 6, sc in next st) 7 times; to **join,** ch 2, tr in first sc (21 sts, 16 ch-6 sps, 2 ch-2 sps, 2 ch-4 sps, 1 ch-7 lp).

NOTE: For **picot,** ch 4, sl st in last sc made.

Rnd 6: Ch 1, sc over joining tr, picot, ch 5, (sc in next ch sp, picot, ch 5) 10 times, skip next ch sp, sc in next sc, ch 5, skip next ch sp, (sc in next ch sp, picot, ch 5) 8 times, join with sl st in first sc, fasten off.

FINISHING

1: Apply fabric stiffener to each Side according to manufacturer's instructions. With wrong side of each Side piece together, place plastic wrap in between, shape pieces at same time. Let dry completely.

2: Using rnds 1-5 of Side as pattern, cut two heart shapes from tulle. Allowing ¼" for seam, sew together leaving small opening. Clip corners. Turn. Fill with potpourri. Sew opening closed.

3: Holding wrong sides of each Side together, glue picots together on last rnd, insert potpourri before closing.

4: Leaving 3" ends, starting at 2nd ch sp from center top, weave 1 yd. of rose ribbon through rnd 5 ending at second from last ch sp at center top. Glue ends together for hanging loop.

5: Leaving 3" ends, starting at center top, weave gold metallic thread through rnd 6. Glue ends to ends of rose ribbon.

6: Starting at center top, weave silver metallic thread through rnd 6, alternating from gold thread. Glue ends together at back of Heart.

7: With remaining rose ribbon, make two 2½" bows. Glue one bow to top of hanging loop. Glue other bow to center front of Heart.

8: Glue ribbon roses diagonally across bow at front of Heart.

9: Cut five 1" pieces of green ribbon. Fold each piece in half and glue ends together. Glue each piece around ribbon roses as desired.

10: Glue baby's breath around ribbon roses as desired.⚜

HEIRLOOM CROCHET TREASURES

SCALLOPED ANTIQUE EDGING

ESSENTIALS

SIZE: Edging is 1¼" wide.
MATERIALS: Size 30 crochet cotton — 120 yds. lt. blue; No. 13 steel crochet hook.

EDGING

Row 1: Ch 14, dc in 6th ch from hook, dc in each of next 2 chs, (ch 2, skip next 2 chs, dc in next ch) 2 times, turn (3 ch sps, 5 dc).

Row 2: Ch 5, skip next ch-2 sp, dc in next dc, ch

INSTRUCTIONS

2, skip next ch-2 sp, dc in each of next 3 dc, (2 dc, ch 3, 3 dc) in last ch sp, turn (9 dc).

Row 3: Ch 3, skip next 2 dc, (3 dc, ch 3, 2 dc) in next ch-3 sp, dc in next 5 dc, skip next ch-2 sp, tr in last ch sp, (ch 2, tr) 6 more times in same ch sp, skip end of row 1, dc in first ch of ch-14 on row 1, turn (7 tr, 11 dc).

Row 4: (Ch 5, sc in next tr) 7 times, dc in next 7 dc, (2 dc, ch 3, 3 dc) in next ch-3 sp, turn (7 ch-5

Continued on page 46

Designed by Carol Smith

HEART DOILY

ESSENTIALS

SIZE: 10" x 10½".

MATERIALS: Size 20 crochet cotton — 50 yds. white and 75 yds. pink variegated; tapestry needle; No. 8 steel crochet hook or size needed to obtain gauge.

GAUGE: One small shell = ½" across; 3 shell rows = 1".

NOTES: For **small shell (sm shell)**, (2 tr, ch 2, 2 tr) in next ch sp.

Ch-5 at beginning of each row counts as (tr, ch 1).

INSTRUCTIONS

DOILY

Row 1: Starting at center, with white, ch 5, sl st in first ch to form ring, ch 5, (2 tr, ch 2, 4 tr, ch 2, 4 tr, ch 2, 2 tr, ch 1, tr) in ring, turn (14 tr, 3 ch-2 sps, 2 ch-1 sps).

Row 2: Sl st in first ch-1 sp, ch 5, sm shell in first ch-2 sp, ch 2, (tr, ch 4, tr) in next ch-2 sp, ch 2, sm shell in next ch-2 sp, ch 1, tr in last ch-5, turn (4 tr, 2 sm shells, 2 ch-1 sps, 1 ch-4 sp).

Row 3: Sl st in first ch-1 sp, ch 5, sm shell in ch-2 sp of first sm shell, ch 1, 21 tr in next ch-4 sp, ch 1, sm shell in next sm shell, ch 1, tr in last ch-5, turn (23 tr, 4 ch-1 sps, 2 sm shells).

Rows 4-5: Ch 5, sm shell in first sm shell, ch 1, (tr in next tr, ch 1) 21 times, sm shell in next sm shell, ch 1, tr in last ch-5, turn (24 ch-1 sps, 23 tr, 2 sm shells).

Row 6: Sl st in first ch-1 sp, ch 5, sm shell in first sm shell, ch 2, skip next ch-1 sp, sc in next ch-1 sp, (ch 3, sc in next ch-1 sp) 19 times, ch 2, skip next ch-2 sp, sm shell in next sm shell, ch 1, tr in last ch-5, turn.

Row 7: Sl st in first ch-1 sp, ch 5, sm shell in first sm shell, ch 3, skip next ch-2 sp, (sc in next ch-3 lp, ch 3) 19 times, skip next ch-2 sp, sm shell in next sm shell, ch 1, tr in last ch-5, turn (20 ch-3 sps, 2 sm shells, 2 tr, 2 ch-1 sps).

Rows 8-23: Ch 5, sm shell in first sm shell, ch 3, skip next ch-3 sp, (sc in next ch-3 sp, ch 3) across to last ch-3 sp, skip last ch-3 sp, sm shell in next sm shell, ch 1, tr in 4th ch of ch-5, turn, ending with 4 ch-3 sps, 2 sm shells, 2 tr and 2 ch-1 sps in last row.

Row 24: Sl st in first ch-1 sp, ch 5; to **tr next 2 sm shells tog,** *yo 2 times, insert hook in ch-2 sp of next shell, yo, draw lp through, (yo, draw through 2 lps on hook) 2 times*, skip next 4 ch-3 sps; repeat between **, yo, draw through all 3 lps on hook; ch 1, tr in last ch-5, turn.

Row 25: Sl st in first ch-1 sp, ch 3, dc in last ch-5, **do not** turn, fasten off.

NOTES: For **beginning large shell (beg lg shell),** (ch 4, 2 tr, ch 2, 3 tr) in same sp.

For **large shell (lg shell),** (3 tr, ch 2, 3 tr) in next sp.

Rnd 26: Working around outer edge, over tr at end of each row, join pink variegated with sl st over dc just made, beg lg shell, (skip next row, lg shell in next row) 9 times, lg shell in each of next 2 rows, skip next row, lg shell in next row, skip next row, sc in next row, sc in ch-5 ring made on row 1, sc in next row, skip next row, lg shell in next row, skip next row, lg shell in each of next 3 rows, skip next row, (lg shell in next row, skip next row) 8 times, lg shell in ch-3 sp of row 25; to **join,** ch 2, sl st in top of ch-4, fasten off (26 lg shells, 3 sc, 1 ch-2 sp).

Rnd 27: Join white with sl st in joining ch-2 sp of last rnd, ch 4, 2 tr in same sp, ch 1, (lg shell in next lg shell, ch 1) 13 times, skip next sc, sc in next sc, ch 1, skip next sc, (lg shell in next lg shell, ch 1) 13 times, 3 tr in joining ch-2 sp of last rnd, join as before, fasten off.

Rnd 28: Join pink variegated with sl st in joining ch-2 sp of last rnd, ch 4, 2 tr in same sp, ch 2, (lg shell in next lg shell, ch 2) 13 times, sc in next sc, ch 2; repeat between ( ) 13 more times, 3 tr in joining ch sp of last rnd, join, fasten off (28 ch-2 sps, 26 lg shells).

Rnds 29-33: Repeat rnd 28, alternating colors and increasing ch sps by one each rnd, ending with white, 26 shells and 28 ch-7 lps on last rnd (**do not** increase joining ch-2 sp).

Rnd 34: Join pink variegated with sl st in joining ch-2 sp of last rnd, ch 4, 2 tr in same sp, (ch 7, sc in next ch-7 lp, ch 7, lg shell in next lg shell) 13 times, ch 8, sc in next sc, ch 8, (lg shell in next lg shell, ch 7, sc in next ch-7 lp, ch 7) 13 times, 3 tr in joining ch sp, join, fasten off.

Continued on next page

SCALLOPED ANTIQUE EDGING

Continued from page 43

sps, 12 dc, 1 ch-3 sp).

Row 5: Ch 3, skip next 2 dc, 3 dc in next ch-3 sp, ch 3, dc in each of next 3 dc, (ch 2, skip next dc, dc in next dc) 2 times leaving remaining sts and ch sps unworked, turn.

Row 6: Ch 5, skip next ch-2 sp, dc in next dc, ch 2, dc in each of next 3 dc, (2 dc, ch 3, 3 dc) in next ch-3 sp leaving remaining sts unworked, turn.

Row 7: Ch 3, skip next 2 dc, (3 dc, ch 3, 2 dc) in next ch-3 sp, dc in next 5 dc, skip next ch-2 sp, tr in next ch-5 sp, (ch 2, tr in same ch sp) 6 times, sc in first dc of row 4, turn.

Row 8: Repeat row 4.

Repeat rows 5-8 consecutively, until desired length is reached. Fasten off at end of last row. ❖

HEART DOILY

Continued from page 45

Rnd 35: Join white with sc in joining ch-2 sp of last rnd, ch 3, sc in same sp, ch 5, (sc in next ch-7 lp, ch 5) 2 times, *(sc, ch 3, sc) in next lg shell, ch 5, (sc in next ch-7 lp, ch 5) 2 times*; repeat between ** 11 times, (sc, ch 3, sc) in next lg shell, ch 6, (sc, ch 3, sc) in next ch-8 lp, ch 5, skip next sc, (sc, ch 3, sc) in next ch-8 lp, ch 6; repeat between ** 13 more times, join with sl st in first sc, fasten off. ❖

SUMMER COLORS

Continued from page 29

chs, (2 tr in next ch, ch 3, tr in next ch, skip next 3 chs) 2 times, skip next sc; repeat from * around, join with sl st in top of ch-4.

Rnd 17: Ch 4, tr in next tr, skip next ch sp, tr in next tr, ch 4, *tr in each of next 2 tr, skip next ch sp, tr in next tr, ch 4; repeat from * around, join.

Rnd 18: Ch 4, tr in next tr, ch 5, tr in next tr, skip next ch sp, *tr in each of next 2 tr, ch 5, tr in next tr, skip next ch sp; repeat from * around, join, fasten off.

Rnd 19: Join pink with sl st in any ch sp, ch 4, 4 tr in same sp, ch 5, sc in next ch sp, ch 5, *5 tr in next ch sp, ch 5, sc in next ch-2 sp, ch 5; repeat from * around, join.

NOTES: For **beginning cluster shell (beg cl shell),** ch 4, ◊yo 2 times, insert hook in same st, *yo, draw lp through, (yo, draw through 2 lps on hook) 2 times*, yo 2 times, insert hook in next tr; repeat between **, yo, draw through all lps on hook, ch 3, [yo 2 times, insert hook in same tr as last st made; repeat between ** one more time, yo 2 times, insert hook in next tr; repeat between ** one more time]; repeat between [ ], yo, draw through all 5 lps on hook, ch 3; repeat between [ ] one more time, yo 2 times, insert hook in same tr as last st made; repeat between ** one more time, yo, draw through all 4 lps on hook◊.

For **cluster shell (cl shell),** yo 2 times, insert hook in next tr, yo, draw lp through, (yo, draw through 2 lps on hook) 2 times; repeat between ◊◊ in beg cl shell.

Rnd 20: Beg cl shell, ch 9, skip next 2 ch sps, *cl shell, ch 9, skip next 2 ch sps; repeat from * around, join with sl st in top of beg cl, fasten off (36 cl shells).

Rnd 21: Join green with sc in any ch-9 sp, 8 sc in same sp, 3 sc in each ch-3 sp and 9 sc in each ch-9 sp around, join with sl st in first sc.

Rnd 22: Sl st in next 4 sts, ch 1, sc in same st, ch 5, skip next 6 sts, tr in next st, ch 3, tr in next st, ch 5, skip next 6 sts, [sc in next st, ch 5, skip next 6 sts, tr in next st, ch 3, tr in next st, ch 5, skip next 6 sts]; repeat between [ ] around, join.

Rnd 23: Ch 7, tr in same st, ch 7, skip next ch-5 sp, sc in next ch-3 sp, ch 7, skip next ch-5 sp, *(tr, ch 3, tr) in next sc, ch 7, skip next ch-5 sp, sc in next ch-3 sp, ch 7, skip next ch-5 sp; repeat from * around, join with sl st in 4th ch of ch-7.

Rnd 24: Sl st in next 2 chs, ch 9, sl st in 4th ch from hook, ch 1, tr in same ch, *ch 8, skip next ch-7 sp, sc in next sc, ch 8, skip next ch-7 sp*, [(tr, ch 5, sl st in 4th ch from hook, ch 1, tr) in next ch-3 sp; repeat between **]; repeat between [ ] around, join with sl st in 4th ch of ch-9, fasten off. ⚜

GALAXY TABLE TOPPER

Continued from page 30

For **joining ch-5 lp,** ch 2, sc in ch-5 lp of next motif, ch 2.

Join motifs according to diagram.

Rnds 1-14: Repeat same rnds of Motif No. 1.

Rnd 15: Repeat same rnd of Motif No. 1 using joining ch-15 lps and joining ch-5 lps when joining motifs.

EDGING

Working around entire outer edge, join with sc in any ch-5 lp, (2 sc, ch 5, 3 sc) in same lp, *ch 5, (sc in next 4 sc, ch 5) 3 times, sc in first 8 chs of next ch-15 lp, ch 5, sc in last 7 chs of same lp, ch 5, (sc in next 4 sc, ch 5) 3 times*, [see diagram, (3 sc, ch 5, 3 sc) in next ch-5 lp — **or** — 2 sc in each of next 2 joining ch-5 lps, ch 5; repeat between **]; repeat between [ ] around, join with sl st in first sc, fasten off. ⚜

JOINING DIAGRAM

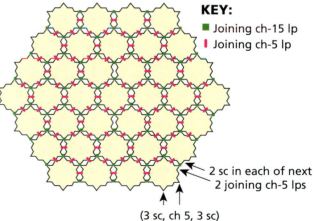

KEY:
- ■ Joining ch-15 lp
- ❙ Joining ch-5 lp

2 sc in each of next 2 joining ch-5 lps

(3 sc, ch 5, 3 sc)

STARFLOWER DOILY

Continued from page 33

lp, ch 15) 7 times, (sc in next ch lp, ch 11) 9 times, (sc in next ch lp, ch 15) 8 times, (sc in next ch lp, ch 11) 4 times, join (33 sc, 18 ch-11 lps, 15 ch-15 lps).

Rnd 7: Ch 3, dc in each ch and in each sc around, join with sl st in top of ch-3 (456 dc).

Rnd 8: Ch 1, sc in same st, ch 7, skip next 3 sts, (sc in next st, ch 7, skip next 3 sts) around, join with sl st in first sc (114 ch-7 lps).

NOTE: For **dc shell**, (4 dc, ch 2, 4 dc) in next ch lp.

Rnd 9: Sl st in next 4 chs, ch 1, sc in same lp, dc shell, (sc in next ch lp, dc shell) around, join (57 dc shells, 57 sc).

Rnd 10: Sl st in next 4 dc, sl st in next ch-2 sp, ch 4, (2 tr, picot, ch 13, sl st in 13th ch from hook, picot, sl st in top of last tr made, 3 tr) in same sp, ch 5, sc in next sc, ch 5, *(3 tr, picot, ch 13, sl st in 13th ch from hook, picot, sl st in top of last tr made, 3 tr) in next ch-2 sp, ch 5, sc in next sc, ch 5; repeat from * around, join with sl st in top of ch-4, fasten off (57 ch-13 lps).

NOTES: For **beginning tr shell (beg tr shell),** ch 4, (4 tr, ch 2, 5 tr) in same lp.

For **tr shell,** (5 tr, ch 2, 5 tr) in next ch lp.

Rnd 11: Join with sl st in any ch-13 lp, beg tr shell, ch 1, (tr shell in next ch-13 lp, ch 1) around, join (57 tr shells, 57 ch-1 sps).

Rnd 12: Sl st in next 4 tr, sl st in ch-2 sp of same tr shell, ch 4, (2 tr, make 3 picots, sl st in top of last tr made, 3 tr) in same sp, ch 7, (sc, ch 5, sc) in next ch-1 sp between shells, ch 7, *(3 tr, make 3 picots, sl st in top of last tr made, 3 tr) in ch-2 sp of next tr shell, ch 7, (sc, ch 5, sc) in next ch-1 sp between shells, ch 7; repeat from * around, join, fasten off.⚜

JOINING DIAGRAM

For left-handed crocheters, join rnd 1 of Border here.

For right-handed crocheters, join rnd 1 of Border here.

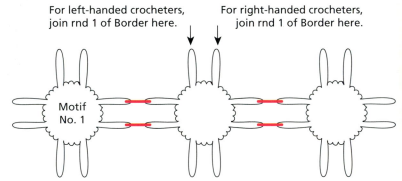

Motif No. 1

NEEDLEWORK TOOL HOLDERS

Continued from page 36

ch-2 sp, dc in next dc, ch 6, skip next 2 dc, dc in next dc, 2 dc in next ch-2 sp, dc in next cl, ch 2, (dc in next dc or in next cl, ch 2) 6 times, dc in last 4 dc, turn (28 dc, 14 ch-2 sps).

Row 6: Ch 3, dc in each of next 3 dc, ch 2, dc in next dc, h-cl, cl, h-cl, dc in next dc, (ch 2, dc in next dc) 3 times, 2 dc in next ch-2 sp, dc in next dc, ch 6, skip next 3 dc, tr in next ch-6 lp, ch 6, skip next 3 dc, dc in next dc, 2 dc in next ch-2 sp, dc in next dc, (ch 2, dc in next dc) 3 times, h-cl, cl, h-cl, dc in next dc, ch 2, dc in last 4 dc, turn (24 dc, 8 ch-2 sps, 4 h-cls, 2 cls).

Row 7: Ch 3, dc in each of next 3 dc, ch 2, dc in next dc, ch 2, skip next h-cl, cl, ch 2, skip next h-cl, dc in next dc, (ch 2, dc in next dc) 2 times, 2 dc in next ch-2 sp, dc in next dc, ch 7, skip next 3 dc, sc in next ch-6 lp, sc in

next tr, sc in next ch-6 lp, ch 7, skip next 3 dc, dc in next dc, 2 dc in next ch-2 sp, (dc in next dc, ch 2) 3 times, skip next h-cl, cl, ch 2, skip next h-cl, dc in next dc, ch 2, dc in last 4 dc, turn (22 dc, 10 ch-2 sps, 2 cls).

Row 8: Ch 3, dc in each of next 3 dc, (ch 2, dc in next dc or in next cl) 4 times, 2 dc in next ch-2 sp, dc in next dc, ch 7, skip next 3 dc, sc in next ch-7 lp, sc in each of next 3 sc, sc in next ch-7 lp, ch 7, skip next 3 dc, dc in next dc, 2 dc in next ch-2 sp, (dc in next dc or in next cl, ch 2) 4 times, dc in last 4 dc, turn.

Row 9: Ch 3, dc in each of next 3 dc, (ch 2, dc in next dc) 3 times, 2 dc in next ch-2 sp, dc in next dc, ch 8, skip next 3 dc, sc in next ch-7 lp, sc in next 5 sc, sc in next ch-7 lp, ch 8, skip next 3 dc, dc in next dc, 2 dc in next ch-2 sp, (dc in next dc, ch 2) 3 times, dc in last 4 dc, turn.

Row 10: Ch 3, dc in each of next 3 dc, ch 2, (dc in next dc, ch 2) 3 times, skip next 2 dc, dc in next dc, 3 dc in next ch-8 lp, ch 7, skip next sc, sc in next 5 sc, ch 7, skip next sc, 3 dc in next ch-8 lp, dc in next dc, ch 2, skip next 2 dc, (dc in next dc, ch 2) 3 times, dc in last 4 dc, turn.

Row 11: Ch 3, dc in each of next 3 dc, ch 2, dc in next dc, h-cl, cl, h-cl, (dc in next dc, ch 2) 2 times, skip next 2 dc, dc in next dc, 3 dc in next ch-7 lp, ch 7, skip next sc, sc in each of next 3 sc, ch 7, skip next sc, 3 dc in next ch-7 lp, dc in next dc, ch 2, skip next 2 dc, dc in next dc, ch 2, dc in next dc, h-cl, cl, h-cl, dc in next dc, ch 2, dc in last 4 dc, turn.

Row 12: Ch 3, dc in each of next 3 dc, ch 2, dc in next dc, ch 2, skip next h-cl, cl, ch 2, skip next h-cl, (dc in next dc, ch 2) 3 times, skip next 2 dc, dc in next dc, 3 dc in next ch-7 lp, ch 4, skip next sc, tr in next sc, ch 4, skip next sc, 3 dc in next ch-7 lp, dc in next dc, ch 2, skip next 2 dc, (dc in next dc, ch 2) 3 times, skip next h-cl, cl, ch 2, skip next h-cl, dc in next dc, ch 2, dc in last 4 dc, turn.

Row 13: Ch 3, dc in each of next 3 dc, ch 2, (dc in next dc or in next cl, ch 2) 6 times, skip next 2 dc, dc in next dc, 3 dc in next ch-4 lp, ch 2, skip next tr, 3 dc in next ch-4 lp, dc in next dc, ch 2, skip next 2 dc, (dc in next dc, ch 2) 6 times, dc in last 4 dc, turn.

Row 14: Ch 3, dc in each of next 3 dc, ch 2, dc in next dc, *h-cl, cl, h-cl, dc in next dc, (ch 2, dc in next dc) 3 times, h-cl, cl, h-cl*, skip next 2 dc, dc in next dc, 2 dc in next ch-2 sp, dc in next dc, skip next 2 dc; repeat between **, dc in next dc, ch 2, dc in last 4 dc, turn.

Row 15: Ch 3, dc in each of next 3 dc, ch 2, dc in next dc, ch 2, skip next h-cl, cl, ch 2, skip next h-cl, (dc in next dc, ch 2) 4 times, skip next h-cl, cl, ch 2, skip next h-cl, dc in next dc, ch 2, skip next 2 dc, dc in next dc, ch 2, skip next h-cl, cl, ch 2, skip next h-cl, (dc in next dc, ch 2) 4 times, skip next h-cl, cl, ch 2, skip next h-cl, dc in next dc, ch 2, dc in last 4 dc, turn.

Row 16: Ch 3, dc in each of next 3 dc, ch 2, (dc in next dc or in next cl, ch 2) across to last 4 dc, dc in last 4 dc, turn.

Row 17: Ch 3, dc in each of next 3 dc, ch 2, (dc in next

dc, ch 2) across to last 4 dc, dc in last 4 dc, turn.

Rows 18-31: Repeat rows 3-16.

Row 32: Ch 3, dc in each dc and 2 dc in each ch-2 sp across, turn (58 dc).

Rnd 33: Working around outer edge, in sts and in ends of rows, ch 3, 6 dc in same st, *skip next 2 sts, (5 dc in next st, skip next 2 sts, sc in next st, skip next 2 sts) across to next corner st, 7 dc in corner st, skip first row, sc in top of next row, (5 dc in top of next row, sc in top of next row) across to next corner*, 7 dc in same corner; repeat between **, join with sl st in top of ch-3, fasten off.

FINISHING

1: For flowers, with one long edge of Case facing you, embroider 4 yellow Lazy-Daisy Stitches (see Stitch Guide) over sc sts on rows 7-11 and over rows 22-26 as shown in diagram. For large French Knot, wrap floss around needle 5 times, complete as regular French Knot. Make one brown large French Knot centered above each flower.

2: For stem, embroider one green Straight Stitch under each flower as shown. With sewing needle and thread, sew one pearl to center of each set of clusters.

3: For lining, cut one piece felt 7" x 8½". For pocket, cut one piece felt 3½" x 8½". To prevent felt from stretching, sew ribbon to one long edge of each piece, wrapping ends under ½" on each side. (For best results, top stitch along both sides of ribbon.)

4: Fold down 1¼" on one long edge of lining, having ribbon on top and facing you (see diagram). Top stitch close to fold. With ribbon on top and facing you, place pocket over lining, having lower edges and sides even. (Ribbon edges are now parallel to each other.) Sew pocket to lining around bottom and sides. Stitch twenty ⅜"-wide sections as shown in diagram.

5: With sewing needle and thread, stitch lining to wrong side of Case around base of rnd 33, making sure top of lining and top of flowers are facing same direction. Cut remaining ribbon in half. Turn one end of each piece under and sew to center of lining on each inside end.⚜

FLOWER DIAGRAM

ASSEMBLY DIAGRAM

FLAP
1¼"
LINING
POCKET

HOLIDAY HEIRLOOMS

Experience the joy of this uplifting array of outstanding crocheted ornaments and table accents that radiate with lasting beauty. These magical designs transform the ordinary into the extraordinary, lending graceful appeal to your seasonal decor. Start a new holiday tradition in your home by decorating with captivating old-fashioned originals.

Designed by Lucille LaFlamme

PINEAPPLE APPEAL

ESSENTIALS

SIZE: 50" x 62½".

MATERIALS: Size 30 cotton thread — 3,150 yds. ecru; No. 12 steel crochet hook or size needed to obtain gauge.

GAUGE: Rnd 1 = 9/16" across. Each Motif is 6¼" square.

INSTRUCTIONS

MOTIF NO. 1

Rnd 1: Ch 8, sl st in first ch to form ring, ch 3, 23 dc in ring, join with sl st in top of ch-3 (24 dc).

Rnd 2: Ch 6, dc in same st, *ch 3, skip next 2 sts, dc in next st, ch 3, skip next 2 sts*, [(dc, ch 3, dc) in next st; repeat between **]; repeat between [ ] around, join with sl st in 3rd ch of ch-6 (12 dc, 12 ch-3 sps).

Rnd 3: Sl st in first ch-3 sp, (ch 4, 4 tr, ch 3, 5 tr) in same sp, *ch 2, skip next ch-3 sp, (dc, ch 3, dc) in next st, ch 2, skip next ch-3 sp*, [(5 tr, ch 3, 5 tr) in next ch-3 sp; repeat between **]; repeat between [ ] around, join with sl st in top of ch-4 (40 tr, 8 dc, 8 ch-2 sps, 4 ch-3 sps).

NOTES: For **beginning large treble cluster (beg lg tr cl),** ch 4, *yo 2 times, insert hook in next st, yo, draw through st, (yo, draw through 2 lps on hook) 2 times; repeat from * 3 times, yo, draw through all 5 lps on hook.

For **large treble cluster (lg tr cl),** *yo 2 times, insert hook in next st, yo, draw through st, (yo, draw through 2 lps on hook) 2 times; repeat from * 4 times, yo, draw through all 6 lps on hook.

Rnd 4: Beg lg tr cl, *ch 3, 9 tr in next ch-3 sp, ch 3, lg tr cl, ch 3, skip next ch-2 sp, (tr, ch 3, tr) in next ch-3 sp*, [ch 3, skip next ch-2 sp, lg tr cl; repeat between **]; repeat between [ ] around; to **join,** dc in top of first cl (44 tr, 20 ch-3 sps, 8 lg tr cl).

Rnd 5: Ch 3, dc in same st, *ch 6, skip next lg tr cl, sc in next st, (ch 3, sc in next st) 8 times, ch 6, skip next lg tr cl, 2 dc in next st, ch 3*, [2 dc in next st; repeat between **]; repeat between [ ] around, join with sl st in top of ch-3 (36 ch-3 sps, 16 dc).

Rnd 6: Ch 3, dc in next st, *ch 6, skip next ch-6 sp, sc in next ch-3 sp, (ch 3, sc in next ch-3 sp) 7 times, ch 6, skip next ch-6 sp, dc in each of next 2 sts, ch 3*, [dc in each of next 2 sts; repeat between **]; repeat between [ ] around, join (32 ch-3 sps, 16 dc).

Rnd 7: Ch 3, dc in same st, *dc in next st, ch 6, skip next ch-6 sp, sc in next ch-3 sp, (ch 3, sc in next ch-3 sp) 6 times, ch 6, skip next ch-6 sp, dc in next st, 2 dc in next st, ch 3*, [2 dc in next st; repeat between **]; repeat between [ ] around, join (28 ch-3 sps, 24 dc).

Rnd 8: Ch 3, dc in each of next 2 sts, *ch 6, skip next ch-6 sp, sc in next ch-3 sp, (ch 4, sc in next ch-3 sp) 5 times, ch 6, skip next ch-6 sp, dc in each of next 3 sts, ch 5*, [dc in each of next 3 sts; repeat between **]; repeat between [ ] around, join (24 dc, 20 ch-4 sps, 4 ch-5 sps).

NOTES: For **beginning small treble cluster (beg sm tr cl),** ch 4, *yo 2 times, insert hook in next st, yo, draw through st, (yo, draw through 2 lps on hook) 2 times; repeat from *, yo, draw through all 3 lps on hook.

For **small treble cluster (sm tr cl),** *yo 2 times, insert hook in next st, yo, draw through st, (yo, draw through 2 lps on hook) 2 times; repeat from * 2 times, yo, draw through all 4 lps on hook.

Rnd 9: Beg sm tr cl, *ch 7, skip next ch-6 sp, sc in next ch-4 sp, (ch 5, sc in next ch-4 sp) 4 times, ch 7, skip next ch-6 sp, sm tr cl, ch 5, tr in 3rd ch of next ch-5 sp, ch 5*, [sm tr cl; repeat between **]; repeat between [ ] around, join with sl st in top of first cl (24 ch-5 sps, 8 sm tr cl, 4 tr).

Rnd 10: (Beg sm tr cl, ch 5, sm tr cl) in top of first cl, *ch 7, skip next ch-7 sp, sc in next ch-5 sp, (ch 5, sc in next ch-5 sp) 3 times, ch 7, skip next ch-7 sp, (sm tr cl, ch 5, sm tr cl) in top of next cl, ch 5, (tr, ch 5, tr) in next tr, ch 5*, [(sm tr cl, ch 5, sm tr cl) in top of next cl; repeat between **]; repeat between [ ] around, join (32 ch-5 sps, 16 sm tr cl, 8 tr).

Rnd 11: Sl st in next ch-5 sp, (beg sm tr cl, ch 5, sm tr cl, ch 5, sm tr cl) in same sp, *ch 9, skip next ch-7 sp, sc in next ch-5 sp, (ch 5, sc in next ch-5 sp) 2 times, ch 9, skip next ch-7 sp, (sm tr cl, ch 5, sm tr cl, ch 5, sm tr cl) in next ch-5 sp, ch 5, 2 tr in next st, ch 5, tr in 3rd ch of next ch-5 sp, ch

Continued on page 64

HEIRLOOM CROCHET TREASURES

SNOW CRYSTALS

GAUGE: Rnds 1-2 = 1¼" across.

ESSENTIALS

SNOWBALLS

SIZE: Each Snowball covers 2½" satin ball ornament.

MATERIALS FOR ONE: *Size 10 bedspread cotton — 50 yds. white; 2½" satin-covered ball ornament; 7" matching ⅛" satin ribbon; 1 yd. matching ¼" satin picot ribbon; two 1"-wide iridescent artificial flowers; two 1"-long pearl-head straight pins; craft glue or hot glue gun; tapestry needle; No. 6 steel crochet hook or size needed to obtain gauge.

INSTRUCTIONS

BLUE SNOWBALL

Rnd 1: Ch 6, sl st in first ch to form ring, ch 1, 12 sc in ring, join with sl st in first sc (12 sc).

Rnd 2: Ch 5, (dc in next st, ch 2) around, join with sl st in 3rd ch of ch-5 (12 dc, 12 ch-2 sps).

Rnd 3: Ch 1, sc in same st, (sc, ch 3, sc) in next ch sp, *sc in next dc, (sc, ch 3, sc) in next ch sp; repeat from * around, join with sl st in first sc (36 sc, 12 ch-3 lps).

Rnd 4: Ch 6, skip next sc, skip next ch lp, skip next sc, *dc in next sc, ch 3, skip next sc, skip next ch lp, skip next sc; repeat from * around, join with sl st in 3rd ch of ch-6 (12 dc, 12 ch-3 sps).

Rnd 5: Repeat rnd 3.

Rnd 6: Ch 7, skip next sc, skip next ch lp, skip next sc, *dc in next sc, ch 4, skip next sc, skip next ch lp, skip next sc; repeat from * around, join with sl st in 3rd ch of ch-7.

Rnd 7: Ch 1, sc in same st, (2 sc, ch 3, 2 sc) in next ch sp, *sc in next dc, (2 sc, ch 3, 2 sc) in next ch sp; repeat from * around, join with sl st in first sc (60 sc, 12 ch-3 lps).

Place ball ornament inside rnds 1-7.

Rnd 8: Working around ornament, ch 7, skip next 2 sc, skip next ch lp, skip next 2 sc, *dc in next sc, ch 4, skip next 2 sc, skip next ch lp, skip next 2 sc; repeat from * around, join with sl st in 3rd ch of ch-7.

Rnd 9: Ch 1, sc in same st, (2 sc, ch 3, sc) in next ch sp, *sc in next dc, (2 sc, ch 3, sc) in next ch sp; repeat from * around, join with sl st in first sc.

Rnd 10: Ch 5, skip next 2 sc, skip next ch lp, skip next sc, *dc in next sc, ch 2, skip next 2 sc, skip next ch lp, skip next sc; repeat from * around, join with sl st in 3rd ch of ch-5.

Rnd 11: Ch 1, sc in same st, 2 sc in each ch sp and sc in each dc around, join with sl st in first sc (36 sc).

Rnd 12: Ch 3, skip next 2 sc, (dc in next sc, skip next 2 sc) around, join with sl st in top of ch-3 (12 dc).

Rnd 13: Ch 1, sc in same st, skip next dc, (sc in next dc, skip next dc) around, join with sl st in first sc, fasten off (6 sc).

FINISHING

1: Fold 14" of picot ribbon into 1½" bow, forming 4 loops. Push pin through center, trim ends.

2: For **hanging loop,** overlap ends of ⅛" satin ribbon, push same pin through overlapped ends. Push pin into top of Snowball through center of rnd 13; glue to secure.

3: Trim stem off one flower, glue over bow.

4: Fold 22" of picot ribbon into 2" bow, forming 8 loops. Push pin through center, trim ends. Push pin into bottom of Snowball through center of rnd 1; glue to secure.

5: Trim stem off 2nd flower, glue over bow.

PEACH SNOWBALL

Rnd 1: Ch 6, sl st in first ch to form ring, ch 1, 10 sc in ring, join with sl st in first sc (10 sc).

Rnd 2: Ch 4, dc in same st, ch 1, *(dc, ch 1, dc) in next st, ch 1; repeat from * around, join with sl st in 3rd ch of ch-4 (20 dc, 20 ch sps).

Rnd 3: Sl st in first ch sp, ch 1, sc in same sp, *ch 2, skip next ch sp, (2 dc, ch 2, 2 dc) in next ch sp, ch 2, skip next ch sp*, [sc in next ch sp; repeat between **]; repeat between [ ] around, join with sl st in first sc (20 dc, 15

ch-2 sps, 5 sc).

Rnd 4: Ch 1, sc in same st, *ch 3, skip next ch-2 sp, (3 dc, ch 3, 3 dc) in next ch-2 sp, ch 3, skip next ch-2 sp*, [sc in next sc; repeat between **]; repeat between [ ] around, join.

Rnd 5: Ch 1, sc in same st, *ch 4, skip next ch-3 sp, (4 dc, ch 4, 4 dc) in next ch-3 sp, ch 4, skip next ch-3 sp*, [sc in next sc; repeat between **]; repeat between [ ] around, join.

Rnd 6: Ch 1, sc in same st, *ch 5, skip next ch-4 sp, (5 dc, ch 5, 5 dc) in next ch-4 sp, ch 5, skip next ch-4 sp*, [sc in next sc; repeat between **]; repeat between [ ] around, join.

Rnd 7: Ch 1, sc in same st, *ch 6, skip next ch-5 sp, (6 dc, ch 3, 6 dc) in next ch-5 sp, ch 6, skip next ch-5 sp*, [sc in next sc; repeat between **]; repeat between [ ] around, join.

Place ball ornament inside rnds 1-7.

Rnd 8: Working around ornament, sl st in next 6 chs, sl st in next 6 dc, sl st in first ch of next ch-6 sp, ch 1, sc in same sp, skip next 2 ch-6 sps, *sc in next ch-3 sp, skip next 2 ch-6 sps; repeat from * around, join, fasten off (5 sc).

FINISHING
Work same as Blue Snowball Finishing.

SNOWFLAKES

SIZE: Each Snowflake is 4" across when stiffened.

MATERIALS FOR ONE: Size 10 bedspread cotton — 25 yds. white; 6" of ¼" satin picot ribbon; silver metallic thread; fabric stiffener; craft glue or hot glue gun; tapestry needle; No. 6 steel crochet hook or size needed to obtain gauge.

GAUGE: Rnds 1-2 = 1¼" across.

BLUE SNOWFLAKE

Rnds 1-4: Repeat same rnds of Blue Snowball.

Rnd 5: Ch 1, sc in same st, (3 sc, ch 3, 2 sc) in next ch sp, *sc in next dc, (3 sc, ch 3, 2 sc) in next ch sp; repeat from * around, join with sl st in first sc.

Rnd 6: Ch 8, skip next 3 sc, skip next ch lp, skip next 2 sc, *dc in next sc, ch 5, skip next 3 sc, skip next ch lp, skip next 2 sc; repeat from * around, join with sl st in 3rd ch of ch-8.

Rnd 7: Ch 1, sc in same st, (4 sc, ch 3, 3 sc) in next ch sp, *sc in next dc, (4 sc, ch 3, 3 sc) in next ch sp; repeat from * around, join with sl st in first sc, fasten off.

FINISHING

1: Apply liquid stiffener to Snowflake according to manufacturer's instructions. Shape; let dry completely.

2: Tie ribbon into small bow, trim ends. Glue over center of rnd 1 on Snowflake.

3: With tapestry needle, thread 8" piece silver thread through any ch lp on last rnd. Tie ends in knot, trim.

Continued on page 61

Designed by Carol Smith

FESTIVE DOILY

ESSENTIALS

SIZE: 11" square after blocking.

MATERIALS: Size 10 bedspread cotton — 175 yds. green and 80 yds. red; No. 8 steel crochet hook or size needed to obtain gauge.

GAUGE: Rnds 1-5 = 2" across.

INSTRUCTIONS

MOTIF NO. 1

Rnd 1: With red, ch 6, sl st in first ch to form ring, ch 1, 16 sc in ring, join with sl st in first sc (16 sc).

Rnd 2: Ch 1, sc in first st, ch 3, skip next st, *sc in next st, ch 3, skip next st; repeat from * around, join (8 ch sps).

Rnd 3: Sl st in first ch sp, (ch 2, 5 dc, hdc) in same sp, (hdc, 5 dc, hdc) in each ch sp around, join with sl st in top of ch-2, fasten off.

Rnd 4: Working behind rnd 3, join red with sc in any unworked sc of rnd 2, ch 5, (sc in next sc of rnd 2, ch 5) around, join.

Rnd 5: Sl st in first ch lp, (ch 3, 7 tr, dc) in same lp, (dc, 7 tr, dc) in each ch lp around, join with sl st in top of ch-3, fasten off (72 sts).

Rnd 6: Join green with sc in center st of any 7-tr group on rnd 5, ch 3, sc in same st, *ch 6, skip next 8 sts, sc in next st, ch 6, skip next 8 sts*, [(sc, ch 3, sc) in next st; repeat between **]; repeat between [ ] around, join with sl st in first sc (8 ch-6 lps, 4 ch-3 sps).

Rnd 7: Sl st in first ch-3 sp, ch 4, 11 tr in same sp, *ch 4, (sc in next ch-6 lp, ch 4) 2 times*, [12 tr in next ch-3 sp; repeat between **]; repeat between [ ] around, join with sl st in top of ch-4 (48 tr, 12 ch-4 sps).

NOTES: For **beginning cluster (beg cl)**, ch 3, yo 2 times, insert hook in next st, yo, draw lp through, (yo, draw through 2 lps on hook) 3 times.

For **cluster (cl)**, *yo 2 times, insert hook in next st, yo, draw lp through, (yo, draw through 2 lps on hook) 2 times; repeat from *, yo, draw through all 3 lps on hook.

Rnd 8: Sl st in next tr, beg cl, *tr in next 6 tr, cl, ch 5, skip next tr, (sc in next ch-4 sp, ch 5) 3 times*, [skip next tr, cl; repeat between **]; repeat between [ ] around, join with sl st in top of beg cl (24 tr, 16 ch-5 lps, 8 cls).

Rnd 9: Sl st in next tr, beg cl, *tr in each of next 2 tr, cl, ch 6, skip next cl, (sc in next ch-5 lp, ch 6) 4 times*, [skip next cl, cl; repeat between **]; repeat between [ ] around, join (20 ch-5 lps, 8 cls, 8 tr).

Rnd 10: Sl st in next tr, beg cl, *ch 7, skip next cl, (sc in next ch-6 lp, ch 7) 5 times, skip next cl, cl; repeat from * around to last 5 ch-6 lps, skip next cl, (ch 7, sc in next ch-6 lp) 5 times; to **join,** ch 3, tr in top of beg cl (24 ch-7 lps, 4 cls).

Rnd 11: Ch 1, sc over joining tr just made, ch 8, (sc in next ch-7 lp, ch 8) around, join, fasten off (24 ch-8 lps).

MOTIFS NO. 2-4

Rnds 1-10: Repeat same rnds of Motif No. 1.

NOTES: For **joining ch-8 lp,** ch 4, sc in ch-8 lp of next motif, ch 4.

Rnd 11: Repeat same rnd of Motif No. 1 using joining ch-8 lps when joining Motifs according to Joining Diagram on page 63.

BORDER

NOTES: For **beginning shell (beg shell),** (ch 4, 2 tr, ch 3, 3 tr) in same lp.

For **shell,** (3 tr, ch 3, 3 tr) in next ch lp.

Rnd 1: Join green with sl st in any corner ch lp, beg shell, ch 4, sc in next ch lp, ch 4, *shell in next ch lp or over sc on next joining ch lp between motifs, ch 4, sc in next ch lp, ch 4; repeat from * around, join with sl st in top of ch-4 (48 ch-4 sps, 24 shells).

Rnd 2: Sl st in next 2 sts, sl st in next ch-3 sp, (beg shell, ch 1, shell) in same sp, [ch 4, (sc in next ch-4 sp, ch 4) 2 times, *shell in ch-3 sp of next shell, ch 4, (sc in next ch-4 sp, ch 4) 2 times; repeat from * around to next corner shell], ◊(shell, ch 1, shell) in next corner shell; repeat between [ ]; repeat from ◊ around, join (72 ch-4 sps, 28 shells, 4 ch-1 sps).

Rnd 3: Sl st in next 2 sts, sl st in first ch-3 sp, ch 1, (sc, ch 3, sc) in same sp, [ch 2, (sc, ch 3, sc) in next ch-1 sp, ch 2, *(sc, ch 3, sc) in next shell, ch 2, sc in next ch-4 sp, (ch 4, sc in next ch-4 sp) 2 times, ch 2; repeat from * around to next corner], ◊(sc, ch 3, sc) in next shell; repeat between [ ]; repeat from ◊ around, join with sl st in first sc, fasten off. ⚜

Designed by Carol Smith

HEIRLOOM CROCHET TREASURES

TABLE ACCENTS

ESSENTIALS	INSTRUCTIONS

NAPKIN RING

SIZE: 3½" across.

MATERIALS FOR ONE: Size 10 bedspread cotton — 25 yds. white; fabric stiffener; rust-proof pins; two 3" foam balls; No. 7 steel crochet hook or size needed to obtain gauge.

GAUGE: Rnds 1-3 = 1" across.

RING

Rnd 1: For **first side,** ch 36, sl st in first ch to form ring, ch 1, sc in same ch, ch 4, skip next 2 chs, *sc in next ch, ch 4, skip next 2 chs; repeat from * around, join with sl st in first sc (12 ch-4 sps).

NOTES: For **beginning shell (beg shell),** (ch 3, 2 dc, ch 2, 3 dc) in same sp.

For **shell,** (3 dc, ch 2, 3 dc) in next ch sp.

Rnd 2: Sl st in next ch sp, beg shell, (ch 4, sc, ch 4) in next ch sp, *shell, (ch 4, sc, ch 4) in next ch sp;

repeat from * around, join with sl st in top of ch-3 (6 shells, 12 ch-4 sps).

Rnd 3: Sl st in next 2 sts, sl st in next ch-2 sp, ch 1, (sc, ch 4, sc) in same sp, (ch 4, sc in next ch-4 sp) 2 times, ch 4; *for **picot,** (sc, ch 4, sc) in next ch-2 sp, (ch 4, sc in next ch-4 sp) 2 times, ch 4; repeat from * around, join. Fasten off.

Rnd 4: For **second side,** working on opposite side of starting ch on rnd 1, join with sl st in first ch, ch 1, sc in same sp, ch 4, skip next 2 chs, *sc in next ch, ch 4, skip next 2 chs; repeat from * around, join.

Rnds 5-6: Repeat rnds 2-3.

FINISHING

1: Apply fabric stiffener to Napkin Ring according to manufacturer's instructions.

2: Pin each side of Napkin Ring to one foam ball, shaping as shown in photo. Allow to dry.

CANDLE HOLDER

SIZE: Holds 8" taper.
MATERIALS FOR ONE: Size 10 bedspread cotton — 40 yds. white; fabric stiffener; craft glue or hot glue gun; 3 soda pop cans; No. 9 steel crochet hook.

MOTIF (make 3)

Rnd 1: Ch 6, sc in first ch to form ring, ch 4, (sc in ring, ch 4) 7 times, join with sl st in first sc (8 ch sps).

Rnd 2: Sl st in next ch sp, ch 1, (sc, ch 4, sc) in same sp, ch 4, *(sc, ch 4, sc) in next ch sp, ch 4; repeat from * around, join (16 ch-4 sps).

NOTES: For **beginning shell,** (ch 3, 2 dc, ch 2, 3 dc) in same sp.

For **shell,** (3 dc, ch 2, 3 dc) in ch-2 sp of next shell or next ch sp.

Rnd 3: Sl st in next ch sp, beg shell, (ch 4, sc, ch 4) in next ch sp, *shell, (ch 4, sc, ch 4) in next ch sp; repeat from * around, join with sl st in top of beg ch-3 (8 shells, 16 ch-4 sps).

Rnd 4: Sl st in next 2 sts, sl st in next ch-2 sp, ch 1, (sc, ch 4, sc) in same sp, (ch 4, sc in next ch-4 sp) 2 times, ch 4, *(sc, ch 4, sc) in next ch-2 sp, (ch 4, sc in next ch-4 sp) 2 times, ch 4; repeat from * around, join. Fasten off.

FINISHING

1: Work Step 1 of Napkin Ring Finishing.

2: Shape one Motif over each soda pop can. Let dry. Arrange Motifs in a triangle shape and glue together as shown in photo.

PLACE MAT

SIZE: 12¾" x 18⅞".
MATERIALS: Size 10 bedspread cotton — 425 yds. white; tapestry needle; No. 9 steel crochet hook or size needed to obtain gauge.
GAUGE: Rnds 1-2 = 1" across.

PLACE MAT

NOTES: For **picot,** ch 4, (sc, ch 4, sc) in next shell or ch sp.

For **beginning shell (beg shell),** sl st in next ch sp, (ch 3, 2 dc, ch 3, 3 dc) in same sp, ch 2, sc in next ch sp.

For **shell,** ch 2, (3 dc, ch 3, 3 dc) in next ch sp, ch 2, sc in next ch sp.

Rnd 1: Ch 20, (sc, ch 4, sc, ch 4, sc) in 2nd ch from hook, *(ch 4, skip next 2 chs, sc in next ch) 6 times*, (ch 4, sc in same ch as last sc) 3 times; working in opposite side of beg ch, repeat between **, ch 4, join with sl st in first sc (18 ch sps).

Rnd 2: Sl st in next ch sp, ch 1, (sc, ch 4, sc) in same sp, picot, *(ch 4, sc in next ch sp) 6 times*, (picot) 3 times; repeat between **, picot, ch 4, join.

Rnd 3: Sl st in last ch sp of previous rnd, ch 1, sc in same sp, ch 4, (sc in next ch sp, ch 4) around, join (24 ch sps).

Rnd 4: Sl st in next ch sp, ch 1, sc in same sp, ch 4, (sc in next ch sp, ch 4) around, join.

Rnd 5: Sl st in next ch sp, ch 1, (sc, ch 4, sc) in same sp, *ch 4, sc in next ch sp, picot, (ch 4, sc in next ch sp) 7 times, picot, ch 4, sc in next sp*, picot; repeat between **, ch 4, join.

Rnd 6: Beg shell, *ch 4, sc in next ch sp, shell, (ch 4, sc in next ch sp) 7 times, shell, ch 4, sc in next ch sp*, shell; repeat between **, ch 2, join with sl st in top of beg ch-3 (18 ch-4 sps, 6 ch-3 sps, 12 ch-2 sps).

Rnd 7: Sl st in each of next 2 sts, sl st in next ch sp of beg shell, ch 1, (sc, ch 4, sc) in same sp, *(ch 4, sc in next ch sp) 3 times, picot, (ch 4, sc in next ch sp) 9 times, picot, (ch 4, sc in next ch sp) 3 times*, picot; repeat between **, ch 4, join with sl st in first sc.

Rnd 8: Sl st in next ch sp, ch 1, (sc, ch 4, sc) in same sp, *(ch 4, sc in next ch sp) 4 times, picot, (ch 4, sc in next ch sp) 10 times, picot, (ch 4, sc in next ch sp) 4 times*, picot; repeat between **, ch 4, join (48 ch sps).

Rnd 9: Beg shell, ch 4, sc in next ch sp, (shell, ch 4, sc in next ch sp) 3 times, (ch 4, sc in next ch sp) 3 times, (shell, ch 4, sc in next ch sp) 7 times, (ch 4, sc in next ch sp) 3 times, (shell, ch 4, sc in next ch sp) 3 times, ch 2, join with sl st in top of beg ch-3 (14 shells).

Rnd 10: Sl st in next 2 sts, sl st in next ch sp of beg shell, ch 1, (sc, ch 4, sc) in same sp, *(ch 4, sc in next ch sp) 3 times, picot, (ch 4, sc in next ch sp) 3 times, picot, (ch 4, sc in next ch sp) 3 times, picot, (ch 4, sc in next ch sp) 6 times, picot, (ch 4, sc in next ch sp) 3 times, picot, (ch 4, sc in next ch sp) 3 times, picot, (ch 4, sc in next ch sp) 3 times*, picot; repeat between **, ch 4, join with sl st in first sc.

Rnd 11: Sl st in next ch sp, ch 1, (sc, ch 4, sc) in same sp, *(ch 4, sc in next ch sp) 4 times, picot, (ch 4, sc in next ch sp) 4 times, picot, (ch 4, sc in next ch sp) 4 times, picot, (ch 4, sc in next ch sp) 7 times, picot, (ch 4, sc in next ch sp) 4 times, picot, (ch 4, sc in next ch sp) 4 times, picot, (ch 4, sc in next ch sp) 4 times*, picot; repeat

Continued on page 64

HEIRLOOM CROCHET TREASURES

CRIMSON ROSE DOILY

ESSENTIALS

SIZE: 12" square after blocking.

MATERIALS: Size 10 bedspread cotton — 150 yds. white; 55 yds. red; 15 yds. green; No. 7 steel crochet hook or size needed to obtain gauge.

GAUGE: Rnds 1-7 = 2¾" across.

INSTRUCTIONS

DOILY

NOTE: Doily may ruffle slightly until blocked.

Rnd 1: For **flower,** with red, ch 6, sl st in first ch to form ring, ch 3, 11 dc in ring, join with sl st in top of ch-3 (12 dc).

Rnd 2: *(Ch 1, dc, tr, dc, ch 1, sl st) in same st, skip next st, sl st in next st; repeat from * around, fasten off (6 petals).

Rnd 3: Working behind petals, join red with sl st in any skipped st on rnd 1, ch 4, (sl st in next skipped st, ch 4) around, join with sl st in first sl st (6 ch-4 lps).

Rnd 4: (Sl st, sc, ch 1, dc, 3 tr, dc, ch 1, sc) in first ch-4 lp, (sc, ch 1, dc, 3 tr, dc, ch 1, sc) in each ch-4 lp around, join with sl st in first sc, fasten off.

Rnd 5: Working behind petals, join red with sl st around post of any sl st on rnd 3, ch 6, (sl st around post of next sl st, ch 6) around, join with sl st in first sl st.

Rnd 6: (Sl st, sc, ch 1, dc, 5 tr, dc, ch 1, sc) in first ch-6 lp, (sc, ch 1, dc, 5 tr, dc, ch 1, sc) in each ch-6 lp around, join with sl st in first sc, fasten off.

NOTE: For **cluster (cl),** *yo 2 times, insert hook in st, yo, draw lp through, (yo, draw through 2 lps on hook) 2 times; repeat from * 2 more times in same st, yo, draw through all 4 lps on hook.

Rnd 7: For **leaves,** *join green with sl st in 3rd tr of next petal on rnd 6, (ch 4, cl, ch 4, sl st) 3 times in same st, fasten off; repeat from * around (18 leaves).

Rnd 8: Join white with sc in first cl on first leaf, *(ch 6, sc in next cl on next leaf) 2 times, ch 1, tr in 2nd sc between next 2 petals on rnd 6, ch 1*, [sc in first cl on next leaf; repeat between **]; repeat between [ ] around, join with sl st in first sc (12 ch-6 lps, 12 ch-1 sps).

Rnd 9: (Sl st, ch 4, 2 tr, ch 2, 3 tr, ch 2) in first ch-6 lp, (3 tr, ch 2, 3 tr, ch 2) in each ch-6 lp around, join with sl st in top of ch-4 (72 tr, 24 ch-2 sps).

Rnd 10: Ch 4, tr in each of next 2 tr, ch 2, tr in each of next 3 tr, ch 3, (tr in each of next 3 tr, ch 2, tr in each of next 3 tr, ch 3) around, join.

Rnd 11: Ch 4, tr in each of next 2 tr, ch 3, tr in each of next 3 tr, ch 4, (tr in each of next 3 tr, ch 3, tr in each of next 3 tr, ch 4) around, join.

Rnd 12: Ch 4, tr in same st, tr in each of next 2 tr, ch 3, tr in each of next 2 tr, 2 tr in next tr, ch 4, (2 tr in next tr, tr in each of next 2 tr, ch 3, tr in each of next 2 tr, 2 tr in

next tr, ch 4) around, join (96 tr, 24 ch sps).

Rnd 13: Ch 4, tr in same st, tr in each of next 3 tr, ch 3, tr in each of next 3 tr, 2 tr in next tr, ch 4, (2 tr in next tr, tr in each of next 3 tr, ch 3, tr in each of next 3 tr, 2 tr in next tr, ch 4) around, join (120 tr, 24 ch sps).

Rnd 14: Ch 4, tr in same st, tr in next 4 tr, ch 3, tr in next 4 tr, 2 tr in next tr, ch 4, (2 tr in next tr, tr in next 4 tr, ch 3, tr in next 4 tr, 2 tr in next tr, ch 4) around, join (144 tr, 24 ch sps).

NOTE: To **tr next 5 sts tog,** *yo 2 times, insert hook in next st, yo, draw lp through, (yo, draw through 2 lps on hook) 2 times*; repeat between ** 4 more times, yo, draw through all 6 lps on hook.

To **tr next 6 sts tog,** repeat between ** above 6 times, yo, draw through all 7 lps on hook.

Rnd 15: Ch 3, tr next 5 tr tog, ch 10, (tr next 6 tr tog, ch 10) around, join with sl st in top of first tr (24 tr, 24 ch-10 lps).

Rnd 16: (Sl st, ch 4, 5 tr, ch 3, 6 tr) in next ch-10 lp, (6 tr, ch 3, 6 tr) in each ch-10 lp around, join with sl st in top of ch-4 (288 tr, 24 ch-3 sps).

Rnd 17: Ch 4, tr in next 5 tr, (2 tr, ch 3, 2 tr) in next ch-3 sp, *tr in next 12 tr, (2 tr, ch 3, 2 tr) in next ch-3 sp; repeat from * around to last 6 sts, tr in last 6 tr, join, fasten off (384 tr, 24 ch-3 sps).

Rnd 18: Join red with sc in first st, (ch 3, sc in next tr) 7 times, (ch 3, sc, ch 3, sc, ch 3, sc) in next ch-3 sp, *(ch 3, sc in next tr) 16 times, (ch 3, sc, ch 3, sc, ch 3, sc) in next ch-3 sp; repeat from * around to last 8 sts, ch 3, (sc in next tr, ch 3) around, join with sl st in first sc, fasten off. ⚜

SNOW CRYSTALS

Continued from page 55

PEACH SNOWFLAKE

Rnd 1: Ch 6, sl st in first ch to form ring, ch 1, 10 sc in ring, join with sl st in first sc (10 sc).

Rnd 2: Ch 4, dc in same st, (dc, ch 1, dc) in each st around, join with sl st in 3rd ch of ch-4 (20 dc, 10 ch sps).

Rnd 3: Sl st in first ch sp, ch 1, sc in same sp, ch 2, (2 dc, ch 2, 2 dc) in next ch sp, ch 2, *sc in next ch sp, ch 2,

(2 dc, ch 2, 2 dc) in next ch sp, ch 2; repeat from * around, join with sl st in first sc (20 dc, 5 sc).

Rnds 4-5: Repeat same rnds of Peach Snowball on page 55. Fasten off at end of last rnd.

FINISHING

Work same as Blue Snowflake Finishing on page 55. ⚜

Designed by Erma Fielder

HEIRLOOM CROCHET TREASURES

DAINTY SNOWFLAKES

ESSENTIALS

SIZE: Snowflakes No. 1, 2 and 3 are 4" across. Snowflake No. 4 is 4½" across.

MATERIALS FOR ONE OF EACH: Size 10 bedspread cotton — 25 yds. white; fabric stiffener; No. 6 steel crochet hook or size needed to obtain gauge.

GAUGE: No. 1, rnds 1-2 = ¾" across. No. 2, rnds 1-2 = 1⅛" across. No. 3, rnd 1 = ⅞" across. No. 4, rnds 1-2 = ⅝" across.

INSTRUCTIONS

SNOWFLAKE NO. 1

Rnd 1: Ch 2, 8 sc in 2nd ch from hook, join with sl st in first sc (8 sc).

Rnd 2: Ch 5, (dc in next st, ch 2) around, join with sl st in 3rd ch of ch-5 (8 ch-2 sps).

NOTES: For **beginning double treble crochet cluster (beg dtr cl),** ch 4, *yo 3 times, insert hook in sp, yo, draw through sp, (yo, draw through 2 lps on hook) 3 times; repeat from * 3 more times in same sp, yo, draw through all 5 lps on hook.

For **double treble crochet cluster (dtr cl),** *yo 3 times, insert hook in sp, yo, draw through sp, (yo, draw through 2 lps on hook) 3 times; repeat from * 4 more times in same sp, yo, draw through all 6 lps on hook.

Rnd 3: Sl st in first ch-2 sp, beg dtr cl, ch 10, (dtr cl in next ch-2 sp, ch 10) around, join with sl st in top of first cl (8 dtr cl).

Rnd 4: Sl st in first ch-10 lp, ch 1, 13 sc in each ch-10 lp around, join (104 sc).

Rnd 5: Sl st in next 6 sts, ch 16, skip next 12 sts, (dc in next st, ch 13, skip next 12 sts) around, join with sl st in 3rd ch of ch-16 (8 ch sps).

Rnd 6: Ch 1, 14 sc in each ch lp around, join with sl st in first sc; for **hanging loop,** ch 15, sl st in same st. Fasten off.

Apply fabric stiffener to Snowflake according to manufacturer's instructions; shape as shown in photo. Let dry.

SNOWFLAKE NO. 2

Rnd 1: Ch 6, sl st in first ch to form ring, ch 1, 12 sc in ring, join with sl st in first sc (12 sc).

Rnd 2: Ch 5, (dc in next st, ch 2) around, join with sl st in 3rd ch of ch-5 (12 dc).

Rnd 3: Ch 3, 2 dc in same st, ch 3, sc in next st, ch 3, *3 dc in next st, ch 3, sc in next st, ch 3; repeat from * around, join with sl st in top of ch-3 (18 dc, 6 sc).

Rnd 4: Ch 3, dc in same st, dc in next dc, 2 dc in next dc, ch 4, sc in next sc, ch 4, *2 dc in next dc, dc in next dc, 2 dc in next dc, ch 4, sc in next sc, ch 4; repeat from * around, join (30 dc, 6 sc).

Rnd 5: Ch 1, sc in same st, ch 7, skip next 3 dc, sc in next dc, *ch 7, skip next sc, sc in next dc, ch 7, skip next 3 dc, sc in next dc; repeat from * around to last sc; to join, ch 3, tr in first sc (12 sc, 12 ch lps).

Rnd 6: Ch 8, (sc in 4th ch of next ch sp, ch 8) around, join with sl st in top of joining tr on last rnd (12 ch lps).

Rnd 7: Sl st in first ch lp, ch 1, (3 sc, ch 3, 3 sc, ch 3, 3 sc, ch 3, 3 sc) in same lp; repeat between ( ) in each ch lp around; for **hanging loop,** ch 15, sl st in same st.

Fasten off.

Apply fabric stiffener to Snowflake according to manufacturer's instructions; shape as shown in photo. Let dry.

SNOWFLAKE NO. 3

Rnd 1: Ch 7, sl st in first ch to form ring, ch 3, 23 dc in ring, join with sl st in top of ch-3 (24 dc).

Rnd 2: (Ch 5, skip next st, sc in next st) around to last st; to **join,** ch 2, dc in first ch of ch-5 (12 ch lps).

Rnd 3: (Ch 5, sc in next ch lp) around, join as before in joining dc on last rnd.

Rnd 4: Ch 5, (sc in next ch lp, ch 5) around, join with sl st in top of joining dc on last rnd.

Rnd 5: (Sl st in first ch lp, ch 1, 7 sc in each ch lp around, join with sl st in first sc (84 sc).

Rnd 6: Sl st in next 3 sts, (ch 6, 5 dc in 3rd ch from hook, ch 2, sl st in same ch, ch 3, skip next 6 sts), *sc in next st; repeat between ( ); repeat from * around, join with sl st in first ch of ch-6; for **hanging loop,** ch 15, sl st in same ch. Fasten off.

Apply fabric stiffener to Snowflake according to manufacturer's instructions; shape as shown in photo. Let dry.

SNOWFLAKE NO. 4

Rnd 1: Ch 2, 5 sc in 2nd ch form hook, join with sl st in first sc (5 sc).

Rnd 2: Ch 1, 2 sc in each st around, join (10).

Rnd 3: Ch 1, sc in each st around, join.

Rnd 4: Ch 1, sc in first st; for **petal,** (ch 10, sc in 2nd ch from hook, hdc in next ch, dc in next 7 chs); *sc in next st on rnd 3; repeat between ( ); repeat from * around, join (10 petals). Fasten off.

Rnd 5: Join with sc in tip of any petal, ch 10, (sc in tip of next petal, ch 10) around, join (10 ch lps).

Rnd 6: Sl st in first ch lp, (5 sc, ch 3, sc, ch 3, sc, ch 3, 5 sc) in same lp; repeat between ( ) in each ch lp around; for **hanging loop,** ch 15, join. Fasten off.

Apply fabric stiffener to Snowflake according to manufacturer's instructions; shape as shown in photo. Let dry. ⚜

FESTIVE DOILY

instructions on page 56

JOINING DIAGRAM

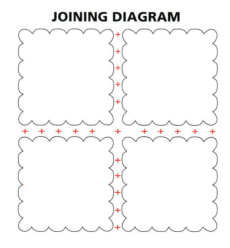

H E I R L O O M   C R O C H E T   T R E A S U R E S

PINEAPPLE APPEAL

Continued from page 53

5, 2 tr in next st, ch 5*, [(sm tr cl, ch 5, sm tr cl, ch 5, sm tr cl) in next ch-5 sp; repeat between **]; repeat between [ ] around, join (40 ch-5 sps, 24 sm tr cl, 20 tr).

Rnd 12: Sl st in next ch-5 sp, (beg sm tr cl, ch 5, sm tr cl) in same sp, *ch 3, (sm tr cl, ch 5, sm tr cl) in next ch-5 sp, ch 9, skip next ch-9 sp, sc in next ch-5 sp, ch 5, sc in next ch-5 sp, ch 9, skip next ch-9 sp, (sm tr cl, ch 5, sm tr cl) in next ch-5 sp, ch 3, (sm tr cl, ch 5, sm tr cl) in next ch-5 sp, ch 5, tr in each of next 2 sts, ch 5, (tr, ch 7, tr) in next st, ch 5, tr in each of next 2 sts, ch 5*, [(sm tr cl, ch 5, sm tr cl) in next ch-5 sp; repeat between **]; repeat between [ ] around, join (36 ch-5 sps, 32 sm tr cl, 24 tr).

Rnd 13: Sl st in next ch-5 sp, (beg sm tr cl, ch 5, sm tr cl) in same sp, *ch 5, sc in next ch-3 sp, ch 5, (sm tr cl, ch 5, sm tr cl) in next ch-5 sp, ch 5, skip next ch-9 sp, dc in next ch-5 sp, ch 5, skip next ch-9 sp, (sm tr cl, ch 5, sm tr cl) in next ch-5 sp, ch 5, sc in next ch-3 sp, ch 5, (sm tr cl, ch 5, sm tr cl) in next ch-5 sp, ch 5, tr in each of next 2 sts, ch 5, skip next st, (dc, ch 11, dc) in 4th ch of next ch-7 sp, ch 5, skip next st, tr in each of next 2 sts, ch 5*, [(sm tr cl, ch 5, sm tr cl) in next ch-5 sp; repeat between **]; repeat between [ ] around, join (56 ch-5 sps, 32 sm tr cl, 16 tr). Fasten off.

MOTIF NO. 2

Rnds 1-12: Repeat same rnds of Motif No. 1.

NOTES: For **joining ch-5 sp,** ch 2, sc in corresponding ch-5 sp on other Motif, ch 2.

For **joining ch-11 lp,** ch 5, sc in corresponding ch-11 lp on other Motif, ch 5.

Rnd 13: Sl st in next ch-5 sp, (beg sm tr cl, ch 5, sm tr cl) in same sp, ◊ch 5, sc in next ch-3 sp, ch 5, (sm tr cl, ch 5, sm tr cl) in next ch-5 sp, ch 5, skip next ch-9 sp, dc in next ch-5 sp, ch 5, skip next ch-9 sp, (sm tr cl, ch 5, sm tr cl) in next ch-5 sp, ch 5, sc in next ch-3 sp, ch 5,

(sm tr cl, ch 5, sm tr cl) in next ch-5 sp, ch 5, tr in each of next 2 sts, ch 5, skip next st◊, dc in 4th ch of next ch-7 sp; to **join,** holding this Motif and last Motif wrong sides together, work joining ch-11 lp, dc in same ch on this Motif as last dc, ch 5, skip next st, tr in each of next 2 sts, ch 5, *sm tr cl in next ch-5 sp, work joining ch-5 sp, sm tr cl in same ch-5 sp on this Motif, ch 5, sc in next ch-3 sp, ch 5, (sm tr cl, joining ch-5 sp, sm tr cl) in next ch-5 sp*, ch 5, skip next ch-9 sp, dc in next ch-5 sp, ch 5, skip next ch-9 sp; repeat between **, ch 5, tr in each of next 2 sts, ch 5, skip next st, (dc, joining ch-11 lp, dc) in 4th ch of next ch-7 sp, [ch 5, skip next st, tr in each of next 2 sts, ch 5, skip next ch sp, (sm tr cl, ch 5, sm tr cl) in next ch-5 sp; repeat between ◊◊, (dc, ch 11, dc) in 4th ch of next ch-7 sp]; repeat between [ ], ch 5, skip next st, tr in each of next 2 sts, ch 5, join (56 ch-5 sps, 32 sm tr cl, 16 tr). Fasten off.

MOTIFS NO. 3-80

Work same as Motif No. 2, joining on two sides where needed to make eight rows of ten Motifs each.

EDGING

Join with sc in any corner ch-11 lp, (7 sc, ch 5, 8 sc) in same lp, [sc in next dc, 5 sc in next ch-5 sp, sc in each of next 2 tr, 5 sc in next ch-5 sp, sc in next sm tr cl, *(4 sc, ch 5, 4 sc) in next ch-5 sp, sc in next sm tr cl, ch 3, sm tr cl in next sc; for **picot, ch 5, sl st in front lp of last cl made;** ch 3, sc in next sm tr cl, (4 sc, ch 5, 4 sc) in next ch-5 sp, sc in next sm tr cl*, 6 sc in each of next 2 ch-5 sps, sc in next sm tr cl; repeat between **, sc in next sm tr cl, 6 sc in next ch-5 sp, sc in each of next 2 tr, 6 sc in next ch-5 sp, sc in next dc], ◊5 sc in each of next 2 ch-11 lps; repeat between [ ]; repeat from ◊ around with (8 sc, ch 5, 8 sc) in each corner ch-11 lp, join with sl st in first sc. Fasten off.❦

TABLE ACCENTS

Continued from page 59

between **, ch 4, join (90 ch-4 sps).

Rnd 12: Beg shell, *(ch 4, sc in next ch sp) 4 times, shell, (ch 4, sc in next ch sp) 4 times, shell, (ch 4, sc in next ch

sp) 4 times, (shell, ch 4, sc in next ch sp) 4 times, (ch 4, sc in next ch sp) 3 times, shell, (ch 4, sc in next ch sp) 4 times, shell, (ch 4, sc in next ch sp) 4 times*, shell; repeat between **, ch 2, join with sl st in top of beg ch-3.

Rnd 13: Skip ch-2 sps on each side of shells, sl st in next 2 sts, sl st in next ch sp of beg shell, ch 1, (sc, ch 4, sc) in same sp, *(ch 4, sc in next ch sp) 4 times, picot, (ch 4, sc in next ch sp) 4 times, picot, (ch 4, sc in next ch sp) 4 times, picot, (ch 4, sc in next ch sp) 4 times, picot, (ch 4, sc in next ch sp, picot) 3 times, (ch 4, sc in next ch sp) 4 times, picot, (ch 4, sc in next ch sp) 4 times, picot, (ch 4, sc in next ch sp) 4 times*, picot; repeat between **, ch 4, join with sl st in first sc.

Rnd 14: Sl st in next ch sp, ch 1, (sc, ch 4, sc) in same sp, *(ch 4, sc in next ch sp) 5 times, picot, (ch 4, sc in next ch sp) 5 times, picot, (ch 4, sc in next ch sp) 5 times, picot, (ch 4, sc in next ch sp) 2 times, picot, (ch 4, sc in next ch sp) 2 times, picot, (ch 4, sc in next ch sp) 2 times, picot, (ch 4, sc in next ch sp) 5 times, picot, (ch 4, sc in next ch sp) 5 times, picot, (ch 4, sc in next ch sp) 5 times*, picot; repeat between **, ch 4, join.

NOTES: For **beginning variation shell (beg V shell),** sl st in next ch sp, (ch 3, 2 dc, ch 3, 3 dc) in same sp, ch 2, skip next ch sp, sc in next ch sp.

For **variation shell (V shell),** ch 2, skip next ch sp, (3 dc, ch 3, 3 dc) in next ch sp, ch 2, skip next ch sp, sc in next ch sp.

Rnd 15: Beg V shell, *(ch 4, sc in next ch sp) 3 times, V shell, (ch 4, sc in next ch sp) 3 times, V shell, (ch 4, sc in next ch sp) 3 times, (V shell) 4 times, (ch 4, sc in next ch sp) 3 times, V shell, (ch 4, sc in next ch sp) 3 times, V shell, (ch 4, sc in next ch sp) 3 times*, V shell; repeat between **, ch 2, skip next ch sp, join with sl st in top of beg ch-3 (18 shells).

Rnd 16: Sl st in next 2 sts, sl st in next ch sp of beg V shell, ch 1, (sc, ch 4, sc) in same sp, *(ch 4, sc in next ch sp) 5 times, picot, (ch 4, sc in next ch sp) 5 times, picot, (ch 4, sc in next ch sp) 5 times, picot, (ch 4, sc in next ch sp) 2 times, picot, (ch 4, sc in next ch sp) 2 times, picot, (ch 4, sc in next ch sp) 2 times, picot, (ch 4, sc in next ch sp) 5 times, picot, (ch 4, sc in next ch sp) 5 times, picot, (ch 4, sc in next ch sp) 5 times*, picot; repeat between **, ch 4, join with sl st in first sc.

Rnd 17: Sl st in next ch sp, ch 1, (sc, ch 4, sc) in same sp, *(ch 4, sc in next ch sp) 6 times, picot, (ch 4, sc in next ch sp) 6 times, picot, (ch 4, sc in next ch sp) 6 times, picot, (ch 4, sc in next ch sp) 3 times, picot, (ch 4, sc in next ch sp) 3 times, picot, (ch 4, sc in next ch sp) 3 times, picot, (ch 4, sc in next ch sp) 6 times, picot, (ch 4, sc in next ch sp) 6 times, picot, (ch 4, sc in next ch sp) 6 times*, picot; repeat between **, ch 4, join.

Rnd 18: Beg V shell, *(ch 4, sc in next ch sp) 4 times, V shell, (ch 4, sc in next ch sp) 4 times, V shell, (ch 4, sc in next ch sp) 4 times, (V shell, ch 4, sc in next ch sp) 4 times, (ch 4, sc in next ch sp) 3 times, V shell, (ch 4, sc in next ch sp) 4 times, V shell, (ch 4, sc in next ch sp) 4 times, V shell, (ch 4, sc in next ch sp) 4

times*, V shell; repeat between **, ch 2, skip next ch sp, join with sl st in top of beg ch-3.

Rnd 19: Sl st in next 2 sts, sl st in next ch sp of beg V shell, ch 1, (sc, ch 4, sc) in same sp, [(ch 4, sc in next ch sp) 6 times, picot, (ch 4, sc in next ch sp) 6 times, picot, (ch 4, sc in next ch sp) 5 times, *ch 4, skip next ch sp, (sc, ch 4, sc) in next ch sp, ch 4, skip next ch sp, sc in next ch sp; repeat from * 3 more times, (ch 4, sc in next ch sp) 4 times, picot, (ch 4, sc in next ch sp) 6 times, picot, (ch 4, sc in next ch sp) 6 times], picot; repeat between [ ], ch 4, join with sl st in first sc.

Rnd 20: Sl st in next ch sp, ch 1, (sc, ch 4, sc) in same sp, *(ch 4, sc in next ch sp) 7 times, picot, (ch 4, sc in next ch sp) 7 times, picot, (ch 4, sc in next ch sp) 6 times, (picot, ch 4, sc in next ch sp, ch 4, sc in next ch sp) 4 times, (ch 4, sc in next ch sp) 4 times, picot, (ch 4, sc in next ch sp) 7 times, picot, (ch 4, sc in next ch sp) 7 times*, picot; repeat between **, ch 4, join.

Rnd 21: Beg V shell, *(ch 4, sc in next ch sp) 5 times, V shell, (ch 4, sc in next ch sp) 5 times, V shell, (ch 4, sc in next ch sp) 4 times, (V shell) 4 times, (ch 4, sc in next ch sp) 4 times, V shell, (ch 4, sc in next ch sp) 5 times, V shell, (ch 4, sc in next ch sp) 5 times*, V shell; repeat between **, ch 4, join with sl st in top of beg ch-3.

Rnd 22: Sl st in next 2 sts, sl st in next ch sp of beg V shell, ch 1, (sc, ch 4, sc) in same sp, [(ch 4, sc in next ch sp) 7 times, picot, (ch 4, sc in next ch sp) 7 times, picot, (ch 4, sc in next ch sp) 6 times, *picot, ch 4, sc in next ch sp, ch 4, sc in next ch sp; repeat from * 3 more times, (ch 4, sc in next ch sp) 4 times, picot, (ch 4, sc in next ch sp) 7 times, picot, (ch 4, sc in next ch sp) 7 times], picot; repeat between [ ], ch 4, join with sl st in first sc.

Rnd 23: Sl st in next ch sp, ch 1, (sc, ch 4, sc) in same sp, [(ch 4, sc in next ch sp) 8 times, picot, (ch 4, sc in next ch sp) 8 times, picot, (ch 4, sc in next ch sp) 6 times, *ch 4, skip next ch sp, (sc, ch 4, sc) in next ch sp, ch 4, skip next ch sp, sc in next ch sp; repeat from * 3 times, (ch 4, sc in next ch sp) 5 times, picot, (ch 4, sc in next ch sp) 8 times, picot, (ch 4, sc in next ch sp) 8 times], picot; repeat between [ ], ch 4, join.

NOTE: Rnd 24 will be worked using shells and V shells.

Rnd 24: Beg V shell, [(ch 4, sc in next ch sp) 6 times, V shell, (ch 4, sc in next ch sp) 6 times, V shell, (ch 4, sc in next ch sp) 5 times, *shell, ch 4, sc in next ch sp; repeat from * 3 times, (ch 4, sc in next ch sp) 5 times, V shell, (ch 4, sc in next ch sp) 6 times, V shell, (ch 4, sc in next ch sp) 6 times], V shell; repeat between [ ], ch 2, join with sl st in top of beg ch-3.

Rnd 25: Sl st in next 2 sts, sl st in next ch sp of beg V shell, ch 1, (sc, ch 4, sc) in same sp, picot in each ch-4 sp, in each V shell and in each shell around, ch 4, join with sl st in first sc. Fasten off. ⚜

ROMANTIC REMEMBRANCE

*Sharing special times with special
people binds our hearts in love and friendship,
evoking cherished memories of times past and exhilarating
anticipation of days to come. When you want your occasions
to be even more memorable, touchable crocheted
accessories and gifts are the perfect
way to say "I care" with eloquent feeling.*

TEATIME DOILY

ESSENTIALS

SIZE: 10" across when blocked.

MATERIALS: Size 20 crochet cotton — 150 yds. each lt. pink and med. pink; tapestry needle; No. 11 steel crochet hook or size needed to obtain gauge.

GAUGE: Rnds 1-2 = 2½" across.

INSTRUCTIONS

DOILY

NOTES: For **picot,** ch 4, sl st in top of last st made.

Doily may ruffle until blocked.

Rnd 1: With med. pink, ch 6, sl st in first ch to form ring, ch 3, 15 dc in ring, join with sl st in top of ch-3 (16 dc).

Rnd 2: Ch 1, sc in same st, sc in next st; for **first petal,** ch 14, dc in 4th ch from hook, 2 dc in next ch, *dc in next ch, picot, 2 dc in next ch, (dc in next ch, 2 dc in next ch) 2 times, picot, dc in each of last 3 chs; sc in each of next 2 sts on rnd 1; for **next petal,** ch 11, **turn,** sl st in 3rd dc above 2nd picot (see photo) on last petal made, **turn,** ch 3, 2 dc in each of next 2 chs; repeat from * 6 more times, dc in next ch, picot, 2 dc in next ch, dc in next ch, 2 dc in next ch, sl st in bottom of ch-3 on end of first petal, dc in next ch of ch-11, 2 dc in next ch, picot, dc in each of last 3 chs, join with sl st in first sc, fasten off (8 petals).

NOTE: When working rnd 3, the ch-3 at beginning of each petal is not used or counted as a dc.

Rnd 3: Join lt. pink with sl st in 3rd dc after first picot on any petal, ch 3, dc in 3rd dc on next petal, ch 11, (dc in 3rd dc after next picot, dc in 3rd dc on next petal, ch 11) around, join with sl st in top of ch-3 (16 dc, 8 ch lps).

Rnd 4: Ch 1, sc in same st, *ch 3, sc in next dc, ch 5, skip first 4 chs on next ch lp, 4 dc in each of next 3 chs on same lp, ch 5, skip last 4 chs*, [sc in next dc; repeat between **]; repeat between [ ] around, join with sl st in first sc (96 dc, 16 sc, 16 ch-5 sps, 8 ch-3 lps).

Rnd 5: Sl st in first ch-3 lp, ch 8, *skip next ch-5 sp, skip next dc, dc in next 10 dc, ch 5, skip next ch-5 sp*, [dc in next ch-3 lp, ch 5; repeat between **]; repeat between [ ] around, join with sl st in 3rd ch of ch-8 (88 dc, 16 ch-5 sps).

NOTES: For **beginning shell (beg shell),** ch 3, (dc, ch 3, 2 dc) in same st or sp.

For **shell,** (2 dc, ch 3, 2 dc) in next st or sp.

Rnd 6: Beg shell, *ch 5, skip next ch-5 sp, skip next dc, dc in next 8 dc, ch 5, skip next dc, skip next ch-5 sp*, [shell in next dc; repeat between **]; repeat between [ ] around, join with sl st in top of ch-3 (64 dc, 16 ch-5 sps, 8 shells).

Rnd 7: Sl st in next dc, sl st in ch sp of same shell, beg shell, *ch 7, skip next ch-5 sp, skip next dc, dc in next 6 dc, ch 7, skip next dc, skip next ch-5 sp*, [shell in ch sp of next shell; repeat between **]; repeat between [ ] around, join (48 dc, 16 ch-7 sps, 8 shells).

Rnd 8: Sl st in next dc, sl st in ch sp of same shell, beg shell, *ch 9, skip next ch-7 sp, skip next dc, dc in next 4 dc, ch 9, skip next dc, skip next ch-7 sp*, [shell in next shell; repeat between **]; repeat between [ ] around, join (32 dc, 16 ch-9 sps, 8 shells).

NOTE: For **cluster (cl),** (yo, insert hook in next dc, yo, draw lp through, yo, draw through 2 lps on hook) 4 times, yo, draw through all 5 lps on hook.

Rnd 9: Sl st in next dc, sl st in ch sp of same shell, beg shell, *ch 13, skip next ch-9 sp, cl, picot, ch 13, skip next ch-9 sp*, [shell in next shell; repeat between **]; repeat between [ ] around, join.

Rnd 10: Sl st in next dc, sl st in ch sp of same shell, ch 3, 6 dc in same sp, *ch 9, dc in 10th ch of next ch-13 sp, ch 7, dc in 4th ch of next ch-13 sp, ch 9*, [7 dc in next shell; repeat between **]; repeat between [ ] around, join.

Rnd 11: Ch 3, dc in same dc, 2 dc in each of next 6 dc, *ch 7, skip next ch-9 sp, skip next dc, 2 dc in each of next 7 chs, ch 7, skip next dc, skip next ch-9 sp*, [2 dc in each of next 7 dc; repeat between **]; repeat between [ ] around, join.

Rnd 12: Ch 5, *skip next dc, dc in next dc, (ch 2, skip next dc, dc in next dc) 2 times, ch 2, dc in next dc, (ch 2, skip next dc, dc in next dc) 3 times, ch 3, sc in next ch-7 sp, ch 3*, [dc in next dc, ch 2; repeat between **]; repeat between [ ] around, join with sl st in 3rd ch of ch-5.

Rnd 13: Ch 5, dc in next dc, (ch 2, dc in next dc) 2 times, *ch 5, dc in next dc, (ch 2, dc in next dc) 3 times*, [dc in next dc, (ch 2, dc in next dc) 3 times;

Continued on page 83

ANTIQUE TEDDY

HEIRLOOM BOOTIES
Instructions on page 72

ANTIQUE TEDDY

ESSENTIALS

SIZE: 8" tall in sitting position.

MATERIALS: Size 10 bedspread cotton — 400 yds. ecru; embroidery floss — 2 yds. brown, small amount white; four ⅝" buttons and matching sewing thread; 18" red ⅜" satin ribbon; polyester fiberfill; sewing and tapestry needles; No. 3 steel crochet hook or size needed to obtain gauge.

GAUGE: 7 sc sts = 1"; 7 sc rows = 1".

NOTE: Entire pattern is worked with 2 strands held together.

INSTRUCTIONS

BODY SIDE PIECE (make 2)

Row 1: Starting at bottom, ch 9, sc in 2nd ch from hook, sc in each ch across, turn (8 sc).

Row 2: Ch 1, 2 sc in first st, sc in each st across with 2 sc in last st, turn (10).

Row 3: For **tummy shaping,** ch 1, 2 sc in first st, sc in each st across, turn (11).

Rows 4-12: Repeat rows 2 and 3 alternately, ending with row 2 and 25 sts.

Rows 13-19: Ch 1, sc in each st across, turn.

Row 20: Ch 1, sc in each st across to last 2 sts, sc last 2 sts tog, turn (24).

Rows 21-25: Repeat rows 13 and 20 alternately, ending with row 13 and 22 sts.

Rows 26-29: Ch 1, sc first 2 sts tog, sc in each st across with sc last 2 sts tog, turn, ending with 14 sts in last row.

Rows 30-32: Ch 1, sc in each st across, turn.

Row 33: Repeat row 2 (16).

Row 34: Ch 1, sc in each st across with 2 sc in last st, turn (17).

Rows 35-36: Repeat rows 2 and 34 (19, 20).

Row 37: Repeat row 3 (21).

Row 38: Ch 1, sc in each st across, turn.

Row 39: Repeat row 3 (22).

Row 40: Repeat row 20 (21).

Row 41: Repeat row 26 (19).

Row 42: Ch 1, sc in each st across, turn.

Row 43: Repeat row 26 (17).

Row 44: Repeat row 20 (16).

Row 45: Repeat row 26 (14).

Row 46: Repeat row 20 (13).

Rows 47-50: Repeat row 26, ending with 5 sts in last row. At end of last row; for first Body Side Piece, **turn**;

for second Body Side Piece, **do not turn.**

Rnd 51: Working around outer edge, ch 1; for first piece, sc first 2 sts tog, sc in each of next 3 sts, sc next 2 sts tog, sc in end of next 17 rows; for **neck,** sc next 2 rows tog; sc in end of each row and in each st around, join with sl st in first sc; for second piece, work pattern in reverse order. Fasten off.

Working in **back lps,** sew Body Pieces together, matching row 40 at front of Body and row 43 at back of Body leaving remaining rows unsewn for Top Head Piece.

TOP HEAD PIECE

Row 1: Starting at bottom, ch 3, sc in 2nd ch from hook, sc in last ch, turn (2 sc).

Row 2: Ch 1, 2 sc in each st across, turn (4).

Row 3: Ch 1, 2 sc in first st, sc in each st across with 2 sc in last st, turn (6).

Row 4: Ch 1, sc in each st across, turn.

Rows 5-12: Repeat rows 3 and 4 alternately, ending with 14 sts in last row.

Rows 13-16: Repeat row 4.

Rows 17-21: Ch 1, sc first 2 sts tog, sc in each st across to last 2 sts, sc last 2 sts tog, turn, ending with 4 sts in last row.

Rnd 22: Working around outer edge, ch 1, sc first 2 sts tog, sc next 2 sts tog, sc in end of each row and in each st around, join with sl st in first sc. Fasten off.

Working in **back lps,** sew top Head Piece to Body according to Sewing Diagram on page 83, stuffing before closing.

MUZZLE

Rnd 1: Ch 6, sl st in first ch to form ring, ch 3, 16 dc in ring, join with sl st in top of ch-3 (17 dc).

Rnd 2: Ch 2, hdc in next 5 sts, 2 hdc in next st, (hdc in next 4 sts, 2 hdc in next st) around, join with sl st in top of ch-2 (20 hdc).

Rnd 3: Ch 1, 2 sc in first st, sc in each st around, join with sl st in first sc (21 sc). Fasten off.

FACIAL FEATURES

Working in **back lps,** sew Muzzle to Head according to Facial Features Diagram on page 83, stuffing before closing.

With brown, using Satin Stitch and Straight Stitches (see Stitch Guide), embroider nose and

Continued on page 73

HEIRLOOM BOOTIES

E S S E N T I A L S

NOTE: Photo on page 70.

SIZE: Instructions given are for 4" sole. Changes for 4½" and 5" are in [ ].

MATERIALS: Size 10 bedspread cotton — 130 yds ecru; 1 yd. ecru ⅛" satin ribbon; tapestry needle; No. 3 steel crochet hook or size needed to obtain gauge.

GAUGE: 9 dc sts = 1"; rnds 1 and 2 are 1½" wide.

I N S T R U C T I O N S

B O O T I E (make 2)

Sole

Rnd 1: Ch 21 [25, 29], 3 dc in 4th ch from hook, (dc in next 16 [20, 24] chs), 6 dc in end ch; working on opposite side of ch; repeat between ( ), join with sl st in top of ch-3 (42 dc) [50 dc, 58 dc].

NOTES: For **beginning cluster (beg cl),** ch 3, *yo 2 times, insert hook in same st, yo, draw through st, (yo, draw through 2 lps on hook) 2 times*; repeat between **, yo, draw through all 3 lps on hook.

For **cluster (cl),** yo 2 times, insert hook in next st, yo, draw through st, (yo, draw through 2 lps on hook) 2 times, *yo 2 times, insert hook in same st, yo, draw through st, (yo, draw through 2 lps on hook) 2 times; repeat from *, yo, draw through all 4 lps on hook.

Rnd 2: Beg cl, (ch 1, cl) in each of next 3 sts, (ch 1, skip next st, cl in next st) 8 [10, 12] times, (ch 1, cl) in each of next 7 sts, ch 1, skip next st, (cl in next st, ch 1, skip next st) around, join with sl st in top of beg cl (26 cls) [30 cls, 34 cls].

Rnd 3: (Sl st, ch 1, sc, ch 3, sc) in next ch, *(sc, ch 3, sc) in sp between last ch and next cl, skip next cl, (sc, ch 3, sc) in next ch*; repeat between ** 3 times, [sc in sp between last ch and next cl, skip next cl, (sc, ch 3, sc) in next ch]; repeat between [ ] 6 [8, 10] times; repeat between ** 7 more times; repeat between [ ] around with (sc, ch 3, sc) in last sp, join with sl st in first sc (38 ch lps) [42 ch lps, 46 ch lps].

Rnd 4: Sl st in next ch lp, beg cl in same lp, *ch 1, skip next lp, cl in next lp*; repeat between ** 3 times, (ch 1, cl) in next 7 [9, 11] ch lps; repeat between ** 7 more times, (ch 1, cl) in each ch lp around leaving last ch lp unworked, join.

Rnd 5: Repeat rnd 3. Fasten off.

Toe

Rnd 1: Ch 6, sl st in first ch to form ring, beg cl in ring, ch 1, (cl, ch 1) 9 times in ring, join with sl st in top of beg cl (10 cls).

Rnd 2: (Sl st, ch 1, sc, ch 3, sc) in next ch, *(sc, ch 3, sc) in sp between last ch and next cl, skip next cl*, [(sc, ch 3, sc) in next ch; repeat between **]; repeat between [ ] around, join (20 ch lps). Fasten off.

NOTES: When joining Toe and Sole, count back from joining on rnd 5 of Sole and place marker in 7th [8th, 9th] ch-3 lp of Sole.

Next place marker in the first ch-3 lp of rnd 2 on Toe. These will be the stitches you join together with a single crochet.

For 4" [4½", 5"] Sole, you will be working in 19 [21, 23] ch-3 lps of rnd 5 on Sole, easing the Toe to fit while crocheting together.

Row 3: Working in rows, hold pieces right sides together with wrong side of bottom on Sole facing you, join with sc through both thicknesses of marked stitches, evenly space 32 sc around to opposite end; turn right side out. Fasten off.

Ankle

Rnd 1: With Toe facing you, join with sl st in first unworked lp on Toe, ch 3, *yo 2 times, insert hook in same st, yo, draw through st, (yo, draw through 2 lps on hook) 2 times*; repeat between **, keeping all lps on hook, (skip next lp; repeat between ** 3 times in next lp) 2 times, yo, draw through all 9 lps on hook, ch 1, cl in same lp as last st of row 3 on toe, ch 1, working in established pattern of rnd 4 on Sole, (cl, ch 1) around, join with sl st in top of first cl.

Rnd 2: (Sl st, ch 1, sc, ch 3, sc) in next ch, working in pattern of rnd 5 on Sole, (sc, ch 3, sc) around, join with sl st in first sc.

Rnd 3: Sl st in next ch lp, beg cl in same lp, working in pattern of rnd 4 on Sole, (cl, ch 1) around, join.

Rnd 4: (Sl st, ch 1, sc, ch 3, sc) in first ch, (sc, ch 3, sc) in each ch and in each sp between ch and cl around leaving each cl unworked, join. Fasten off. Cut ribbon in half, weave one through ch lps of rnd 2, tie in bow at front of Bootie. ⚜

ANTIQUE TEDDY

Continued from page 71

mouth lines over rnd 1 according to diagram.

With brown and white, using Satin Stitch, embroider eyes ¾" apart above Muzzle according to diagram.

E A R (make 2)
Row 1: Ch 4, 9 dc in 4th ch from hook, turn (10 dc).

Row 2: Ch 2, hdc in same st, hdc in next st, (2 hdc in next st, hdc in next st) across, **do not** turn (15 hdc).

Rnd 3: Working around outer edge, ch 1, sc in end of each row and in each st around, join with sl st in first sc (19 sc). Fasten off.

Sew Ears ¾" apart across top of Head.

L E G   P I E C E (make 4)
Row 1: Starting at foot, ch 17, sc in 2nd ch from hook, sc in each ch across, turn (16 sc).

Row 2: Ch 1, sc in each st across, turn.

Row 3: Ch 1, sc in each st across with sc last 2 sts tog, turn (15).

Row 4: Ch 1, sc first 2 sts tog, sc in each st across, turn (14).

Rows 5-8: Repeat rows 3 and 4 alternately, ending with 10 sts in last row.

Rows 9-10: Repeat row 2.

Row 11: Ch 1, 2 sc in first st, sc in each st across with 2 sc in last st, turn (12).

Rows 12-17: Repeat row 2.

Row 18: Ch 1, 2 sc in first st, sc in each st across with sc last 2 sts tog, turn (12).

Row 19: Ch 1, sc first 2 sts tog, sc in each st across with 2 sc in last st, turn (12).

Row 20: Repeat row 18.

Rows 21-22: Repeat row 2.

Row 23: Repeat row 11 (14).

Rows 24-26: Repeat row 2.

Rows 27-31: Ch 1, sc first 2 sts tog, sc in each st across with sc last 2 sts tog, turn, ending with 4 sts in last row. At end of last row; for **first and third pieces,** turn; for **second and fourth pieces,** do not turn.

Rnd 32: For **first and third pieces,** working around outer edge, ch 1, sc in each stitch and in end of each row around, join with sl st in first sc; for **second and fourth pieces,** work pattern in reverse order. Fasten off.

Working in **back lps,** sew first and second Leg Pieces together, leaving row 1 free. Repeat with third and fourth Leg Pieces.

S O L E (make 2)
Rnd 1: Ch 9, 2 sc in 2nd ch from hook, sc in next 6 chs, 5 sc in end ch; working on opposite side of ch, sc in last 7 chs,

join with sl st in first sc, **turn** (20 sc).

Rnd 2: Ch 1, sc in first st, 2 sc in next st, sc in next 6 sts, (2 sc in next st, sc in next st) 3 times, sc in next 5 sts, 2 sc in last st, join, **turn** (25).

Rnd 3: Ch 1, sc in first 5 sts, hdc in next 4 sts, (2 hdc in next st, hdc in each of next 2 sts, 2 hdc in next st) 2 times, hdc in next 4 sts, sc in last 4 sts, join (29). Fasten off.

Stuff Leg; sew Sole to bottom of each Leg.

To **attach Legs,** with bedspread cotton, run tapestry needle through Body between rows 8 and 9. Draw through Leg between rows 26 and 27, make small stitch. Draw back through Body and through second Leg making small stitch; go back and forth twice making a small stitch each time. Draw thread tight, secure. Sew buttons over stitches of each Leg between rows 26 and 27.

A R M   P I E C E (make 4)
Row 1: Starting at hand, ch 4, sc in 2nd ch from hook, sc in each ch across, turn (3 sc).

Rows 2-5: Ch 1, 2 sc in first st, sc in each st across with 2 sc in last st, turn, ending with 11 sts in last row.

Rows 6-7: Ch 1, sc in each st across, turn.

Row 8: Ch 1, sc first 2 sts tog, sc in each st across with sc last 2 sts tog, turn (9).

Rows 9-10: Repeat row 7.

Rows 11-12: Repeat row 2 (11, 13).

Rows 13-15: Repeat row 7.

Row 16: For **back shoulder shaping,** ch 2, hdc in each of next 2 sts, sc in each st across, turn.

Row 17: Ch 1, sc in each st across to last 4 sts, hdc in last 4 sts, turn.

Row 18: Ch 2, hdc in next 4 sts, sc in each st across, turn.

Row 19: Repeat row 7.

Rows 20-23: Repeat row 8, ending with 5 sts.

Rnd 24: For **first and third pieces,** working around outer edge, ch 1, sc in each stitch and in end of each row around, join with sl st in first sc; for **second and fourth pieces,** work pattern in reverse order. Fasten off.

Working in **back lps,** sew first and second Arm Pieces together, leaving row 1 free, stuffing before closing. Repeat with third and fourth Arm Pieces.

To **attach Arms,** with bedspread cotton, run needle through Body between rows 23 and 24. Draw through Arm between rows 20 and 21, make small stitch. Draw back through Body and through second Arm making small stitch; go back and forth twice making a small stitch each time. Draw thread tight, secure. Sew buttons over stitches of each Arm between rows 20 and 21.

Tie ribbon in bow around neck. ⚜

H E I R L O O M   C R O C H E T   T R E A S U R E S

CAMELLIA DOILY

ESSENTIALS

SIZE: 14$\frac{1}{2}$" across, after blocking.

MATERIALS: Size 10 bedspread cotton — 75 yds. white and 25 yds. pink; No. 8 steel crochet hook or size needed to obtain gauge.

GAUGE: Rnds 1 - 3 = 3$\frac{1}{2}$"across.

INSTRUCTIONS

DOILY

Rnd 1: With pink, ch 7, sl st in first ch to form ring, ch 3, 17 dc in ring, join with sl st in top of ch-3 (18 dc).

Rnd 2: Ch 1; for **petal,** *2 sc in next st, ch 15, **turn,** sl st back into first sc made, ch 1, **turn,** (4 sc, 2 hdc, 9 dc, 2 hdc, 4 sc) over ch-15 lp just made, sc in each of next 2 sts on rnd 1; repeat from * around, join with sl st in first sc (6 petals).

Rnd 3: Working in sts of petals, sl st in first 7 sts, *ch 4, skip next 2 sts, dc in next st, ch 2; for **V-st, (dc ch 2, dc)** in next st; ch 2, dc in next st, ch 4, skip next 2 sts, sl st in next 3 sts, skip first 4 sc on next petal*, [sl st in next 3 sts; repeat between **];** repeat between [ ] around, join with sl st in 5th sl st of first petal (12 dc, 6 V-sts). Fasten off.

Rnd 4: Join white with sl st in first dc; for **beginning V-st (beg V-st), ch 5, dc in same st;** *(ch 2, V-st in next dc) 3 times, ch 4*, [V-st in next dc; repeat between **]; repeat between [ ] around, join with sl st in 3rd ch of ch-5 (24 V-sts).

Rnd 5: (Sl st, beg V-st) in first V-st, *(ch 3, V-st in next V-st) 3 times, ch 2, sc in next ch-4 sp, ch 2*, [V-st in next V-st; repeat between **]; repeat between [ ] around, join (24 V-sts, 6 sc).

Rnd 6: (Sl st, beg V-st) in first V-st, *ch 4, V-st in next V-st, ch 6, V-st in next V-st, ch 4, V-st in next V-st, (ch 3, sc, ch 3) in next sc*, [V-st in next V-st; repeat between **]; repeat between [ ] around, join.

Rnd 7: (Sl st, beg V-st) in first V-st, *ch 4, V-st in next V-st, ch 4, (dc, ch 4) 2 times in next ch-6 lp, (V-st in next V-st, ch 4) 2 times, skip next sc*, [V-st in next V-st; repeat between **]; repeat between [ ] around, join (24 V-sts, 12 dc).

Rnds 8-9: (Sl st, beg V-st) in first V-st, *ch 4, V-st in next V-st, ch 4, skip next ch-4 sp, (dc, ch 4) 2 times in next ch-4 sp, (V-st in next V-st, ch 4) 2 times*, [V-st in next V-st; repeat between **]; repeat between [ ] around, join.

Rnd 10: (Sl st, beg V-st) in first V-st, *ch 5, V-st in next V-st, ch 5, skip next ch-4 sp, 9 dc in next ch-4 sp, ch 5, (V-st in next V-st, ch 5) 2 times*, [V-st in next V-st; repeat between **]: repeat between [ ] around, join (54 dc, 24 V-sts).

Rnd 11: (Sl st, beg V-st) in first V-st, *ch 5, V-st in next V-st, ch 2, dc in next dc, (ch 1, dc in next dc) 8 times, ch 2, V-st in next V-st, ch 5, V-st in next V-st, ch 2, sc in next ch-5 sp, ch 2*, [V-st in next V-st; repeat between **]; repeat between [ ] around, join.

Rnd 12: (Sl st, beg V-st) in first V-st, *ch 5, V-st in next V-st, ch 5, sc in next dc, ch 5, skip next 2 dc, dc in next dc, ch 2, V-st in next dc, ch 2, dc in next dc, ch 5, skip next 2 dc, sc in next dc, (ch 5, V-st in next V-st) 2 times, ch 3, sc in next sc, ch 3*, [V-st in next V-st; repeat between **]; repeat between [ ] around, join (30 V-sts, 18 sc, 12 dc).

Rnd 13: (Sl st, beg V-st) in first V-st, *ch 5, V-st in next V-st, ch 5, skip next sc, dc in next dc, ch 2, dc in next dc, ch 5, dc in next dc, ch 2, dc in next dc, (ch 5, V-st in next V-st) 2 times, ch 4, sc in next sc, ch 4*, [V-st in next V-st; repeat between **]; repeat between [ ] around, join (24 V-sts, 24 dc, 6 sc).

Rnd 14: (Sl st, beg V-st) in first V-st, *ch 5, V-st in next V-st, ch 5, dc in next dc, ch 2, dc in next dc, 10 dc in next ch-5 sp, dc in next dc, ch 2, dc in next dc, (ch 5, V-st in next V-st) 2 times, ch 4, sc in next sc, ch 4*, [V-st in next V-st; repeat between **]; repeat between [ ] around, join (84 dc, 24 V-sts, 6 sc).

Rnd 15: (Sl st, beg V-st) in first V-st, *ch 5, V-st in next V-st, ch 5, dc in next dc, ch 2, dc in next dc, (ch 1, dc in next dc) 11 times, ch 2, dc in next dc, (ch 5, V-st in next V-st) 2 times, ch 4, sc in next sc, ch 4*, [V-st in next V-st; repeat between **]; repeat between [ ] around, join. Fasten off.

MOTIF NO. 1

Rnd 1: With pink, ch 6, sl st in first ch to form ring, ch 1, 14 sc in ring, join with sl st in first sc (14).

Rnd 2: Ch 1, sc in first st, ch 3; to attach Motif to Doily, with rnd 15 towards you, sc in first V-st on rnd 15 of Doily, (see Motif Joining Diagram) *ch 3, skip next sc on Motif, sc in next sc on Motif*, ch 3, sc in next sc on rnd 15 of Doily; repeat between **, ch 3, sc in next V-st on rnd 15 of Doily; repeat between **, ch 7, skip next sc on Motif, (sc in next sc on Motif, ch 7, skip next sc on Motif) 3 times, join with sl st in first sc. Fasten off.

MOTIFS NO. 2-6

Work same as Motif No. 1, joining Motif between each (V-st, ch 5, sc, ch 5, V-st) group around, ending with 6 Motifs.

BORDER

Rnd 1: With right side of Doily facing you, join white with sl st in first V-st on rnd 15 of doily, ch 8, *V-st in next V-st, ch 5, dc in next dc, ch 2, (tr in next dc, ch 2) 13 times, dc in next dc, ch 5, V-st in next V-st, ch 5, dc in next V-st, ch 5; working in ch-7 lps of next Motif, V-st in first lp, (ch 2, V-st in next lp) 3 times, ch 5*, [dc in next V-st on rnd 15 of Doily, ch 5; repeat between **]; repeat between [ ] around, join with sl st in 3rd ch of ch-8.

Rnd 2: Ch 8, *V-st in next V-st, ch 5, dc in next dc, ch 2, (tr in next tr, ch 2) 13 times, dc in next dc, ch 5, V-st in next V-st, ch 5, dc in next dc, ch 5, V-st in next V-st, (ch 2, V-st in next V-st) 3 times, ch 5*, [dc in next dc, ch 5; repeat between **]; repeat between [ ] around, join. Fasten off.

Rnd 3: Join pink with sc in any ch-5 sp, 5 sc in same sp, (6 sc in each ch-5 sp and 3 sc in each ch-2 sp) around, join with sl st in first sc. Fasten off. ⚜

MOTIF JOINING DIAGRAM

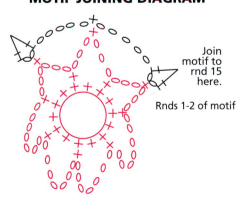

Join motif to rnd 15 here.

Rnds 1-2 of motif

HEIRLOOM CROCHET TREASURES

VICTORIAN LADY

ESSENTIALS

SIZE: 7" tall.

MATERIALS: Size 20 crochet cotton — 200 yds. ecru; 9" burgundy $\frac{3}{8}$" satin ribbon, 12" burgundy $\frac{1}{16}$" satin ribbon; two small silk flowers; $3\frac{1}{2}$" strand 2-mm. pearls; acrylic doll hair; chenille stem; $3\frac{1}{2}$" x $5\frac{1}{2}$" piece unbleached muslin fabric; $6\frac{1}{2}$" ecru $\frac{3}{4}$" flat lace; fabric stiffener; empty thread spool or $\frac{3}{4}$" tall x $1\frac{1}{2}$" across round wooden cylinder; $4\frac{1}{2}$"-long wooden dowel to fit in spool hole; craft glue or hot glue gun; polyester fiberfill; off-white sewing thread; sewing and tapestry

needles; No. 10 steel crochet hook or size needed to obtain gauge.

GAUGE: 10 dc sts = 1"; 5 dc rows = 1".

INSTRUCTIONS

DOLL

Rnd 1: Starting at head, ch 5, sl st in first ch to form ring, ch 1, 8 sc in ring, join with sl st in first sc (8 sc).

Rnd 2: Ch 1, 2 sc in each st around, join (16).

Rnd 3: Ch 1, sc in each st around, join.

Rnd 4: Ch 1, (sc in next st, 2 sc in next st) around, join (24).

Rnds 5-11: Ch 1, sc in each st around, join.

Rnd 12: Ch 1, (sc in next st, sc next 2 sts tog) around, join (16). Stuff head only.

Rnd 13: Ch 1, sc in each of first 2 sts, sc next 2 sts tog, (sc in each of next 3 sts, sc next 2 sts tog) 2 times, sc in each of last 2 sts, join (13).

Rnds 14-16: Ch 1, sc in each st around, join.

Rnd 17: For **back,** ch 1, 2 sc in each of first 2 sts, sc in each st around with 2 sc in each of last 2 sts, join (17).

Rnd 18: Ch 1, 2 sc in each of first 2 sts, sc in each st around with 2 sc in last st, join (20).

Rnds 19-20: Ch 1, sc in each st around, join.

Rnd 21: Ch 1, sc in first 8 sts; for **bust,** 6 dc in next st, sc in each of next 3 sts, 6 dc in next st; sc in last 7 sts, join.

Rnd 22: Ch 1, sc in each sc and hdc in each dc around, join.

NOTE: To **hdc next 2 hdc tog,** (yo, insert hook in next st, yo, draw lp through) 2 times, yo, draw through all 5 lps on hook.

Rnd 23: Ch 1, sc in first 8 sc, (hdc next 2 hdc tog) 3 times, sc in each of next 3 sc, (hdc next 2 hdc tog) 3 times, sc in last 7 sc, join (24 sts).

Rnds 24-25: Ch 1, sc in each st around, join.

Rnd 26: Ch 1, (sc next 2 sts tog) 2 times, sc in each st around, join (22).

Rnd 27: Ch 1, sc in each st around, join.

Rnd 28: Repeat rnd 17 (26).

Rnds 29-30: Ch 1, sc in each st around, join.

Rnd 31: Repeat rnd 17 (30).

Rnds 32-33: Ch 1, sc in each st around, join.

Rnd 34: Ch 1, sc in first st, 2 sc in next st, (sc in each of next 3 sts, 2 sc in next st) around, join (38).

Rnds 35-39: Ch 1, sc in each st around, join.

NOTES: Ch-3 at beginning of each rnd counts as first st.

For **raised treble crochet (rtr),** yo 2 times, insert hook from front to back around post of next st on rnd before last, complete as tr, skip next st on the row you are working.

For **front post (fp,** see Stitch Guide), yo, insert hook around post of next rtr or dc fp, complete as dc.

Rnd 40: For **skirt,** ch 3, dc in next 12 sts, rtr, dc in **back lps** of next 13 sts, rtr, dc in **both lps** of each st around, join with sl st in top of ch-3.

Rnd 41: Ch 3, dc in same st, dc in next 12 sts, fp, dc in **back lps** of next 13 sts, fp, dc in **both lps** of each st around, join (39 sts).

Rnd 42: Ch 3, dc in next 13 sts, fp, dc in **back lps** of next 13 sts, fp, dc in **both lps** of each st around, join.

Rnd 43: Ch 3, dc in each of next 2 sts, 2 dc in next st, (dc in next 4 sts, 2 dc in next st) 2 times, fp, dc in **back lps** of next 13 sts, fp; working in **both lps;** repeat between ( ) 2 more times, join (44).

Rnds 44-46: Ch 3, dc in next 16 sts, fp, dc in **back lps** of next 13 sts, fp, dc in **both lps o**f each st around, join.

Rnd 47: Ch 3, dc in next 16 sts, fp; working in **back lps,** 2 dc in next st, dc in next 11 sts, 2 dc in next st, fp, dc in **both lps** of each st around, join (46).

Rnds 48-49: Ch 3, dc in next 16 sts, fp, dc in **back lps** of next 15 sts, fp, dc in **both lps** of each st around, join.

Rnd 50: Ch 3, dc in next 15 sts, 2 dc in next st, fp, dc in **back lps** of next 15 sts, fp; working in **both lps,** 2 dc in next st, dc in each st around, join (48).

Rnd 51: Ch 3, dc in next 16 sts, 2 dc in next st, fp, dc in **back lps** of next 15 sts, fp; working in **both lps,** 2 dc in next st, dc in each st around, join (50).

Rnds 52-54: Ch 3, dc in next 18 sts, fp, dc in **back lps** of next 15 sts, fp, dc in **both lps** of each st around, join.

Rnd 55: Ch 1, sc in **both lps** of each st around, join with sl st in first sc, fasten off.

For **ruffles,** join with sc over post of first fp on rnd 40; working in **front lps** of rnd 39, (dc, ch 1, dc) in each st across, sc over post of last fp, fasten off. Repeat on every other rnd.

SLEEVE (make 2)

Rnd 1: Starting at wrist, ch 7, sl st in first ch to form ring, ch 1, 9 sc in ring, join with sl st in first sc (9 sc).

Rnds 2-8: Ch 1, sc in each st around, join.

Row 9: Working in rows; for **elbow,** ch 1, sc in first 4 sts leaving remaining sts unworked, turn (4).

Row 10: Ch 1, sc in each st across, turn.

Rnd 11: Working in rnds, ch 1, sc in first 4 sts, sc in each unworked st of rnd 8, join (9).

Rnds 12-14: Ch 1, sc in each st around, join.

Rnd 15: Ch 1, (sc in each of next 2 sts, 2 sc in next st) around, join (12).

Rnds 16-18: Ch 1, sc in each st around, join.

Rnd 19: Ch 1, sc in each of first 2 sts, 2 sc in each of next 2 sts, (sc in next st, 2 sc in each of next 3 sts) around, join (20).

Rnd 20: Ch 1, sc in each st around, join.

Rnd 21: Working this rnd in **back lps,** ch 1, sc in each st around, join.

Rnd 22: Ch 1, sc in each st around, join.

Rnd 23: Ch 1, sc first 2 sts tog, (sc in next st, sc next 2 sts tog) around, join (13).

Rnd 24: Ch 1, sc first 2 sts tog, sc in each st around, join (12).

Rnds 25-26: Ch 1, sc in each st around, join. Fasten off at end of last rnd, leaving 6" for sewing.

For **Sleeve ruffle,** working in **front lps** of rnd 20, join with sl st in first st, ch 4, dc in same st, (dc, ch 1, dc) in next 13 sts leaving remaining sts unworked, fasten off.

For **arms,** insert chenille stem through rnd 19 on one side of body, push through to opposite side of body. Place Sleeve over one end, lightly stuffing, sew rnd 26 to body. Repeat with other Sleeve on opposite end. Bend at elbows.

Continued on page 82

ROMANTIC LINENS

SIZE: 4" wide.

MATERIALS: Size 20 crochet cotton — 2,000 yds. white; one white flat sheet with matching pillowcases; white sewing thread; five $\frac{3}{8}$"-wide craft sticks; sewing and tapestry needles; No. 7 steel crochet hook or size needed to obtain gauge.

GAUGE: 8 dc sts = 1"; 4 dc rows = 1".

NOTES: For **beginning tall sc (beg tall sc),** insert hook in ch or st, yo, draw through, yo, draw through 2 lps on hook drawing up $\frac{1}{2}$" long lp; without twisting, place long lp on hook over craft stick, drop lp from hook, draw lp down snuggly over stick.

For **tall sc,** insert hook in ch or st, yo, draw through, yo, draw through lp on hook drawing up $\frac{1}{2}$" long lp, place long lp on hook over craft stick, drop lp from hook, draw lp down snuggly over stick.

Long lp of tall sc can be drawn up any length to comfortably be placed over craft stick, but the height of the finished lp needs to be $\frac{3}{8}$".

INSTRUCTIONS

EDGING

Row 1: Ch 57, dc in 4th ch from hook, dc in next 8 chs, skip next ch, dc in next 5 chs, skip next ch, dc in next 8 chs, *ch 4, skip next 4 chs, 3 dc in next ch, ch 4, skip next 4 chs*, [(beg tall sc, 3 tall sc, sl st) in next ch; repeat between **]; repeat between [ ] across to last ch, dc in last ch, turn (33 dc, 6 ch-4 sps, 8 lps).

Row 2: Ch 7, 2 dc in first ch-4 sp, dc in next dc, ch 1, skip next dc, dc in next dc, ch 4, *sc in next 4 lps while removing from stick, ch 4, skip next dc, dc in next dc, ch 4, skip next dc; repeat from *, dc in each of next 3 dc, ch 4, skip next 4 dc, sl st in next dc leaving remaining sts unworked, turn (10 dc, 8 sc).

Row 3: Sl st in first ch-4 sp, (ch 1, beg tall sc, 9 tall sc, sl st) in same sp, dc in each of next 3 dc, ch 4, (beg tall sc, 3 tall sc, sl st) in next dc, *ch 4, skip next sc, 3 dc in next sc, ch 4, skip next 2 sc, (beg tall sc, 3 tall sc, sl st) in next dc; repeat from *, ch 4, skip next 2 dc, dc in next dc, 2 dc in next ch-7 lp, ch 4, dc in 3rd ch of same ch-7 lp, turn (22 lps, 13 dc).

Row 4: Ch 7, 2 dc in first ch-4 sp, dc in next dc, ch 1, skip next dc, dc in next dc, ch 4, sc in next 4 lps, *ch 4, skip next dc, dc in next dc, ch 4, skip next dc, sc in next 4 lps; repeat from *, ch 4, dc in each of next 3 dc, sc in next 5 lps, ch 4, sc in next 5 lps, skip next 4 dc on unworked row, sl st in next dc leaving remaining sts unworked, turn (22 sc, 10 dc).

Row 5: (Sl st, ch 1, beg tall sc) in first sc, tall sc in next 4 sc, 8 tall sc in next ch-4 sp, tall sc in next 5 sc, sl st in same st as last st made, dc in each of next 3 dc, *ch 4, skip next sc, 3 dc in next sc, ch 4, skip next 2 sc, (beg tall sc, 3 tall sc, sl st) in next dc; repeat from * 2 times, ch 4, skip next 2 dc, dc in next dc, 2 dc in next ch-7 lp, ch 4, dc in 3rd ch of same lp, turn (30 lps, 10 dc).

Row 6: Ch 7, 2 dc in first ch-4 sp, dc in next dc, ch 1, skip next dc, dc in next dc, ch 4, *sc in next 4 lps, ch 4, skip next dc, dc in next dc, ch 4; repeat from * 2 times, dc in each of next 3 dc, sc in next 9 lps, ch 4, sc in next 9 lps, skip next 4 dc on unworked row, sl st in next dc leaving remaining sts unworked, turn (30 sc, 11 dc).

Row 7: (Sl st, ch 1, beg tall sc) in first sc, tall sc in next 8 sc, 8 tall sc in next ch-4 sp, tall sc in next 9 sc, sl st in same sc as last st made, dc in each of next 3 dc, ch 4, (beg tall sc, 3 tall sc, sl st) in next dc, *ch 4, skip next sc, 3 dc in next sc, ch 4, skip next 2 sc, (beg tall sc, 3 tall sc, sl st) in next dc; repeat from * 2 times, ch 4, skip next 2 dc, dc in next dc, 2 dc in next ch-7 lp, ch 4, dc in 3rd ch of same lp, turn (42 lps, 16 dc).

Row 8: Ch 7, 2 dc in first ch-4 sp, dc in next dc, ch 1, skip next dc, dc in next dc, ch 4, sc in next 4 lps, *ch 4, skip next dc, dc in next dc, ch 4, skip next dc, sc in next 4 lps; repeat from * 2 times, ch 4, dc in each of next 3 dc, sc in next 13 lps, ch 4, sc in next 13 lps, skip next 4 dc on unworked row, sl st in top of ch-3, turn (42 sc, 11 dc).

Row 9: Ch 3, sc in first sc, (sc in next sc, ch 3, sc in next sc) 6 times, (sc, ch 3, sc) 2 times in next ch-4 sp, (sc in next sc, ch 3, sc in next sc) 6 times, ch 3, sc in next sc, dc in each of next 3 dc, 2 dc in next ch-4 sp, dc in next 4 sc, 2 dc in next ch-4 sp, dc in next dc, 3 dc in next ch-4 sp, dc in next 4 sc, 3 dc in next ch-4 sp, dc in next dc, *ch 4, skip next sc, 3 dc in next sc, ch 4, skip next 2 sc, (beg tall sc, 3 tall

Continued on page 81

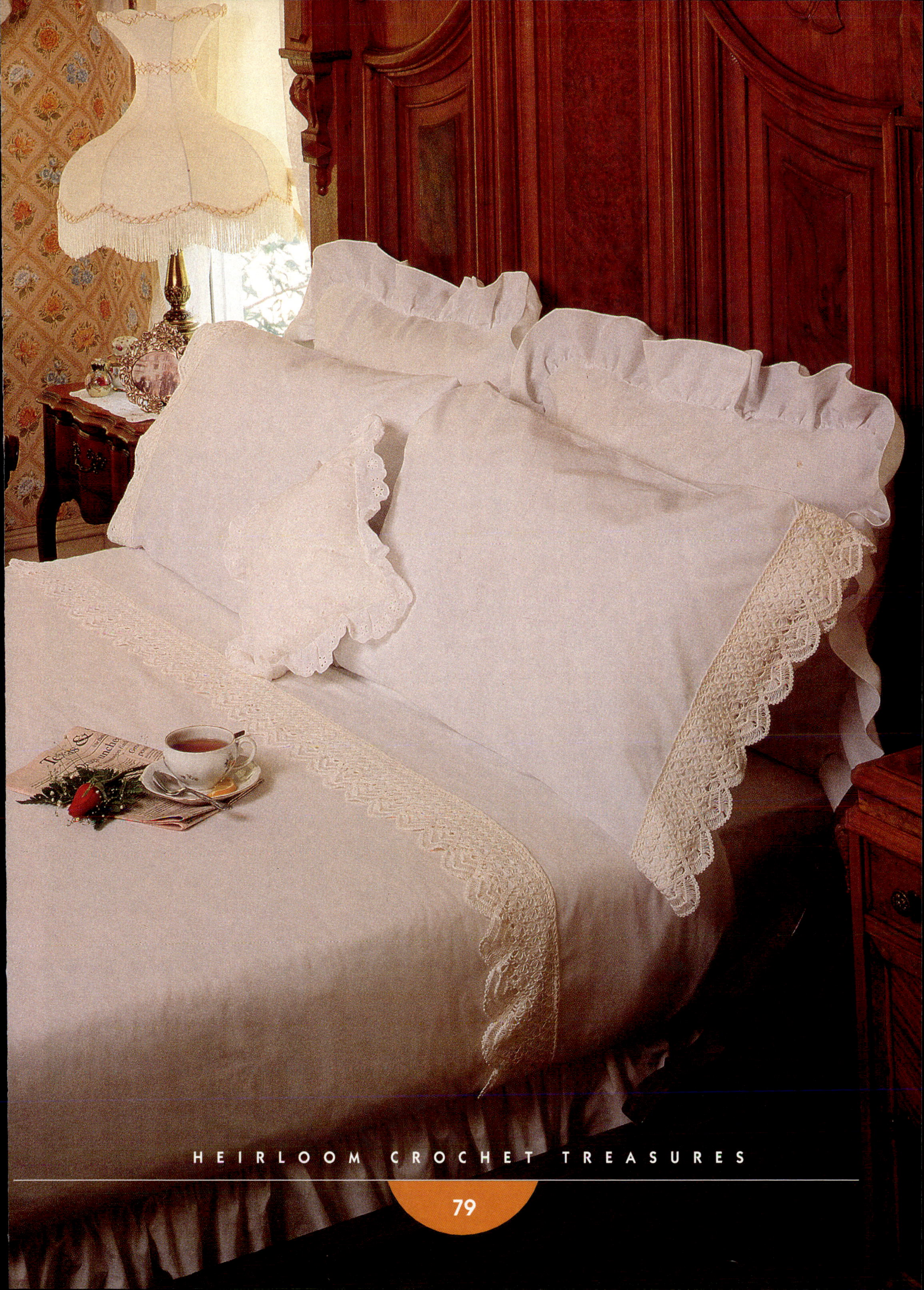

HEIRLOOM CROCHET TREASURES

FANCY MOTIF

SIZE: With size 10 bedspread cotton and No. 6 steel hook, motif is 6" x 6¾". With size 20 crochet cotton and No. 9 steel hook, motif is 4" x 4½".

MATERIALS FOR ONE: Size 10 or 20 crochet cotton — 75 yds.; No. 6 or 9 steel crochet hook or size needed to obtain gauge.

GAUGE: Larger thread and hook, 11 dc sts = 1". Smaller thread and hook, 14 dc sts = 1".

MOTIF

Rnd 1: Ch 8, sl st in first ch to form ring, ch 3, 15 dc in ring, ch 5, join with sl st in top of ch-3 (16 dc, 1 ch-5 lp).

Rnd 2: Ch 3, dc in same st, 2 dc in each of next 15 sts, ch 5, sc in next ch-5 lp, ch 5, join (32 dc, 2 ch-5 lps).

Rnd 3: Ch 3, dc in each of next 2 sts, ch 4, skip next 2 sts, (dc in each of next 3 sts, ch 4, skip next 2 sts) 5 times, dc in next st, 2 dc in last dc, ch 5, (sc in next ch-5 lp, ch 5) 2 times, join (21 dc, 3 ch-5 lps).

Rnd 4: Sl st across to ch-4 sp; for **beg shell, ch 3, (2 dc, ch 3, 3 dc)** in same sp; *ch 6; for **shell, (3 dc, ch 3, 3 dc)** in next ch-4 sp, repeat from * 4 more times, ch 5, (sc in next ch-5 lp, ch 5) 3 times, join (6 shells, 4 ch-5 lps).

Rnd 5: Sl st across to ch-4 sp, beg shell in same sp, (ch 8, shell in next shell) 5 times, ch 5, (sc in next ch-5 lp, ch 5) 4 times, join (6 shells, 5 ch-5 lps).

Rnd 6: Sl st across to ch-4 sp, beg shell in same sp, (ch 10, shell in next shell) 5 times, ch 5, (sc in next ch-5 lp, ch 5) 5 times, join (6 shells, 6 ch-5 lps).

Rnd 7: Ch 1, sc in same st, ch 5, sc in next ch-3 sp, (ch 8, working over ch lps of rnds 5 and 6, sc in ch lp of rnd 4, ch 8, sc in next ch-3 sp) 5 times, ch 5, skip next 2 dc, sc in next dc, ch 5, (sc in next ch-5 lp, ch 5) 6 times, join with sl st in first sc (10 ch-8 lps, 9 ch-5 lps).

Rnd 8: Sl st in ch-5 lp, ch 1, (sc, hdc, 5 dc) in same lp, dc in next sc, *(11 dc, hdc, sc) in next ch-8 lp, (sc, hdc, 11 dc) in next ch-8 lp, dc in next sc; repeat from * 4 times, (5 dc, hdc, sc) in next ch-5 lp, ch 5, (sc in next ch-

5 lp, ch 5) 7 times, join.

Rnd 9: Sl st in next 2 sts, ch 3, dc in each of next 2 sts, ch 7, skip next 5 sts, dc in each of next 3 sts, *ch 7, skip next 16 sts, dc in each of next 3 sts, ch 7, skip next 5 sts, dc in each of next 3 sts; repeat from * 4 times, ch 5, (sc in next ch-5 lp, ch 5) 8 times, join (36 dc, 11 ch-7 lps, 9 ch-5 lps).

Rnd 10: Sl st across to ch-7 lp, beg shell in same lp, (ch 7, shell in next ch-7 lp) 10 times, ch 5, (sc in next ch-5 lp, ch 5) 9 times, join (11 shells, 10 ch-7 lps, 10 ch-5 lps).

Rnd 11: Sl st across to ch-3 sp, beg shell in same sp, (ch 7, shell in next shell) 10 times, ch 4, (sc in next ch-5 lp, ch 4) 10 times, join (11 shells, 10 ch-7 lps, 11 ch-4 lps).

Rnd 12: Ch 1, sc in same st, ch 3, (sc in next dc, ch 3) 2 times, [sc in next ch-3 sp, (ch 3, sc in next dc) 3 times], *ch 3, working over next ch lp of rnd 11, sc in ch lp of rnd 10, ch 3, (sc in next dc, ch 3) 3 times; repeat between [ ]; repeat from * 8 times, ch 4, (sc in next ch-4 lp, ch 4) 11 times, join. Fasten off.❧

ROMANTIC LINENS

Continued from page 78

sc, sl st) in next dc; repeat from *, ch 4, skip next 2 dc, dc in next dc, 2 dc in next ch-7 lp, ch 4, dc in 3rd ch of same lp, turn (33 dc, 16 ch-3 sps, 8 lps).

Repeat rows 2-9 consecutively until desired length is reached. At end of last row, **do not fasten off.**

For **border,** working across long straight edge, ch 1, 3 sc in each ch-3 sp and over each dc across to row 1. Fasten off.

Using sewing needle and thread, sew Edging to desired item.❧

VICTORIAN LADY

Continued from page 77

Hand

Row 1: Flatten rnd 1 of Sleeve; working through both thicknesses, skip first ch, join with sc in next ch, sc in each of next 2 chs, turn (3 sc).

Row 2: Ch 1, sc in each st across, turn.

Row 3: Ch 1, sc first 3 sts tog, fasten off.

NECK RUFFLE

Row 1: Ch 14, sc in 2nd ch from hook, sc in each ch across, turn (13 sc).

Rows 2-3: Ch 1, sc in each st across, turn.

Row 4: Ch 1, (sc, ch 3, sc) in each st across, fasten off, leaving 6" for sewing.

Place Ruffle around neck, sew ends together at back. Tie $\frac{1}{16}$" ribbon into $\frac{5}{8}$" bow. With collar up towards chin, glue or sew bow to front over row 3. Place pearl strand around neck, glue ends together at back.

Styling as desired, glue hair to head.

BUSTLE

Row 1: Ch 30, dc in 4th ch from hook, dc in each ch across, turn (28 dc).

NOTE: Work remaining rows in **back lps** unless otherwise stated.

Row 2: Ch 3, dc in each of next 2 sts, 2 dc in next st, (dc in each of next 3 sts, 2 dc in next st) across, turn (35).

Row 3: Ch 3, dc in each of next 3 sts, 2 dc in next st, (dc in next 4 sts, 2 dc in next st) across, turn (42).

Row 4: Ch 3, dc in next 4 sts, 2 dc in next st, (dc in next 5 sts, 2 dc in next st) across, turn (49).

Row 5: Ch 3, dc in next 5 sts, 2 dc in next st, (dc in next 6 sts, 2 dc in next st) across, turn (56).

Row 6: Ch 3, dc in next 6 sts, 2 dc in next st, (dc in next 7 sts, 2 dc in next st) across, turn (63).

Row 7: Ch 3, dc in next 7 sts, 2 dc in next st, (dc in next 8 sts, 2 dc in next st) across, turn (70).

Row 8: Working this row in **both lps,** sl st in each st across, fasten off.

Place Bustle around Doll's waist with ends of rows in front. Gather ends of rows together, sew in place. Make $1\frac{1}{2}$" bow from $\frac{3}{8}$" ribbon, trim ends. Glue over front of Bustle.

PURSE

Rnd 1: Ch 20, sl st in first ch to form ring, ch 1, sc in each ch around, join with sl st in first sc (20 sc).

Rnd 2: Ch 2, hdc in each st around, join with sl st in top of ch-2.

Rnds 3-4: Ch 1, sc in each st around, join.

Rnd 5: Ch 1, sc in each of first 2 sts, (2 sc in next st, sc in each of next 2 sts) around, join (26).

Rnds 6-12: Ch 1, sc in each st around, join.

Row 13: Flatten rnd 12; working in rows, through both thicknesses, ch 1, sc in each st across, fasten off.

For **trim,** working on opposite side of rnd 1, join with sc in any st, sc in same st, 2 sc in each st around, join, fasten off (40 sc).

For **draw-string,** fold 8" of crochet cotton in half, weave through hdc sts of rnd 2, tie ends in knot to secure. Trim ends. Stuff Purse lightly. Pull drawstring closed. Make two loops with remaining $\frac{1}{16}$" ribbon, glue or sew to one side of Purse. Glue one silk flower over bow.

DOWEL CAP

NOTE: For remainder of pattern, **do not** join rnds unless otherwise stated. Mark first st of each rnd.

Rnd 1: Ch 5, sl st in first ch to form ring, ch 1, 8 sc in ring (8 sc).

Rnds 2-8: Sc in each st around. At end of last rnd, join with sl st in first sc, fasten off.

Leaving rnds 6-8 free, glue Cap over dowel.

For **skirt lining,** with sewing needle and thread, sew lace to one long edge of fabric. Machine or hand sew short sides together. Hand baste around top edge leaving ends long. Pull ends to gather, sew to rnd 8 of Dowel Cap.

HAT

Rnd 1: Ch 4, sl st in first ch to form ring, ch 1, 12 sc in ring (12 sc).

Rnd 2: (Sc in next 5 sts, 2 sc in next st) around (14).

Rnd 3: Sc in each of first 2 sts, (2 sc in next st, sc in each of next 2 sts) around (18).

Rnd 4: (2 sc in next st, sc in next st) around (27).

Rnd 5: Sc in each st around.

Rnd 6: Sc in each of first 6 sts, 2 sc in next st, (sc in next 4 sts, 2 sc in next st) around, join with sl st in first sc (32).

Rnd 7: Working this rnd in **back lps,** ch 1, sc in each st around, join.

Rnds 8-9: Working in **both lps,** ch 1, sc in each st around, join.

Rnd 10: Repeat rnd 6 (38).

Rnds 11-14: Ch 1, sc in each st around, join.

Rnd 15: Ch 1, 2 sc in each st around, join (76).

Rnds 16-19: Ch 1, sc in each st around, join.

Rnd 20: Sl st in each st around, join, fasten off.

Apply fabric stiffener to Hat according to manufacturer's instructions; allow to dry, shaping brim as it dries. When completely dry, form bow with remaining $\frac{3}{8}$" ribbon and glue to back of Hat. Glue silk flower over bow. Place hat on doll's head.

FINISHING
1: Finish stuffing and shaping upper body.

2: Insert Dowel Cap through center of fiberfill. Glue or tack Dowel Cap to fiberfill. Glue dowel inside wooden cylinder.

3: Stuff around dowel for skirt shaping.❧

ANTIQUE TEDDY

Instructions on page 71

FACIAL FEATURES DIAGRAM

SEWING DIAGRAM

TEATIME DOILY

Continued from page 69

repeat between **]; repeat between [ ] around, join, fasten off.

Rnd 14: Join med. pink with sl st in center ch of any ch-5 sp, beg shell, ch 2, (dc in next dc, ch 2) 3 times, skip next 2 dc, (dc in next dc, ch 2) 3 times, [shell in center ch of next ch-5 sp, ch 2, (dc in next dc, ch 2) 3 times, skip next 2 dc, (dc in next dc, ch 2) 3 times]; repeat between [ ] around, join with sl st in top of ch-3.

Rnd 15: Ch 1, sc in same st, sc in next dc, *2 sc in ch sp of same shell, ch 4, sl st in 4th ch from hook, ch 6, sl st in 6th ch from hook, ch 4, sl st in 4th ch from hook, 2 sc in ch sp of same shell, sc in each of next 2 dc, skip next ch-2 sp, dc in next dc, (2 dc in next ch-2 sp, dc in next dc) 2 times, (dc, picot, dc) in next ch-2 sp, dc in next dc, (2 dc in next ch-2 sp, dc in next dc) 2 times, skip next ch-2 sp*, [sc in each of next 2 dc; repeat between **]; repeat between [ ] around, join with sl st in first sc, fasten off.❧

FILET ARTISTRY

If you have a taste for the finer things in life, then this dazzling assembly of crochet masterpieces is just for you. Prime examples of an age-old art form, these spectacular designs are refreshingly simple, yet splendidly detailed. Why not indulge the connoisseur within and lavish yourself and your home with timeless needlework treasures.

HEIRLOOM CROCHET TREASURES

WILD ROSE FILET

ESSENTIALS

SIZE: 13" x 15".
MATERIALS: Size 10 bedspread cotton — 325 yds. ecru; No. 7 steel crochet hook or size needed to obtain gauge.
GAUGE: 9 dc sts = 1"; 4 dc rows = 1".

INSTRUCTIONS

DOILY
NOTES: For **beginning mesh (beg mesh)**, ch 5, skip next 2 chs or sts, dc in next ch or dc.

For **mesh**, ch 2, skip next 2 chs or sts, dc in next ch or dc.

For **block**, dc in each of next 2 ch sps or sts, dc in next ch or dc.

Row 1: Ch 127, dc in 8th ch from hook (beg mesh made), complete row according to graph on next page, turn (40 mesh). Back of row 1 is right side of work.

Rows 2-62: Work according to graph, turn. Fasten off at end of last row.

EDGING

Rnd 1: Working in ch sps around outer edge, join ecru with sl st in any mesh, ch 3, dc in same mesh, 2 dc over each mesh around with (3 dc, ch 2, 3 dc) in each corner, join with sl st in top of ch-3.

Rnd 2: (Ch 3, dc; for **picot,** ch 3, sc in 2nd ch from hook; 2 dc) in same st, ch 1, skip next 3 sts, *2 dc, picot, 2 dc) in next st, ch 1, skip next 3 sts; repeat from * around with (3 dc, picot, 3 dc) in each corner, join, fasten off. ⚜

WILD ROSE FILET GRAPH

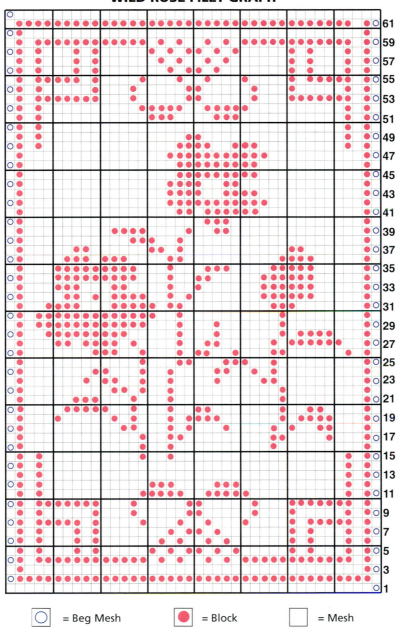

○ = Beg Mesh   ● = Block   ☐ = Mesh

Designed by Carol Smith

HEIRLOOM CROCHET TREASURES

FLOWER BASKET

ESSENTIALS

SIZE: 14⅛" x 16⅜".

MATERIALS: Size 10 bedspread cotton — 325 yds. white; No. 7 steel crochet hook or size needed to obtain gauge.

GAUGE: 4 dc and 2 ch sps = 1"; 4 dc rows = 1".

NOTES: For **beginning mesh (beg mesh),** ch 5, skip first 2 sts or chs, dc in next st or ch.

For **mesh,** ch 2, skip next 2 sts or chs, dc in next st or ch.

For **block,** dc in each of next 2 sts or chs, dc in next st or ch.

INSTRUCTIONS

DOILY

Row 1: Ch 134, dc in 8th ch from hook (beg mesh made), complete row according to Graph A, turn.

Rows 2-34: Work according to graph. At end of last row, fasten off.

Row 35: Working in starting ch on opposite side of row 1, join with sl st in first ch, complete row according to Graph B, turn.

Rows 36-65: Work according to graph. At end of last row, fasten off. ⚜

FLOWER BASKET GRAPH

GRAPH A

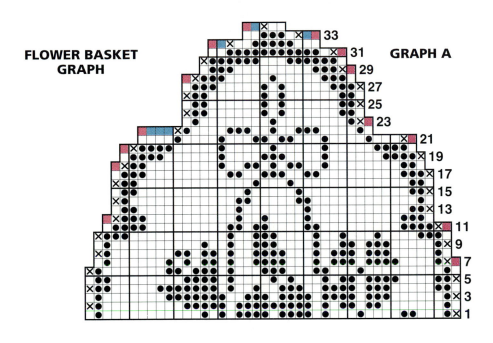

GRAPH B

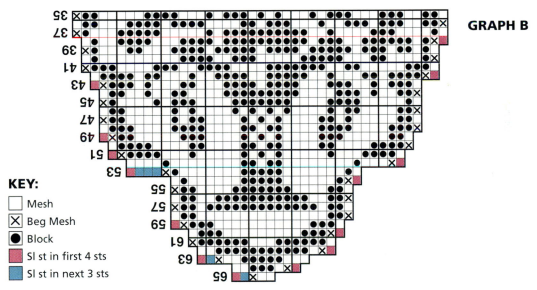

KEY:
- ☐ Mesh
- ☒ Beg Mesh
- ● Block
- 🟥 Sl st in first 4 sts
- 🟦 Sl st in next 3 sts

HEIRLOOM CROCHET TREASURES

HUMMINGBIRD CENTERPIECE

ESSENTIALS

SIZE: 19" x 25".

MATERIALS: Size 10 bedspread cotton — 675 yds.; No. 7 steel crochet hook or size needed to obtain gauge.

GAUGE: 4 dc and 3 ch sps = 1"; 4 dc rows = 1".

NOTES: For **mesh,** ch 2, skip next 2 sts or chs, dc in next st or ch.

For **beginning block (beg block),** ch 3, dc in each of next 2 sts or chs, dc in next st or ch.

For **block,** dc in each of next 2 sts or chs, dc in next st or ch.

INSTRUCTIONS

CENTERPIECE

Row 1: Ch 225, dc in 4th ch from hook (beg mesh made); complete row according to row 1 of graph, turn.

Rows 2-54: Work according to graph. At end of last row, fasten off.

Row 55: Working in starting ch on opposite side of row 1, join with sl st in first ch, complete row according to graph, turn.

Rows 56-108: Work according to graph. At end of last row, fasten off. ⚜

HUMMINGBIRD GRAPH

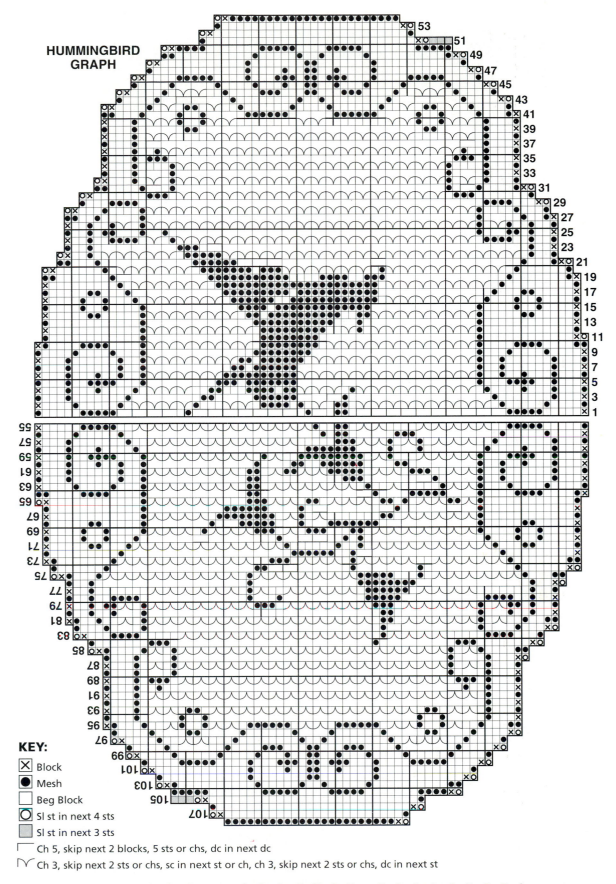

KEY:
- ☒ Block
- ● Mesh
- ☐ Beg Block
- ⭘ Sl st in next 4 sts
- ▨ Sl st in next 3 sts
- ⌐ Ch 5, skip next 2 blocks, 5 sts or chs, dc in next dc
- ⋎ Ch 3, skip next 2 sts or chs, sc in next st or ch, ch 3, skip next 2 sts or chs, dc in next st

HEIRLOOM CROCHET TREASURES

LACY PILLOWS

SIZE: 12" square, not including Ruffle.

MATERIALS FOR ALL THREE: Size 10 bedspread cotton — 1,500 yds. white; three 12" square pillows in desired colors with 3" ruffles; white sewing thread; sewing and tapestry needles; No. 7 steel crochet hook or size needed to obtain gauge.

GAUGE: 4 dc and 3 ch sps = 1"; 4 dc rows = 1".

NOTES: For **beginning block (beg block),** ch 3, dc in each of next 3 sts.

For **block,** dc in each of next 2 sts or chs, dc in next dc.

For **mesh,** ch 2, skip next 2 sts or chs, dc in next st or ch.

PILLOW FRONT (make 3)

Row 1: Ch 123, dc in 4th ch from hook, dc in

each ch across, turn (121 dc).

Rows 2-50: Work according to desired graph. At end of last row, fasten off.

Ruffle

Rnd 1: With right side facing you, working around outer edge, join with sl st in any st, ch 6, (dc, ch 3) in each st around with (dc, ch 2) 2 times in end of each row, join with sl st in 3rd ch of ch-6.

Rnds 2-6: Ch 7, (dc, ch 3) in each st around, join with sl st in 3rd ch of ch-6.

Rnd 7: For picot, ch 6, sl st in 3rd ch from hook; ch 3, *sl st in next st, picot, ch 3; repeat from * around, join with sl st in first ch of ch-6. Fasten off.

Sew Pillow Front to one side of pillow leaving ruffle free.❖

Graphs continued on next page

LOVE GRAPH

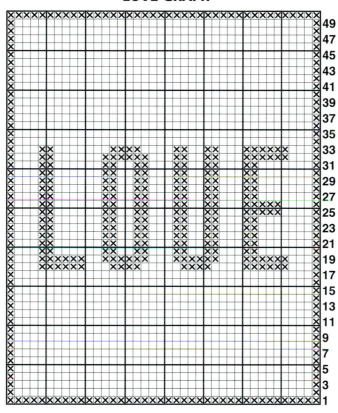

KEY:

☒ = Block

☐ = Mesh

LACY PILLOWS

Instructions on page 92

FAITH GRAPH

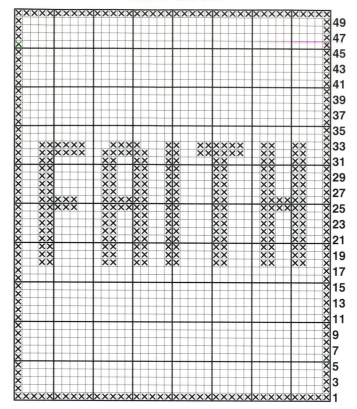

KEY:
☒ = Block
☐ = Mesh

JOY GRAPH

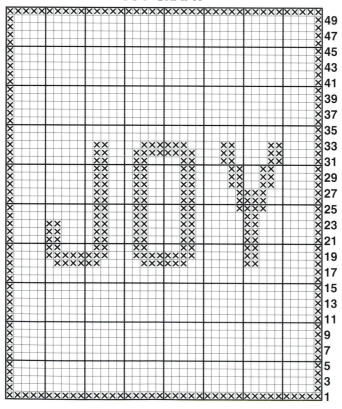

Designed by Carol Smith

H E I R L O O M   C R O C H E T   T R E A S U R E S

PENNSYLVANIA DUTCH

ESSENTIALS

SIZE: 20⅜" long including rod loops x 36" wide.

MATERIALS: Size 20 crochet cotton — 1,215 yds. white; No. 11 steel crochet hook or size needed to obtain gauge.

GAUGE: 14 dc = 1"; 5 dc rows = 1".

CURTAIN

INSTRUCTIONS

NOTES: For **beginning mesh (beg mesh),** ch 5, skip next 2 sts or chs, dc in next dc or ch.

For **mesh,** ch 2, skip next 2 sts or chs, dc in next dc or ch.

For **beginning block (beg block),** ch 3, dc in each of next 3 sts or ch.

For **block,** dc in each of next 2 sts or chs, dc in next dc.

Row 1: Ch 542, dc in 8th ch from hook (beg mesh made), complete row according to graph on next two pages, turn.

Rows 2-96: Work according to graph. **Do not** fasten off at end of last row, turn.

Continued on next page

PENNSYLVANIA DUTCH

Continued from page 95

For **trim,** ch 1, sc in same st; for **rod loop,** ch 32; 2 sc in first mesh, *sc in next dc, (2 sc in next mesh, sc in next dc) 8 times, ch 32, 2 sc in next mesh; repeat from * 18 times, sc in next dc, (2 sc in next mesh, sc in next dc) 6 times, 3 sc in next mesh, ch 32; working along sides of curtain and across bottom, (2 sc in each mesh, sc in each dc) around with 3 sc in each corner st, join with sl st in first sc. Fasten off. ❖

PENNSYLVANIA DUTCH GRAPH

Graph is worked across two pages

KEY:
☐ Mesh
Ⓞ Beg Mesh
● Block
☒ Beg Block

Graph is worked across two pages

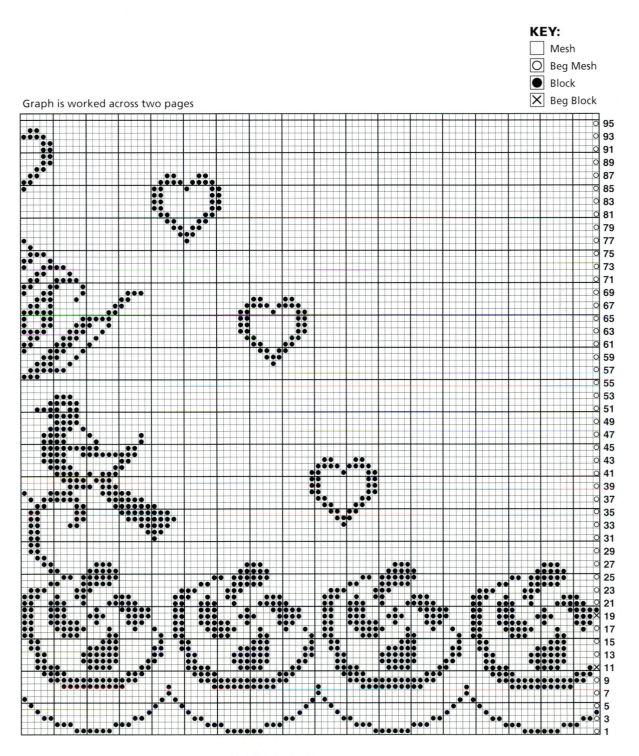

HEIRLOOM CROCHET TREASURES

SPRINGTIME SERENADE

Flirty blooms dance gayly among gossamer strands in a symphony of color and style sure to capture any flower-lover's heart. These captivating creations are liberally sprinkled with vibrant renditions of Mother Nature's handiwork, giving them the feel of eternal Spring. Cultivate your own crochet garden filled with an exotic medley of uncommonly lovely offerings.

LAVENDER POSIES

ESSENTIALS

SIZE: 12" across after blocking.

MATERIALS: Size 10 bedspread cotton — 165 yds. green, 40 yds. lavender and small amount yellow; tapestry needle; No. 7 steel crochet hook or size needed to obtain gauge

GAUGE: Rnds 1-2 = 2¼" across.

NOTE: Doily is designed to ruffle slightly.

INSTRUCTIONS

DOILY

Rnd 1: With green, ch 8, sl st in first ch to form ring, ch 4, 2 tr in ring, ch 3, (3 tr in ring, ch 3) 7 times, join with sl st in top of ch-4 (24 tr, 8 ch-3 sps).

NOTES: For **beginning shell (beg shell)**, (ch 4, 2 tr, ch 3, 3 tr) in same ch sp.

For **shell,** (3 tr, ch 3, 3 tr) in next ch sp or next shell.

Rnd 2: Sl st in each of next 2 sts, sl st in next ch-3 sp, beg shell, *(ch 4, sc, ch 4) in next ch sp*, [shell in next ch sp; repeat between **]; repeat between [ ] around, join (4 shells, 4 sc, 8 ch-4 sps).

Rnd 3: Sl st in each of next 2 sts, sl st in next ch-3 sp, ch 4, 7 tr in same sp, *ch 4, (sc in next ch sp, ch 4) 2 times*, [8 tr in ch sp of next shell; repeat between **]; repeat between [ ] around, join (32 tr, 12 ch-4 sps).

Rnd 4: Ch 4, tr in each of next 2 sts, *2 tr in each of next 2 sts, tr in each of next 3 sts, ch 4, sc in next ch-4 sp, ch 4, 8 tr in next ch-4 sp, ch 4, sc in next ch-4 sp, ch 4*, [tr in each of next 3 sts; repeat between **]; repeat between [ ] around, join (72 tr, 8 sc, 16 ch sps).

NOTES: For **beginning cluster (beg cl),** ch 4, *yo 2 times, insert hook in next st, yo, draw lp through, (yo, draw through 2 lps on hook) 2 times; repeat from * 8 more times, yo, draw through all 10 lps on hook.

For **cluster (cl),** *yo 2 times, insert hook in next st, yo, draw lp through, (yo, draw through 2 lps on hook) 2 times; repeat from * 9 more times, yo, draw through all 11 lps on hook.

Rnd 5: Beg cl, *ch 8, (sc in next ch-4 sp, ch 4) 2 times, tr in each of next 3 sts, 2 tr in each of next 2 sts, tr in each of next 3 sts, (ch 4, sc in next ch-4 sp) 2 times*, [ch 8, cl; repeat between **]; repeat between

[ ] around; **to join,** (ch 4, tr) in top of beg cl (40 tr, 4 cls, 16 sc, 8 ch-8 sps, 16 ch-4 sps).

Rnd 6: *Ch 4, sc in next ch-8 sp, ch 4, shell in next ch-4 sp, ch 4, sc in next ch-4 sp, ch 8, cl, ch 8, sc in next ch-4 sp, ch 4, shell in next ch-4 sp*, [ch 4, sc in next ch-8 sp; repeat between **]; repeat between [ ] around to last ch-8 sp, join with ch 4, sl st in top of joining tr (8 shells, 16 sc, 4 cls, 20 ch-4 sps, 8 ch-8 sps).

Rnd 7: Sl st in next 2 chs, beg shell, *ch 4, sc in next ch-4 sp, ch 4, shell in next shell, ch 4, sc in next ch-4 sp, ch 4, (sc in next ch-8 sp, ch 4) 2 times, sc in next ch-4 sp, ch 4, shell in next shell, ch 4, sc in next ch-4 sp, ch 4*, [shell in next ch sp; repeat between **]; repeat between [ ] around, join with sl st in top of ch-4 (12 shells, 24 sc, 36 ch-4 sps).

Rnd 8: Sl st in next 2 sts, sl st in next ch sp, beg shell, ◊*ch 4, (sc in next ch-4 sp, ch 4) 2 times, shell in next shell, ch 4, (sc in next ch-4 sp, ch 4) 2 times*, shell in next ch-4 sp; repeat between **◊, [shell in next shell; repeat between ◊◊]; repeat between [ ] around, join (16 shells, 48 ch-4 sps).

Rnd 9: Sl st in next 2 sts, sl st in next ch sp, beg shell, ◊*ch 4, (sc in next ch-4 sp, ch 4) 3 times, 8 tr in next shell, ch 4, (sc in next ch-4 sp, ch 4) 3 times*, shell in next shell; repeat between **◊, [shell in next shell; repeat between ◊◊]; repeat between [ ] around, join (8 shells, 64 tr, 64 ch-4 sps).

Rnd 10: Sl st in next 2 sts, sl st in next ch sp, ch 4, 7 tr in same sp, ◊*ch 4, (sc in next ch-4 sp, ch 4) 4 times, tr in each of next 3 sts, 2 tr in each of next 2 sts, tr in each of next 3 sts, ch 4, (sc in next ch-4 sp, ch 4) 4 times*, shell in next shell; repeat between **◊, [8 tr in next shell; repeat between ◊◊]; repeat between [ ] around, join (4 shells, 112 tr, 80 ch-4 sps).

Rnd 11: Ch 4, tr in each of next 2 sts, 2 tr in each of next 2 sts, tr in each of next 3 sts, ◊*(ch 4, sc in next ch-4 sp) 5 times, ch 6, cl, ch 6, (sc in next ch-4 sp, ch 4) 5 times*, 8 tr in next shell; repeat between **◊, [tr in each of next 3 sts, 2 tr in each of next 2 tr, tr in each of next 3 sts; repeat between ◊◊]; repeat between [ ] around, join (72 tr, 8 cls, 80 ch-4 sps, 16 ch-6 sps).

Rnd 12: Beg cl, ◊ch 6, *(sc in next ch-4 sp, ch 4) 5 times, sc in next ch-6 sp, ch 4, sc in top of next cl, ch 4, sc in next ch-6 sp, ch 4*, (sc in next ch-4 sp, ch 4) 5 times, tr in each of next 3 sts, 2 tr in each of next 2 sts, tr in each of next 3 sts, ch 4; repeat between **,

Continued on page 112

FANS & LACE

ESSENTIALS

SIZE: 36" across.
MATERIALS: Size 10 bedspread cotton – 1,575 yds. blue; No. 7 steel crochet hook or size needed to obtain gauge.
GAUGE: Rnds 1-2 = 1⅛" across.

INSTRUCTIONS

TABLECLOTH

Rnd 1: Ch 5, sl st in first ch to form ring, ch 1, sc in ring, (ch 6, sc) 9 times in ring; to **join,** ch 3, dc in first st (10 ch-6 lps).

Rnds 2-3: (Ch 6, sc in next ch lp) around to last ch lp, join with ch 3, dc in top of joining dc.

Rnd 4: *Ch 6, (sc, ch 6, sc) in next ch lp; repeat from * around to last ch sp, ch 6, sc in last ch sp, join as before (20 ch-6 lps).

Rnds 5-7: Repeat rnd 2.

Rnd 8: Repeat rnd 4 (40 ch-6 lps).

Rnds 9-12: Repeat rnd 2.

Rnd 13: Ch 4, 5 tr over joining dc just made, sc in next ch lp, [*(ch 6, sc in next ch lp) 3 times], 12 tr in next ch lp, sc in next ch lp; repeat from * 6 times; repeat between [ ], 6 tr in last ch lp, join with sl st in top of ch 4 (96 tr, 24 ch-6 lps).

Rnd 14: Ch 5, tr in next tr, (ch 1, tr in next tr) 4 times, *[sc in next ch lp, (ch 6, sc in next ch lp) 2 times, tr in next tr], (ch 1, tr in next tr) 11 times; repeat from * 6 times; repeat between [ ], ch 1, (tr in next tr, ch 1) 5 times, join with sl st in 4th ch of ch-5.

Rnd 15: Ch 6, tr in next tr, (ch 2, tr in next tr) 4 times, *[sc in next ch lp, ch 6, sc in next ch lp, tr in next tr], (ch 2, tr in next tr) 11 times; repeat from * 6 times; repeat between [ ], ch 2, (tr in next tr, ch 2) 5 times, join with sl st in 4th ch of ch-6.

Rnd 16: (Ch 6, sc in next tr) 5 times, [*ch 6, sc in next ch lp], (ch 6, sc in next tr) 12 times; repeat from * 6 times; repeat between [ ], (ch 6, sc in next tr) 6 times, join with ch 3, dc in first ch (104 ch-6 lps).

Rnd 17: (Ch 6, skip next ch lp, sc in next ch lp) 3 times, *ch 6, sc in next ch lp, (ch 6, skip next ch lp, sc in next ch lp) 6 times; repeat from * 6 times, ch 6, sc in next ch lp, (ch 6, skip next ch lp, sc in next ch lp) 2 times, join with ch 3, dc in next dc (60 ch lps).

Rnds 18-22: Repeat rnd 2.

Rnd 23: (Ch 6, sc in next ch lp) 2 times, [*ch 6, (sc, ch 6, sc) in next ch lp], (ch 6, sc in next ch lp) 6 times; repeat from * 6 times; repeat between [ ], (ch 6, sc in next ch lp) 3 times, join.

Rnds 24-25: Repeat rnd 2.

Rnd 26: [*12 tr in next ch lp, sc in next ch lp, ch 6, (sc, ch 6, sc) in next ch lp], ch 6, sc in next ch lp; repeat from * 14 times; repeat between [ ], join with ch 3, dc in next dc.

Rnd 27: [*Tr in next tr, (ch 1, tr in next tr) 11 times, sc in next ch lp, ch 6, (sc, ch 6, sc) in next ch lp], ch 6, sc in next ch lp; repeat from * 14 more times; repeat between [ ], join as before.

Rnd 28: *[Tr in next tr, (ch 2, tr in next tr) 11 times, sc in next ch lp], (ch 6, sc in next ch lp) 2 times; repeat from * 14 times; repeat between [ ], ch 6, sc in next ch lp, join.

Rnd 29: [*(Ch 6, sc in next tr) 12 times], (ch 6, sc in next ch lp) 2 times; repeat from * 14 times; repeat between [ ], ch 6, sc in next ch lp, join (224 ch-6 lps).

Rnd 30: Ch 6, sc in next ch lp, *[(ch 6, skip next ch lp, sc in next ch lp) 6 times], (ch 6, sc in next ch lp) 2 times; repeat from * 14 times; repeat between [ ], join (128 ch-6 lps).

Rnds 31-35: Repeat rnd 2.

Rnd 36: Ch 6, (sc in next ch lp, ch 6) 2 times, [*(sc, ch 6, sc) in next ch lp, ch 6], (sc in next ch lp, ch 6) 7 times; repeat from * 14 times; repeat between [ ], sc in next ch lp, (ch 6, sc in next ch lp) 3 times, join.

Rnds 37-38: Repeat rnd 2.

Rnd 39: Ch 4, 5 tr over joining dc, 6 tr in next ch lp, [*(ch 6, sc in next ch lp) 3 times, 12 tr in next ch lp], (sc in next ch lp, ch 6,) 3 times], 6 tr in each of next 2 ch lps; repeat from * 14 times; repeat between [ ], (sc in next ch lp, ch 6) 2 times, sc in next ch lp, join with ch 2, tr in top of ch-4.

Rnd 40: Tr in same st, [*(ch 1, tr in next tr) 11 times, sc in next ch lp], (ch 6, sc in next ch lp) 2 times, tr in next tr; repeat from * 30 times;

Continued on page 112

HEIRLOOM CROCHET TREASURES

SPRING BASKETS

ESSENTIALS

SIZE: 11" x 19½" after blocking.
GAUGE: 41 tr and chs = 4"; 9 tr rows = 4".
MATERIALS: Size 10 bedspread cotton — 300 yds. white, 36 yds. lt. pink, 24 yds. pink, 20 yds. lt. green, 12 yds. each lt. blue, blue and yellow; white sewing thread; sewing and tapestry needles; No. 6 steel crochet hook or size needed to obtain gauge.

INSTRUCTIONS

MAT

Row 1: With white, ch 117, tr in 5th ch from hook, (ch 5, skip next 5 chs, tr in each of next 2 chs) across, turn (34 tr, 16 ch sps).

Row 2: Ch 4, tr in next st, (ch 5, sc in next ch sp, ch 5, tr in each of next 2 sts) across, turn (34 tr, 32 ch sps, 16 sc).

Rows 3-4: Ch 4, tr in next tr, (ch 5, skip next 2 ch sps, tr in each of next 2 tr) across, turn.

Rows 5-28: Repeat rows 2-4 consecutively. Fasten off at end of last row.

BASKET (make 2)
Row 1: With white, ch 30, dc in 4th ch from hook, dc in each ch across, turn (28 dc).

Row 2: Ch 3, dc in each of next 3 sts, (ch 1, dc in next 4 sts) across, turn (28 dc, 6 ch sps).

Row 3: Ch 3, dc in each of next 3 dc, (ch 3, dc in next 4 dc) across, turn.

Row 4: Ch 1, sc in first st, ch 3, skip next 2 sts, sc in next st, (ch 3, sc in next ch sp, ch 3, sc in next st, ch 3, skip next 2 sts, sc in next st) across, turn (20 sc, 19 ch sps).

NOTE: For **shell,** (2 dc, ch 2, 2 dc) in next ch sp.

Row 5: Ch 3, (dc, ch 2, 2 dc) in next ch sp, ch 2, sc in next ch sp, ch 3, sc in next ch sp, ch 2, (shell, ch 2, sc in next ch sp, ch 3, sc in next ch sp, ch 2) across to last ch sp, (2 dc, ch 2, dc) in next ch sp, dc in last st, turn (12 sc, 12 ch-2 sps, 6 ch-3 sps, 7 shells).

Row 6: Ch 3, shell, (ch 3, skip next ch sp, sc in next ch sp, ch 3, skip next ch sp, shell) across with dc in top of ch-3, turn (12 ch sps, 7 shells, 2 dc).

Row 7: Ch 1, sc in each of first 3 sts, sc in next ch sp, (ch 7, skip next 2 ch sps, sc in next ch sp) across with sc in each of last 3 sts, turn (13 sc, 6 ch sps).

Row 8: Ch 3, dc in each of next 3 sts, ch 3, 3 dc in 4th ch of next ch-7, ch 3, (dc in next sc, ch 3, 3 dc in 4th ch of next ch-7, ch 3) across with dc in last 4 sts, turn (31 dc, 12 ch sps).

Row 9: Ch 3, dc in each of next 3 dc, ch 5, dc next 3 dc tog, (ch 3, 3 dc in next dc, ch 3, dc next 3 dc tog) across to last 4 sts, ch 5, dc in last 4 dc, turn (29 dc, 10 ch-3 sps, 2 ch-5 sps).

Row 10: Ch 3, dc in each of next 3 sts, ch 5, dc in next dc 3 tog, (ch 3, dc next 3 sts tog, ch 3, dc in next dc 3 tog) across with ch 5, dc in last 4 sts, turn (19 dc, 10 ch-3 sps, 2 ch-5 sps).

Row 11: Ch 3, dc in each of next 3 sts, ch 3, shell in next dc, ch 3, (skip next dc 3 tog, shell in next dc, ch 3) across with dc in last 4 sts, turn (8 dc, 7 ch-3 sps, 6 shells).

Row 12: Ch 3, dc in each of next 3 sts, ch 5, shell in next shell, (ch 3, shell in next shell) across with ch 5, dc in last 4 sts, turn (8 dc, 6 shells, 5 ch-3 sps, 2 ch-5 sps).

NOTE: For **V-stitch (V-st),** (dc, ch 3, dc) in next ch sp.

Row 13: Ch 3, dc in each of next 3 sts, ch 3, dc in next ch sp, ch 3, (V-st, ch 3, dc in next ch sp, ch 3) across with dc in last 4 sts, turn (15 dc, 14 ch-3 sps, 6 V-sts).

NOTE: For **picot,** ch 4, sl st in last st made.

Row 14: Ch 3, dc in each of next 3 sts, ch 3, sc in next dc, picot, ch 3, *(3 dc, picot, 3 dc) in next V-st, ch 3, sc in next dc, picot, ch 3; repeat from * across with dc in last 4 sts, turn.

Row 15: For **handle,** ch 3, dc in each of next 3 sts leaving remaining sts unworked, turn (4 dc).

Rows 16-65: Ch 3, dc in each of last 3 sts, turn. Fasten off at end of last row.

Matching sts, sew row 65 to last 4 sts on row 14.

Sew row 14 and handle of one Basket over center of rows 1-11 of Mat and row 14 and handle of second Basket over center of rows 18-28 of Mat according to Assembly Diagram.

ROSE (make 6 lt. pink, 4 pink)
Rnd 1: Ch 6, sl st in first ch to form ring, ch 1, (sc, ch 3) 6 times in ring, join with sl st in first sc (6 sc, 6 ch lps).

Rnd 2: Sl st in first ch lp, ch 1, (sc, hdc, dc, hdc, sc) in each ch lp around, join (6 petals).

Rnd 3: Ch 4, skip next petal, (sl st in next sc on rnd 1, ch 4, skip next petal) around, join with sl st in first ch of first ch-4 lp (6 ch lps).

Rnd 4: Ch 1, (sc, hdc, dc, 2 tr, dc, hdc, sc) in each ch lp around, join with sl st in first sc, fasten off.

MEDIUM FLOWER (make 4 each blue and lt. blue)
NOTE: For **treble cluster (tr cl),** *yo 2 times, insert hook in ring, yo, draw lp through, (yo, draw through 2 lps on hook) 2 times; repeat from *, yo, draw through all 3 lps on hook.

Ch 6, sl st in first ch to form ring, (ch 4, tr cl, ch 3, sl st in top of tr cl just made, ch 4, sc in ring) 5 times, join with sl st in first ch of ch-4, fasten off.

SMALL FLOWER (make 6)
With yellow, ch 6, sl st in first ch to form ring, ch 1, (sc, ch 4, sc, ch 8) 5 times in ring, join with sl st in first sc, fasten off.

LEAF (make 8)
With lt. green, ch 15, sc in 2nd ch from hook, (hdc in next ch, dc in each of next 3 chs, tr in next 4 chs, dc in each of next 3 chs, hdc in next ch, sc in last ch), ch 3; working on opposite side of ch, sc in next ch; repeat between ( ), join with sl st in first sc, fasten off.

Sew Roses, Flowers and Leaves across Mat and Flower Baskets according to Assembly Diagram.✠

ASSEMBLY DIAGRAM

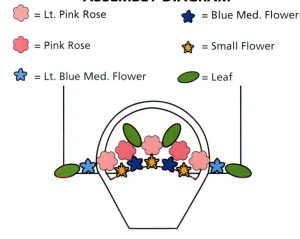

= Lt. Pink Rose   = Blue Med. Flower

= Pink Rose   = Small Flower

= Lt. Blue Med. Flower   = Leaf

EARLY BLOOMS

ESSENTIALS

SIZE: 17" across after blocking.
GAUGE: Rnds 1-2 = 2" across.
MATERIALS: Size 10 bedspread cotton — 300 yds. green, 50 yds. each yellow, dk. yellow, pink and dk. pink; sewing thread; sewing and tapestry needles; No. 6 steel crochet hook or size needed to obtain gauge.

INSTRUCTIONS

DOILY

Rnd 1: With green, ch 9, sl st in first ch to form ring, ch 3, 31 dc in ring, join with sl st in top of ch-3 (32 dc).

Rnd 2: Ch 7, skip next st, (tr in next st, ch 3, skip next st) around, join with sl st in 4th ch of ch-7 (16 tr, 16 ch sps).

NOTE: For **picot,** ch 4, sl st in top of st just made.

Rnd 3: Sl st in next ch sp, ch 4, (2 tr, picot, 3 tr) in same sp, ch 5, skip next ch sp, *(3 tr, picot, 3 tr) in next ch sp, ch 5, skip next ch sp; repeat from * around, join with sl st in top of ch-4 (48 tr, 8 ch sps, 8 picots).

Rnd 4: Ch 11, *skip next 4 tr, tr in next tr, ch 7, skip next ch sp*, [tr in next tr, ch 7; repeat between **]; repeat between [ ] around, join with sl st in 4th ch of ch-11 (16 tr, 16 ch sps).

NOTE: For **cluster (cl),** *yo 2 times, insert hook in next st, yo, draw lp through, (yo, draw through 2 lps on hook) 2 times; repeat from * 2 times in same st, yo, draw through all 4 lps on hook.

Rnd 5: Ch 4, 4 tr in same st, *ch 7, cl in next tr, ch 7*, [5 tr in next tr; repeat between **]; repeat between [ ] around, join with sl st in top of ch-4 (40 tr, 16 ch sps, 8 cls).

Rnd 6: Ch 4, tr in next 4 tr, ch 9, cl in next cl, ch 9, (tr in next 5 tr, ch 9, cl in next cl, ch 9) around, join.

NOTE: For **V-stitch (V-st),** (tr, ch 3, tr) in st or ch sp.

Rnd 7: Ch 4, tr in next tr, *V-st in next tr, tr in each of next 2 tr, ch 9, cl in next cl, ch 9*, [tr in each of next 2 tr; repeat between **]; repeat between [ ] around, join (32 tr, 16 ch-9 sps, 8 cls, 8 V-sts).

Rnd 8: Ch 4, tr in same tr, *tr in next tr, 2 tr in next tr, ch 3, 2 tr in next tr, tr in next tr, 2 tr in next tr, ch 9, cl in next cl, ch 9*, [2 tr in next st; repeat between **]; repeat between [ ] around, join (80 tr, 16 ch-9 sps, 8 cls, 8 ch-3 sps).

Rnd 9: Ch 4, tr in same tr, *(tr in next tr, 2 tr in next tr) 2 times, ch 5, 2 tr in next tr, (tr in next tr, 2 tr in next tr) 2 times, ch 6, cl in next cl, ch 6*, [2 tr in next tr; repeat between **]; repeat between [ ] around, join (128 tr, 16 ch-6 sps, 8 cls, 8 ch-5 sps).

Rnd 10: Ch 4, tr in next 7 tr, *ch 3, tr in next ch sp, ch 3, tr in next 8 tr, ch 7, sc in next cl, ch 7*, [tr in next 8 tr; repeat between **]; repeat between [ ] around, join (136 tr, 16 ch-3 sps, 16 ch-7 sps, 8 sc).

Rnd 11: Ch 4, tr in next 7 tr, *ch 3, (tr in next ch sp, ch 3) 2 times, tr in next 8 sts, ch 7, sc in next sc, ch 7*, [tr in next 8 tr; repeat between **]; repeat between [ ] around, join (144 tr, 24 ch-3 sps, 16 ch-7 sps, 8 sc).

Rnd 12: Ch 4, tr in next 7 tr, *ch 3, (tr in next ch sp, ch 3) 3 times, tr in next 8 tr, ch 5, sc in next ch sp, ch 3, sc in next ch sp, ch 5*, [tr in next 8 tr; repeat between **]; repeat between [ ] around, join (152 tr, 40 ch-3 sps, 16 sc, 16 ch-5 sps).

Rnd 13: Ch 4, tr in next 7 tr, *ch 5, tr in next ch sp, (ch 3, tr in next ch sp) 3 times, ch 5, tr in next 8 tr, ch 4, skip next ch sp, tr in next ch sp, ch 4, skip next ch sp*, [tr in next 8 tr; repeat between **]; repeat between [ ] around, join (168 tr, 24 ch-3 sps, 16 ch-5 sps, 16 ch-4 sps).

Rnd 14: Ch 4, tr in next st, *(tr next 2 sts tog) 2 times, tr in each of next 2 sts, ch 5, tr in next ch sp, (ch 3, tr in next ch sp) 4 times, ch 5, tr in each of next 2 sts, (tr next 2 sts tog) 2 times, tr in each of next 2 sts, ch 9, skip next 2 ch sps*, [tr in each of next 2 sts; repeat between **]; repeat between [ ] around, join (136 tr, 32 ch-3 sps, 16 ch-5 sps, 8 ch-9 sps).

Rnd 15: Ch 4, tr next 5 sts tog, *ch 5, V-st in next ch sp, ch 3, (tr in next ch sp, ch 3) 4 times, V-st in next ch sp, ch 5, tr next 6 sts tog, ch 7, tr in 5th ch of next ch-9, ch 7*, [tr next 6 sts tog;

Continued on page 113

HEIRLOOM CROCHET TREASURES

PINK PINEAPPLES

ESSENTIALS

SIZE: 14½" across, after blocking.
MATERIALS: Size 10 bedspread cotton — 250 yds. pink; No. 7 steel crochet hook or size needed to obtain gauge.
GAUGE: Rnds 1-3 = 2" across.
NOTE: Doily will ruffle slightly until blocked.

INSTRUCTIONS

DOILY

Rnd 1: Ch 4, sl st in first ch to form ring, ch 4, 19 tr in ring, join (20 tr).

Rnd 2: (Ch 4, skip next st, sc in next st) around to last st, skip last st; to **join,** ch 2, dc in first ch of ch-4 (10 ch lps).

Rnd 3: *Ch 4, (sc ch 4, sc) in next lp; repeat from * 8 times, ch 4, sc in last ch sp, join as before in joining dc on previous rnd (20 ch lps).

Rnds 4-5: (Ch 4, sc in next ch lp) around, join as before.

Rnd 6: *Ch 4, (sc, ch 4, sc) in next ch lp*, [ch 4, sc in next ch lp; repeat between **]; repeat between [ ] around, join as before (30 ch lps).

Rnds 7-8: Repeat rnd 4.

Rnd 9: *Ch 4, (sc in next ch lp, ch 4) 2 times*, [(sc, ch 4, sc) in next ch lp; repeat between **]; repeat between [ ] 8 times, sc in last ch lp, join as before (40 ch lps).

Rnds 10-11: Repeat rnd 4.

Rnd 12: *Ch 5, (sc, ch 5, sc) in next ch lp*, [(ch 5, sc in next ch lp) 3 times; repeat between **]; repeat between [ ] 8 times, (ch 5, sc in next ch lp) 2 times, join as before (50 ch lps).

Rnd 13: *(Skip next ch lp, 18 dtr in next ch lp, skip next ch lp, sc in next ch lp), ch 4, sc in next ch lp; repeat from * 8 times; repeat between ( ), join as before (180 dtr, 10 ch lps).

NOTES: For **treble cluster (tr cl),** *yo 2 times, insert hook in sp, yo, draw through sp, (yo, draw through 2 lps on hook) 2 times; repeat from * 2 times in same sp, yo, draw through all 4 lps on hook.

For **beginning treble cluster (beg tr cl),** ch 4, *yo 2 times, insert hook in sp, yo, draw through sp, (yo, draw through 2 lps on hook) 2 times; repeat from * in same space, yo, draw

through all 3 lps on hook.

Rnd 14: *[Tr cl in next st, (ch 2, skip next st, tr cl in next st) 8 times, skip next 2 sts], sc in next ch lp; repeat from * 8 times; repeat between [ ], join with sl st in top of first tr cl (90 tr cl).

Rnd 15: Sl st in first ch-2 sp, beg tr cl, *(ch 2, tr cl in next ch-2 sp) 7 times*, [ch 4, tr cl in next ch-2 sp; repeat between **]; repeat between [ ] 8 times; to **join,** ch 2, dc in top of beg tr cl (80 tr cl).

Rnd 16: *Ch 4, tr cl in next ch-2 sp, (ch 2, tr cl in next ch-2 sp) 6 times*, [ch 4, sc in next ch-4 lp; repeat between **]; repeat between [ ] around, join as before in joining dc on previous rnd (70 tr cl).

Rnd 17: *Ch 4, sc in next ch-4 lp, ch 4, tr cl in next ch-2 sp, (ch 2, tr cl in next ch-2 sp) 5 times*, [ch 4, sc in next ch-4 lp; repeat between **]; repeat between [ ] around, join as before (60 tr cl).

Rnd 18: *Ch 4, (sc, ch 4, sc) in next ch-4 lp, ch 4, sc in next ch-4 lp, ch 4, tr cl in next ch-2 sp, (ch 2, tr cl in next ch-2 sp) 4 times*, [ch 4, sc in next ch-4 lp; repeat between **]; repeat between [ ] around, join as before (50 tr cl).

Rnd 19: Ch 4, (sc in next ch-4 lp, ch 4) 4 times, *tr cl in next ch-2 sp, (ch 2, tr cl in next ch-2 sp) 3 times*, [ch 4, (sc in next ch-4 lp, ch 4) 5 times; repeat between **]; repeat between [ ] around, join as before (40 tr cl).

Rnd 20: Ch 4, (sc in next ch-4 lp, ch 4) 5 times, *tr cl in next ch-2 sp, (ch 2, tr cl in next ch-2 sp) 2 times*, [ch 4, (sc in next ch-4 lp, ch 4) 6 times; repeat between **]; repeat between [ ] around, join as before (30 tr cl).

Rnd 21: Ch 4, (sc in next ch-4 lp, ch 4) 2 times, *(sc, ch 4, sc) in next ch-4 lp, ch 4, (sc in next ch-4 lp, ch 4) 3 times, tr cl in next ch-2 sp, ch 3, tr cl in next ch-2 sp*, [ch 4, (sc in next ch-4 lp, ch 4) 3 times; repeat between **]; repeat between [ ] around, join as before (20 tr cl).

Rnd 22: Ch 4, (sc in next ch-4 lp, ch 4) around with (sc, ch 3, sc) in each ch-3 sp, join as before (110 ch lps).

Rnd 23: Ch 4, (sc in next ch-4 lp, ch 4) around with (sc, ch 4, sc) in each ch-3 lp, join as before (120 ch lps). Fasten off. ⚜

H E I R L O O M   C R O C H E T   T R E A S U R E S

DELIGHTFUL DAISIES

ESSENTIALS

SIZE: 12" x 17".

MATERIALS: Size 10 bedspread cotton — 300 yds. ecru, 150 yds. green and 60 yds. yellow; No. 9 steel crochet hook or size needed to obtain gauge.

GAUGE: Dc in next ch, (ch 1, skip next ch, dc in next ch) 5 times = 1"; 5 dc rows = 1".

NOTE: For **beginning cluster (beg cl),** ch 4, *yo 2 times, insert hook in same st or sp, yo, draw lp through, (yo, draw through 2 lps on hook) 2 times; repeat from *, yo, draw through all 3 lps on hook.

For **cluster (cl),** yo 2 times, insert hook in next st or sp, *yo, draw lp through, (yo, draw through 2 lps on hook) 2 times*, [yo 2 times, insert hook in same st or sp; repeat between **]; repeat between [ ], yo, draw through all 4 lps on hook.

Doily may ruffle until blocked.

INSTRUCTIONS

D A I S Y (make 20)

Rnd 1: With yellow, ch 9, sl st in first ch to form ring, beg cl in ring, ch 5, (cl in ring, ch 5) 7 times, join with sl st in top of beg cl, fasten off (8 cls, 8 ch lps).

Rnd 2: Join green with sc in any ch lp, (2 sc, ch 3, 3 sc) in same lp, (3 sc, ch 3, 3 sc) in each ch lp around, join with sl st in first sc, fasten off.

DOILY

Rnd 1: With ecru, ch 38, dc in 6th ch from hook, ch 1, skip next ch, (dc in next ch, ch 1, skip next ch) across with (dc, ch 5, dc, ch 5, dc) in end ch; working on opposite side of ch, (ch 1, skip next ch, dc in next ch) 15 times, ch 1; working in chs of first ch-5, skip next ch, (dc, ch 5) 2 times in next ch, skip next ch, join with sl st in next ch (36 dc, 4 ch-5 lps).

Rnd 2: Ch 4, dc in next dc, (ch 1, dc in next dc) 15 times, *ch 5, dc in 3rd ch of next ch-5, ch 3, dc in next dc, ch 3, dc in 3rd ch of next ch-5, ch 5*, dc in next dc, (ch 1, dc in next dc) 16 times; repeat between **, join with sl st in 3rd ch of ch-4 (40 dc, 4 ch-5 lps, 4 ch-3 sps).

Rnd 3: Ch 4, dc in next dc, (ch 1, dc in next dc) 15 times, *ch 1, dc in 2nd ch of next ch-5, ch 5, dc in next dc, ch 5, (cl, ch 5, cl) in next dc, ch 5, dc in next dc, ch 5, dc in 4th ch of next ch-5*, (ch 1, dc in next dc) 17 times; repeat between **, ch 1, join, fasten off (42 dc, 10 ch-5 lps, 4 cls).

Rnd 4: Join green with sl st in same st as joining on last rnd, (beg cl, ch 5, cl) in same st, [*ch 3, skip next 3 dc, (cl, ch 5, cl) in next dc; repeat from * 3 times, ch 3, skip next dc, (cl, ch 5, cl) in next dc, ch 7, skip next ch-3 sp, skip next cl, (cl, ch 5, cl) in 3rd ch of next ch-5, ch 7, skip next cl, skip next ch-3 sp, (cl, ch 5, cl) in next dc, ch 3, skip next dc], (cl, ch 5, cl) in next dc; repeat between [ ], join with sl st in top of beg cl, fasten off (16 ch-5 lps, 12 ch-3 sps, 4 ch-7 lps).

Rnd 5: Join ecru with sc in first ch-5 lp, 4 sc in same lp, 3 sc in each ch-3 sp, 5 sc in each ch-5 lp and 7 sc in each ch-7 lp around, join with sl st in first sc (144 sc).

NOTE: Joining counts as ch lp.

Rnd 6: Sl st in next 2 sc, ch 1, sc in same st, (ch 5, skip next 3 sc, sc in next sc) 10 times, (ch 7, skip next 3 sc, sc in next sc) 6 times, (ch 5, skip next 3 sc, sc in next sc) 12 times, (ch 7, skip next 3 sc, sc in next sc) 6 times, ch 5, skip next 3 sc, sc in next sc; to **join,** ch 2, dc in first sc (24 ch-5 lps, 12 ch-7 lps).

Rnd 7: Working in ch-5 and ch-7 lps, ch 1, sc over joining dc just made, (ch 5, sc in next ch lp) 10 times, (ch 7, sc in next ch lp) 7 times, (ch 5, sc in next ch lp) 11 times, (ch 7, sc in next ch lp) 7 times, join as before.

Rnd 8: Ch 1, sc over joining dc just made, ch 5, (sc in next ch lp, ch 5) 10 times, *dc in next sc, ch 5, sc in next ch lp, (ch 9, sc in next ch lp) 6 times, ch 5, dc in next sc*, ch 5, (sc in next ch lp, ch 5) 11 times; repeat between **, join.

Rnd 9: Ch 1, sc over joining dc just made, ch 5, (sc in

next ch lp, ch 5) 12 times, *dc in next sc, ch 5, sc in next ch lp, (ch 9, sc in next ch lp) 5 times, ch 5, dc in next sc, ch 5*, (sc in next ch lp, ch 5) 14 times; repeat between **, sc in last ch lp, join.

Rnd 10: Ch 1, sc over joining dc just made, ch 5, (sc in next ch lp, ch 5) 14 times, *dc in next sc, ch 5, sc in next ch lp, (ch 9, sc in next ch lp) 4 times, ch 5, dc in next sc*, ch 5, (sc in next ch lp, ch 5) 17 times; repeat between **, (ch 5, sc in next ch lp) 2 times, join.

Rnd 11: Ch 1, sc over joining dc just made, ch 5, (sc in next ch lp, ch 5) 16 times, *dc in next sc, ch 5, sc in next ch lp, (ch 11, sc in next ch lp) 3 times, ch 5, dc in next sc, ch 5*, (sc in next ch lp, ch 5) 20 times; repeat between **, (sc in next ch lp, ch 5) 3 times, join with sl st in first sc, fasten off (46 ch-5 lps, 6 ch-11 lps).

NOTE: For **double treble (dtr),** yo 3 times, insert hook in next st, yo, draw lp through, (yo, draw through 2 lps on hook) 4 times.

Rnd 12: Join green with sl st in first ch-5 lp after last dc made, (beg cl, ch 5, cl) in same lp, ch 5, skip next ch-5 lp, *(cl, ch 5, cl) in next ch-5 lp, ch 5, skip next ch-5 lp*; repeat between ** 9 times, [dtr in next sc, ch 5, ◊(cl, ch 5, cl) in 6th ch of next ch-11 lp, ch 5; repeat from ◊ 2 times, dtr in next sc, ch 5, skip next ch-5 lp]; repeat between ** 11 more times; repeat between [ ], join with sl st in top of beg cl, fasten off (60 ch lps).

Rnd 13: Join ecru with sc in first ch lp, 4 sc in same lp, 5 sc in each ch lp around, join with sl st in first sc (300 sc).

Rnd 14: Sl st in next 2 sc, ch 1, sc in same st, (ch 7, skip next 4 sc, sc in next sc) around to last 2 sc, skip last 2 sc; to **join,** ch 3, tr in first sc (60 ch lps).

Rnds 15-17: Ch 1, sc over joining tr just made, (ch 7, sc in next ch lp) around, join as before. At end of last rnd; to **join,** ch 7, sl st in first sc.

Rnd 18: To **join Daisies,** sl st in first 4 chs, ch 1, sc in same ch, ch 4, dc in any ch sp of first Daisy, dc in any ch sp of next Daisy, ch 4, sc in next ch lp on Doily, *(ch 3, sl st in next ch sp on same Daisy, ch 3, sc in next ch lp on Doily) 2 times, ch 4, dc in next ch sp on same Daisy, dc in any ch sp on next Daisy, ch 4, sc in next ch sp on Doily; repeat from * around to last ch lp on Doily; repeat between ( ), ch 3, sl st in next ch sp on same Daisy, ch 3, join with sl st in first sc, fasten off.

NOTE: For **picot,** ch 6, sl st in 4th ch from hook.

Rnd 19: Working in remaining ch sps on Daisies, join green with sl st in first ch sp, beg cl, [ch 5, *(cl, picot, ch 2, cl) in next ch sp, ch 5; repeat from * one more time, cl in last ch sp of same daisy], ◊cl in first ch sp on next daisy; repeat between [ ]; repeat from ◊ around, join with sl st in top of beg cl, fasten off. ⚜

LAVENDER POSIES

Continued from page 101

(sc in next ch-4 sp, ch 4) 4 times, sc in next ch-4 sp, ch 6◊, [cl; repeat between ◊◊]; repeat between [ ] around, join with sl st in top of beg cl (40 tr, 4 cls, 104 ch-4 sps, 8 ch-6 sps).

Rnd 13: Ch 1, sc in same st, *ch 4, sc in next ch-6 sp, (ch 4, sc in next ch-4 sp) 13 times, ch 6, cl, ch 6, sc in next ch-4 sp, (ch 4, sc in next ch-4 sp) 12 times, ch 4, sc in next ch-6 sp*, [ch 4, sc in top of next cl; repeat between **]; repeat between [ ] around, join with ch 1, dc in first sc (4 cls, 112 ch-4 sps, 8 ch-6 sps).

Rnd 14: *Ch 4, (sc in next ch-4 sp, ch 4) 14 times, sc in next ch-6 sp, ch 4, sc in top of next cl, ch 4, sc in next ch-6 sp, (ch 4, sc in next ch-4 sp) 13 times*, [ch 4, sc in next ch-4 sp; repeat between **]; repeat between [ ] around, join with ch 1, dc in top of joining dc (124 ch-4 sps).

Rnd 15: Ch 4, (sc in next ch sp, ch 4) around, join with sl st in top of joining dc.

Rnd 16: Sl st in first ch sp, ch 1, 3 sc in same sp, ◊ch 3, *3 sc in each of next 7 ch sps, (3 sc, ch 3, 3 sc) in next ch sp; repeat from * 2 more times, 3 sc in each of next 6 ch sps ◊, [3 sc in next ch sp; repeat between ◊◊]; repeat between [ ] around, join with sl st in first sc, fasten off.

FLOWER (make 24)

With lavender, ch 2, sc in 2nd ch from hook, ch 3, *(2 tr, ch 3, sc, ch 3) in same ch as first sc; repeat from * 3 times, join with sl st in first sc, fasten off (4 petals).

FINISHING

Sew eight Flowers in center of Doily over rnds 1 and 2; sew one Flower on each shell of rnds 8 and 9.

With yellow, embroider one French Knot (see Stitch Guide) in center of each Flower.⚜

FANS & LACE

Continued from page 102

repeat between [ ], ch 6, sc in next ch lp, join with ch 2, tr in joining tr.

Rnd 41: [*Tr in next tr, (ch 2, tr in next tr) 11 times, sc in next ch lp], ch 6, sc in next ch lp; repeat from * 30 times; repeat between [ ], join with ch 3, dc in joining tr.

Rnd 42: [*(Ch 6, sc in next tr) 12 times], ch 6, sc in next ch lp; repeat from * 30 times; repeat between [ ], join with ch 3, dc in joining dc (416 ch-6 lps).

Rnd 43: Ch 6, sc in next ch lp, *(ch 6, skip next ch lp, sc in next ch lp) 6 times, ch 6, sc in next ch lp; repeat from * 30 times, (ch 6, skip next ch lp, sc in next ch lp) 5 times, join as before.

Rnds 44-50: Repeat rnd 2..times, join.

Rnd 52: Ch 6, sc in next ch lp, [*12 tr in next ch lp, sc in next ch lp], (ch 6, sc in next ch lp) 2 times; repeat from * 62 times; repeat between [ ], join.

Rnd 53: [*Ch 6, sc in next ch lp, tr in next tr, (ch 1, tr in next tr) 11 times], sc in next ch lp; repeat from * 62 times; repeat between [ ], join with sl st in joining dc.

Rnd 54: Ch 1, sc over joining dc just made, [*tr in next tr, (ch 2, tr in next tr) 11 times], sc in next ch lp; repeat from * 62 times; repeat between [ ], join with sl st in first sc.

Rnd 55: Ch 6, skipping ch-2 sps, (sc, ch 6) in each st around, join with sl st in first ch. Fasten off. ⚜

EARLY BLOOMS

Continued from page 106

repeat between **]; repeat between [ ] around, join with sl st in top of tr 5 tog (56 tr, 40 ch-3 sps, 16 V-sts, 16 ch-7 sps, 16 ch-5 sps).

Rnd 16: Ch 9, tr in next ch sp, *(ch 3, tr in next ch sp) 8 times, ch 5, tr in next st, ch 5, (tr in next ch sp, ch 5) 2 times*, [tr in next st, ch 5; repeat between **]; repeat between [ ] around, join with sl st in 4th ch of ch-9.

Rnd 17: Ch 4, 6 tr in same st, *ch 4, skip next ch sp, tr in next ch sp, (ch 3, tr in next ch sp) 7 times, ch 4, skip next ch sp, 7 tr in next st, ch 3, skip next ch sp, 7 tr in 3rd ch of next ch-5, ch 3, skip next ch sp*, [7 tr in next st; repeat between **]; repeat between [ ] around, join with sl st in top of ch-4.

Rnd 18: Sl st in next 3 sts, ch 4, (2 tr, picot, 3 tr) in same st, *ch 3, (tr in next ch sp, ch 3) 9 times, (3 tr, picot, 3 tr) in 4th tr of next 7-tr group, ch 5, sc in 4th tr of next 7-tr group, ch 5*, [(3 tr, picot, 3 tr) in 4th tr of next 7-tr group; repeat between **]; repeat between [ ] around, join, fasten off.

T U L I P (make 2 each yellow, dk. yellow, pink and dk. pink)
Center Petal
Row 1: Starting at top, ch 4, 4 dc in 4th ch from hook, turn (5 dc).

Row 2: Ch 3, dc in same st, 2 dc in each of last 4 sts, turn (10).

Rows 3-6: Ch 3, dc in each st across, turn.

Row 7: Ch 3, dc next 3 sts tog, dc in each of next 2 sts, dc next 3 sts tog leaving last st unworked, turn (5).

Row 8: Ch 3, dc last 4 sts tog, ch 1 tightly to close, **do not** turn.

Rnd 9: Working in ends of rows around outer edge, (3 sc in each of next 2 rows, 3 hdc in next row, 3 dc in each of next 2 rows, 3 hdc in next row, 3 sc in each of last 2 rows), 3 sc in next ch; working on opposite side; repeat between ( ), sl st in next st, fasten off.

Side Petal (make 2)
Row 1: Starting at top, ch 4, 2 dc in 4th ch from hook, turn (3 dc).

Row 2: Ch 3, dc in same st, 2 dc in each of last 2 sts, turn (6).

Rows 3-7: Ch 3, dc in each st across, turn.

Row 8: Ch 3, dc next 4 sts tog leaving last st unworked, ch 1 tightly to close, **do not** turn.

Rnd 9: Working in sts and ends of rows around outer edge, 3 sc in each of next 8 rows, 3 sc in next ch; working on opposite side, 3 sc in each of next 8 rows, sl st in next st, fasten off.

Matching sts on ends of rows 6-8, sew two Side Petals together according to photo. Sew rows 6-7 of Side Petals over rows 7-8 of Center Petal.

Sew Tulips over rnds 15-18 of Doily as shown in photo. ⚜

ANTIQUE LACE

Once coveted more than precious
metals or jewels, lace has been a favorite for
decorating and personal adornment for centuries.
Nothing adds warmth and elegance like the rich, ageless
beauty of sumptuous thread crochet. Stitch your own
treasury of luxurious heirlooms with fashionable
patterns that celebrate the heritage
of this creative craft.

LYRIC TABLECLOTH

ESSENTIALS

SIZE: 50" square.

MATERIALS: Size 10 bedspread cotton — 3,384 yds. ecru; No. 9 steel crochet hook or size needed to obtain gauge.

GAUGE: Rnds 1-2 of Motif = 1¾". Each Motif is 5½" across.

INSTRUCTIONS

MOTIF NO. 1

Rnd 1: Ch 5, sl st in first ch to form ring, ch 11, tr in ring, ch 11, (tr in ring, ch 7, tr in ring, ch 11) 3 times, join with sl st in 4th ch of first ch-11 (4 ch-11 lps, 4 ch-7 lps).

Rnd 2: Sl st in first ch-7 lp, ch 1, 9 sc in same lp, *ch 3, sc in next ch-11 lp, ch 3, (sc in same lp, ch 3) 5 times*, [9 sc in next ch-7 lp; repeat between **]; repeat between [ ] around, join with sl st in first sc (60 sc, 28 ch-3 sps).

Rnd 3: Sl st in next 4 sc, ch 1, sc in same st, *ch 5, skip next 2 ch-3 sps, sc in next ch-3 sp, (ch 4, sc in next ch-3 sp) 2 times, ch 5, skip next 2 ch-3 sps*, [sc in 5th sc of next 9-sc group; repeat between **]; repeat between [ ] around, join (16 sc, 8 ch-5 sps, 8 ch-4 sps).

Rnd 4: Ch 1, sc in same st, *ch 9, skip next ch-5 sp, sc in next ch-4 sp, ch 11, sc in next ch-4 sp*, [ch 9, skip next ch-5 sp, sc in next sc; repeat between **]; repeat between [ ] around to last ch-5 sp, skip last sp; to **join,** ch 5, tr in first sc (8 ch-9 lps, 4 ch-11 lps).

Rnd 5: *Ch 7, sc in 3rd ch of next ch-9 lp, ch 11, (2 tr, ch 7, 2 tr) in 6th ch of next ch-11 lp, ch 11*, [sc in 7th ch of next ch-9 lp; repeat between **]; repeat between [ ] around; to **join,** sc in joining dc of last rnd (8 ch-11 lps, 8 ch-7 lps).

Rnd 6: *Ch 5, sc in next ch-7 lp, ch 5, sc in same lp, ch 5, sc in next sc, ch 7, (2 tr, ch 5, 2 tr) in 9th ch of next ch-11 lp, ch 3, (2 tr, ch 5, 2 tr) in 4th ch of next ch-7 lp, ch 3, (2 tr, ch 5, 2 tr) in 3rd ch of next ch-11 lp, ch 7*, [sc in next sc; repeat between **]; repeat between [ ] around, join with sl st in joining sc of last rnd (24 ch-5 sps, 8 ch-7 lps, 8 ch-3 sps).

Rnd 7: Sl st in next 3 chs, ch 1, sc in same sp, *(ch 5, sc in next ch-5 sp) 2 times, ch 7, skip next ch-7 lp, (2 tr, ch 5, 2 tr) in 3rd ch of next ch-5 sp, ch 3, skip next ch-3 sp, (2 tr, ch 5, 3 tr, ch 5, 2 tr) in next ch-5 sp, ch 3, skip next ch-3 sp, (2 tr, ch 5, 2 tr) in 3rd ch of next ch-5 sp, ch 7, skip next ch-7 lp*, [sc in next ch-5 sp; repeat between **]; repeat between [ ] around, join with sl st in first sc.

Rnd 8: Sl st in next 3 chs, ch 1, sc in same sp, *ch 21, sc in next ch-5 sp, ch 9, skip next ch-7 lp, (2 tr, ch 5, 2 tr) in 3rd ch of next ch-5 sp, ch 3, skip next ch-3 sp, (2 tr, ch 5, 2 tr) in 3rd ch of next ch-5 sp, tr in 2nd tr of next 3-tr group, ch 7, sl st in top of tr just made, (2 tr, ch 5, 2 tr) in 3rd ch of next ch-5 sp, ch 3, skip next ch-3 sp, (2 tr, ch 5, 2 tr) in 3rd ch of next ch-5 sp, ch 9, skip next ch-7 lp*, [sc in next ch-5 sp; repeat between **]; repeat between [ ] around, join, fasten off (16 ch-5 sps, 8 ch-9 lps, 8 ch-3 sps, 4 ch-21 lps).

MOTIFS NO. 2-81

Rnds 1-7: Repeat same rnds of Motif No. 1.

NOTES: For **joining ch-21 lp,** ch 10, sl st in ch-21 lp of next motif, ch 10.

For **joining ch-5 sp,** ch 2, sl st in ch-5 sp of next motif, ch 2.

For **joining ch-7 lp,** ch 3, sl st in ch-7 lp of next motif, ch 3.

Join Motifs according to diagram in 9 rows of 9 motifs each.

Rnd 8: Repeat same rnd of Motif No. 1, using joining ch-21 lps, joining ch-5 sps and joining ch-7 lps when joining Motifs according to Joining Diagram on page 124.

BORDER

NOTE: For **picot,** ch 5, sl st in top of last st made.

Join with sl st in any corner ch-7 lp, ch 4, (2 tr, picot, 3 tr) in same lp, [ch 7, sc in next ch-5 sp, picot, *ch 7, (3 tr, picot, 3 tr) in next ch-5 sp, ch 11, (2 sc, picot, 2 sc) in next ch-21 lp, ch 11, (3 tr, picot, 3 tr) in next ch-5 sp*, ◊ch 7, (3 tr, picot, 3 tr) in next ch-5 sp, ch 5, skip next 2 joining ch-7 lps, (3 tr, picot, 3 tr) in next ch-5 sp; repeat between **; repeat from ◊ 7 times, ch 7, sc in next ch-5 sp, picot, ch 7], •(3 tr, picot, 3 tr) in corner ch-7 lp; repeat between [ ]; repeat from • around, join with sl st in top of first ch-4, fasten off. ❧

HEIRLOOM CROCHET TREASURES

SAPPHIRE CENTERPIECE

ESSENTIALS

SIZE: 16" after blocking.

MATERIALS: Size 10 bedspread cotton — 250 yds. blue; No. 7 steel crochet hook or size needed to obtain gauge.

GAUGE: Rnds 1-2 = 2".

NOTE: Doily may ruffle until blocked.

INSTRUCTIONS

DOILY

Rnd 1: Ch 9, sl st in first ch to form ring, ch 7, (tr, ch 3) 11 times in ring, join with sl st in 4th ch of ch-7 (12 tr, 12 ch sps).

Rnd 2: Ch 3, dc in each tr around with 3 dc in each ch sp, join with sl st in top of ch-3 (48 dc).

Rnd 3: Ch 1, (sc in next st, ch 11, skip next 7 sts) around, join with sl st in first sc (6 ch lps).

Rnd 4: Ch 1, *skip next sc, (3 sc, hdc, 5 dc, 3 tr, 5 dc, hdc, 2 sc) in next ch lp; repeat from * around, join (126 sts).

Rnd 5: Ch 1, *sc in next st, (ch 3, skip next st, sc in next st) 10 times, ch 1; repeat from * around, join (60 ch-3 lps, 6 ch-1 sps).

Rnd 6: Sl st in first ch, ch 1, sc in same lp, *(ch

4, sc in next ch-3 lp) 9 times, ch 1, skip next ch-1 sp*, [sc in next ch-3 lp; repeat between **]; repeat between [ ], join (54 ch-4 lps 6 ch-1 sps).

Rnd 7: Sl st in first 2 chs, ch 1, sc in same lp, *(ch 4, sc in next ch-4 lp) 8 times, ch 1, skip next ch-1 sp*, [sc in next ch-4 lp; repeat between **]; repeat between [ ] around, join (48 ch-4 lps, 6 ch-1 sps).

Rnd 8: Sl st in first 2 chs, ch 1, sc in same lp, *(ch 5, sc in next ch-4 lp) 7 times, ch 1, skip next ch-1 sp*, [sc in next ch-4 lp; repeat between **]; repeat between [ ] around, join (42 ch-5 lps, 6 ch-1 sps).

Rnd 9: Sl st in first 3 chs, ch 1, sc in same lp, *(ch 5, sc in next ch-5 lp) 6 times, ch 1, skip next ch-1 sp*, [sc in next ch-5 lp; repeat between **]; repeat between [ ] around, join (36 ch-5 lps, 6 ch-1 sps).

NOTE: For **cluster (cl),** *yo 2 times, insert hook in sp, yo, draw lp through, (yo, draw through 2 lps on hook) 2 times; repeat from * 2 times in same sp, yo, draw through all 4 lps on hook.

Rnd 10: Sl st in first 3 chs, ch 1, sc in same lp, *(ch 7, sc in next ch-5 lp) 5 times, ch 3, cl in next ch-1 sp, ch 3*, [sc in next ch-5 lp; repeat between **]; repeat between [ ] around, join (30 ch-7 lps, 12 ch-3 sps, 6 cls).

Rnd 11: Sl st in first 4 chs, ch 1, sc in same lp, *(ch 7, sc in next ch-7 lp) 4 times, ch 3, cl in next ch-3 sp, ch 5, cl in next ch-3 sp, ch 3*, [sc in next ch-7 lp; repeat between **]; repeat between [ ] around, join (24 ch-7 lps, 12 cls, 12 ch-3 sps, 6 ch-5 sps).

Rnd 12: Sl st in first 4 chs, ch 1, sc in same lp, *(ch 7, sc in next ch-7 lp) 3 times, ch 3, cl in next ch-3 sp, ch 3, (cl, ch 3) 3 times in next ch-5 sp, cl in next ch-3 sp, ch 3*, [sc in next ch-7 lp; repeat between **]; repeat between [ ] around, join (36 ch-3 sps, 30 cls, 18 ch-7 lps).

Rnd 13: Sl st in first 4 chs, ch 1, sc in same lp, *(ch 7, sc in next ch-7 lp) 2 times, (ch 3, cl in next ch-3 sp) 3 times, ch 9, (cl in next ch-3 sp, ch 3) 3 times*, [sc in next ch-7 lp; repeat between **]; repeat between [ ] around, join (36 cls, 36 ch-3 sps, 12 ch-7 lps, 6 ch-9 sps).

Rnd 14: Sl st in first 4 chs, ch 1, sc in same lp, *ch 7, sc in next ch-7 lp, (ch 3, cl in next ch-3 sp) 3 times, (ch 4, sc) 5 times in next ch-9 lp, ch 4, (cl in next ch-3 sp, ch 3) 3 times*, [sc in next ch-7 lp; repeat between **]; repeat between [ ] around, join (36 cls, 36 ch-3 sps, 36 ch-4 sps, 6 ch-7 lps).

Rnd 15: Sl st in next 3 chs, (sl st, ch 4, 4 tr) in next ch, *ch 3, (cl in next ch-3 sp, ch 3) 3 times, cl in next ch-4

sp, ch 5, sc in next ch-4 lp, (ch 4, sc in next ch-4 lp) 3 times, ch 5, cl in next ch-4 sp, ch 3, (cl in next ch-3 sp, ch 3) 3 times*, [5 tr in 4th ch of next ch-7 lp; repeat between **]; repeat between [ ] around, join with sl st in top of ch-4 (48 cls, 48 ch-3 sps, 30 tr, 18 ch-4 sps, 12 ch-5 sps).

Rnd 16: Ch 4, tr in next tr, *ch 5, skip next tr, tr in each of next 2 tr, ch 3, skip next ch-3 sp, cl in next ch-3 sp, (ch 3, cl in next ch-3 sp) 2 times, ch 9, skip next ch-5 sp, sc in next ch-4 lp, (ch 4, sc in next ch-4 lp) 2 times, ch 9, skip next ch-5 sp, (cl in next ch-3 sp, ch 3) 3 times, skip next ch-3 sp*, [tr in each of next 2 tr; repeat between **]; repeat between [ ] around, join (36 cls, 36 ch-3 sps, 24 tr, 12 ch-9 lps, 12 ch-4 sps).

Rnd 17: Ch 4, tr in next tr, *ch 11, skip next ch-5 sp, tr in each of next 2 tr, ch 3, skip next ch-3 sp, cl in next ch-3 sp, ch 3, cl in next ch-3 sp, ch 11, skip next ch-9 lp, sc in next ch-4 lp, ch 7, sc in next ch-4 lp, ch 11, skip next ch-9 lp, (cl in next ch-3 sp, ch 3) 2 times, skip next ch-3 sp*, [tr in each of next 2 tr; repeat between **]; repeat between [ ] around, join (24 tr, 24 cls, 24 ch-3 sps, 18 ch-11 lps, 6 ch-7 lps).

Rnd 18: Ch 4, tr in next tr, *ch 5, 3 sc in next ch-11 lp, ch 5, tr in each of next 2 tr, ch 3, skip next ch-3 sp, cl in next ch-3 sp, ch 15, skip next ch-11 lp, 3 tr in 4th ch of next ch-7 lp, ch 15, skip next ch-11 lp, cl in next ch-3 sp, ch 3, skip next ch-3 sp*, [tr in each of next 2 tr; repeat between **;] repeat between [ ] around, join (42 tr, 18 sc, 12 ch-15 lps, 12 ch-5 sps, 12 ch-3 sps, 12 cls).

Rnd 19: Ch 1, sc in each of first 2 tr, *ch 7, skip next ch-5 sp, skip next sc, (sc, ch 5, sc) in next sc, ch 7, skip next sc, skip next ch-5 sp, sc in each of next 2 tr, ch 5, skip next ch-3 sp, skip next cl, dc in next 15 chs, ch 4, skip next tr, (sc, ch 5, sc) in next tr, ch 4, dc in next 15 chs, ch 5, skip next cl, skip next ch-3 sp*, [sc in each of next 2 tr; repeat between **]; repeat between [ ] around, join with sl st in first sc (180 dc, 48 sc, 24 ch-5 sps, 12 ch-7 lps, 12 ch-4 sps).

Rnd 20: Ch 1,*sc in next sc, ch 5, sc in next sc, ch 11, tr in 4th ch of next ch-7 lp, skip next ch-5 lp, tr in 4th ch of next ch-7 lp, ch 11, (sc in next sc, ch 5) 2 times, skip next ch-5 sp, ◊sc in next dc, (ch 3, skip next dc, sc in next dc) 3 times, ch 7, skip next dc, sc in next dc, (ch 3, skip next dc, sc in next dc) 3 times◊, ch 7, skip next ch-4 sp, skip next ch-5 lp, skip next ch-4 sp; repeat between ◊◊, ch 5, skip next ch-5 sp; repeat from * around, join, fasten off (72 ch-3 sps, 24 ch-5 sps, 18 ch-7 lps, 12 ch-11 lps, 12 tr). ⚜

HEIRLOOM CROCHET TREASURES

PINEAPPLE CENTERPIECE

ESSENTIALS

SIZE: 19" across.
MATERIALS: Size 10 bedspread cotton — 300 yds. white, 120 yds. each purple and green; No. 7 steel crochet hook or size needed to obtain gauge.
GAUGE: One shell = ¾"; 5 shell rows = 2".

INSTRUCTIONS

PINEAPPLE NO. 1
Row 1: With white, ch 4, sl st in first ch to form ring, ch 5, (3 tr in ring, ch 1) 4 times, tr in ring, turn (14 tr, 5 ch-1 sps).
NOTE: For **shell,** (3 tr, ch 1, 3 tr) in next sp.
Row 2: Ch 5, skip first ch-1 sp, skip next 3 tr, shell in next ch-1 sp, ch 1, (tr, ch 3, tr) in next ch-1 sp, ch 1, shell in next ch-1 sp, ch 1, tr in 4th ch of last ch-5, turn (4 tr, 4 ch-1 sps, 2 shells, 1 ch-3 sp).
Row 3: Ch 5, shell in ch sp of next shell, ch 1, skip next ch-1 sp, 15 tr in next ch-3 sp, ch 1, skip next ch-1 sp, shell in ch sp of next shell, ch 1, tr in 4th ch of last ch-5, turn (17 tr, 4 ch-1 sps, 2 shells).
Row 4: Ch 5, shell in next shell, ch 1, skip next 3 tr of same shell, (tr in next tr, ch 1) 15 times, shell in next shell, ch 1, tr in 4th ch of last ch-5, turn (17 tr, 18 ch-1 sps, 2 shells).
Row 5: Ch 5, shell in next shell, ch 1, skip next ch-1 sp, sc in next ch-1 sp, (ch 3, sc in next ch-1 sp) 13 times, ch 1, shell in next shell, ch 1, tr in 4th ch of last ch-5, turn (13 ch-3 lps, 4 ch-1 sps, 2 shells, 2 tr).
Row 6: Ch 5, shell in next shell, ch 2, skip next ch-1 sp, sc in next ch-3 lp, (ch 3, sc in next ch-3 lp) across to next shell, ch 2, shell in next shell, ch 1, tr in 4th ch of last ch-5, turn (12 ch-3 lps).
Rows 7-17: Ch 5, shell in next shell, ch 2, skip next ch-2 sp, sc in next ch-3 lp, (ch 3, sc in next ch-3 lp) across to next shell, ch 2, shell in next shell, ch 1, tr in 4th ch of last ch-5, turn, ending with one ch-3 lp in last row.
NOTE: For **double treble crochet (dtr),** yo 3 times, insert hook in next st or sp, yo, draw lp through, (yo, draw through 2 lps on hook) 4 times.
Row 18: Ch 5, shell in next shell, (dtr, ch 2, dtr) in next ch-3 lp, shell in next shell, ch 1, tr in 4th ch of last ch-5, turn.
Row 19: Ch 5, 3 tr in next shell, ch 1, skip next ch-2 sp, 3 tr in next shell, ch 1, tr in 4th ch of last ch-5, turn (8 tr, 3 ch-1 sps).
Row 20: Ch 5, skip next 3 tr, 3 tr in next ch-1 sp, ch 1, skip next 3 tr, tr in 4th ch of last ch-5, turn.
Row 21: Ch 5, skip next 3 tr, sc in 4th ch of last ch-5, fasten off.

Border
Rnd 1: Working around outer edge, in ch-5 sps and over tr on ends of rows, join purple with sc in ch-4 ring on row 1, (sc, hdc, 2 dc, 2 tr) in next sp, shell in each of next 8 sps, sc in next sp, (shell in next sp, sc in next sp) 5 times; for **point,** (shell, ch 1, shell) in ch-5 lp on row 21, sc in next sp, (shell in next sp, sc in next sp) 5 times, shell in each of next 8 sps, (2 tr, 2 dc, hdc, sc) in last sp, join with sl st in first sc, fasten off.
Rnd 2: Join green with sc in first st, ch 4, skip next 3 sts, (sc, ch 4, sc) in next st, ch 4, skip next 2 sts, sc in next sp between sts, ch 4, (sc, ch 4, sc) in ch sp of next shell, ch 4, *sc in next sp between shells, ch 4, (sc, ch 4, sc) in next shell, ch 4*; repeat between ** 6 times, [sc in next sc, ch 4, (sc, ch 4, sc) in next shell, ch 4]; repeat between [ ] 5 times; for **point,** (sc, ch 4, sc) in next ch-1 sp, ch 4, (sc, ch 4, sc) in next shell, ch 4; repeat between [ ] 6 more times; repeat between ** 7 more times, skip next 3 sts of same shell, sc in next sp between sts, ch 4, skip next 2 sts, (sc, ch 4, sc) in next st, ch 4, join with sl st in first sc, fasten off.

PINEAPPLES NO. 2-6
Work same as Pineapple No. 1.

Border
Rnd 1: Repeat same rnd of Pineapple No. 1 Border.
NOTES: For **joining ch-4 sp,** ch 2, sl st in next ch-4 sp on corresponding Pineapple, ch 2.

Join Pineapples in seven ch-4 sps on each side of point as shown in Joining Diagram on page 127.

Rnd 2: Repeat same rnd of Pineapple No. 1 Border, using joining ch-4 sps to join Pineapples according to diagram. ⚜

HEIRLOOM CROCHET TREASURES

SPRING TEATIME

ESSENTIALS

SIZE: 40" across.
MATERIALS: Size 20 crochet cotton — 1,000 yds. ecru; No. 12 steel crochet hook or size needed to obtain gauge.
GAUGE: Rnds 1-3 = 1⅞" across.
NOTES: For **scallop,** (sc, hdc, 6 dc, tr, 6 dc, hdc, sc) in next ch lp.

For **cluster (cl),** *yo 2 times, insert hook in ch lp, yo, draw lp through, (yo, draw through 2 lps on hook) 2 times; repeat from * 2 times in same lp, yo, draw through all 4 lps on hook.

Tablecloth may ruffle until blocked.

INSTRUCTIONS

TABLECLOTH

Rnd 1: Ch 10, sl st in first ch to form ring, ch 1, 24 sc in ring, join with sl st in first sc (24 sc).

Rnd 2: Ch 1, sc in same st, ch 10, skip next 3 sts, (sc in next st, ch 10, skip next 3 sts) around, join with sl st in first sc (6 ch lps).

Rnd 3: Sl st in first ch lp, ch 1, scallop in same lp and in each ch lp around, join (6 scallops).

NOTE: Joining (ch 2, dc) counts as ch lp.

Rnd 4: Sl st in next 2 sts, ch 1, sc in same st, (ch 5, skip next 3 sts, sc in next st) 3 times, *ch 5, sc in 3rd st of next scallop, (ch 5, skip next 3 sts, sc in next st) 3 times; repeat from * around to last 4 sts, skip last 4 sts; to join, ch 2, dc in first sc (24 ch lps).

Rnd 5: (Ch 5, sc in next ch lp) around, join as before in joining dc on last rnd.

Rnd 6: Ch 10, sc in next ch lp, *(ch 5, sc in next ch lp) 3 times, ch 10, sc in next ch lp; repeat from * around to last 2 ch lps, (ch 5, sc in next ch lp) 2 times, join as before.

Rnd 7: Ch 1, sc over dc just made, *scallop in next ch-10 lp, sc in next ch-5 lp, ch 5, (cl, ch 3, cl) in next ch-5 lp*, [ch 5, sc in next ch-5 lp; repeat between **]; repeat between [ ] around, join as before in first sc (12 ch-5 lps, 6 scallops, 6 ch-3 lps).

Rnd 8: Ch 5, sc in 3rd st of next scallop, (ch 5, skip next 3 sts, sc in next st) 3 times, *ch 5, (sc in next ch-5 lp or ch-3 lp, ch 5) 3 times, sc in 3rd st of next scallop, (ch 5, skip next 3 sts, sc in next st)

3 times; repeat from * around to last 2 ch-5 and ch-3 lps, (ch 5, sc in next ch-5 lp or ch-3 lp) 2 times, join as before in joining dc on last rnd (42 ch lps).

Rnds 9-10: Repeat rnd 5.

Rnd 11: Ch 10, sc in next ch lp, *(ch 5, sc in next ch lp) 6 times, ch 10, sc in next ch lp; repeat from * around to last 5 ch lps, (ch 5, sc in next ch lp) 5 times, join as before (36 ch-5 lps, 6 ch-10 lps).

Rnd 12: Ch 1, sc over dc just made, *scallop in next ch-10 lp, sc in next ch-5 lp, ch 5, (cl, ch 3, cl) in next ch-5 lp, ch 5, (sc in next ch-5 lp, ch 5) 2 times, (cl, ch 3, cl) in next ch-5 lp*, [ch 5, sc in next ch-5 lp; repeat between **]; repeat between [ ] around, join as before in first sc (30 ch-5 lps, 12 ch-3 lps, 6 scallops).

Rnd 13: Ch 5, sc in 3rd st of next scallop, (ch 5, skip next 3 sts, sc in next st) 3 times, *ch 5, (sc in next ch-5 lp or ch-3 lp, ch 5) 7 times, sc in 3rd st of next scallop, (ch 5, skip next 3 sts, sc in next st) 3 times; repeat from * around to last 6 ch-5 and ch-3 lps, (ch 5, sc in next ch-5 lp or ch-3 lp) 6 times, join as before in joining dc on last rnd (66 ch-5 lps).

Rnds 14-15: Repeat rnd 5.

Rnd 16: (Ch 5, sc in next ch-5 lp) 9 times, ch 10, sc in next ch-5 lp, *(ch 5, sc in next ch-5 lp) 10 times, ch 10, sc in next ch-5 lp; repeat from * around, join (60 ch-5 lps, 6 ch-10 lps).

Rnd 17: Ch 5, (sc in next ch-5 lp, ch 5) 2 times, *(cl, ch 3, cl) in next ch-5 lp, ch 5, (sc in next ch-5 lp, ch 5) 2 times, (cl, ch 3, cl) in next ch-5 lp, (ch 5, sc in next ch-5 lp) 3 times, scallop in next ch-10 lp*, [(sc in next ch-5 lp, ch 5) 3 times; repeat between **]; repeat between [ ] around, join with sl st in top of joining dc on last rnd (54 ch-5 lps, 12 ch-3 lps, 6 scallops).

Rnd 18: Sl st in next 3 chs of first ch-5 lp, ch 1, sc in same lp, ch 5, (sc in next ch-5 lp or ch-3 lp, ch 5) 10 times, *sc in 3rd st of next scallop, (ch 5, skip next 3 sts, sc in next st) 3 times*, [ch 5, (sc in next ch-5 lp, ch 5) 11 times; repeat between **]; repeat between [ ] around; to join, ch 2, dc in first sc (90 ch lps).

Rnd 19: Repeat rnd 5.

Rnd 20: Ch 10, sc in next ch-5 lp, ch 5, (sc in next ch-5 lp, ch 10, sc in next ch-5 lp, ch 5)

Continued on next page

SPRING TEATIME

Continued from page 123

around, join with sl st in top of joining dc on last rnd.

Rnd 21: (Scallop in next ch-10 lp, sc in next ch-5 lp) around, join with sl st in first sc (45 scallops, 45 sc).

Rnd 22: Sl st in next 2 sts, ch 1, sc in same st, (ch 5, skip next 3 sts, sc in next st) 3 times, *sc in 3rd st of next scallop, (ch 5, skip next 3 sts, sc in next st) 3 times; repeat from * around, join with sl st in first sc (135 ch lps).

Rnd 23: Sl st in next 3 chs of first ch lp, ch 1, sc in same lp, (ch 5, sc in next ch lp) around; to join, ch 2, dc in first sc.

Rnds 24-25: Repeat rnd 5.

Rnd 26: Ch 5, (cl, ch 3, cl) in next ch lp, *ch 5, (sc in next ch lp, ch 5) 8 times, (cl, ch 3, cl) in next ch lp; repeat from * around to last 7 ch lps, (ch 5, sc in next ch lp) 7 times, join (135 ch-5 lps, 15 ch-3 lps).

Rnds 27-30: Repeat rnd 5 (150 ch lps).

Rnd 31: Ch 5, (sc in next ch lp, ch 5) 8 times, (cl, ch 3, cl) in next ch lp, *ch 5, (sc in next ch lp, ch 5) 9 times, (cl, ch 3, cl) in next ch lp; repeat from * around, join (150 ch-5 lps, 15 ch-3 lps).

Rnds 32-36: Repeat rnd 5 (165 ch lps).

Rnd 37: Ch 5, (sc in next ch lp, ch 5) 6 times, (cl, ch 3,

cl) in next ch lp, *ch 5, (sc in next ch lp, ch 5) 10 times, (cl, ch 3, cl) in next ch lp; repeat from * around to last 3 ch lps, (ch 5, sc in next ch lp) 3 times, join (165 ch-5 lps, 15 ch-3 lps).

Rnds 38-42: Repeat rnd 5 (180 ch lps).

Rnds 43-66: Repeat rnds 20-42, ending with 360 ch lps in last rnd.

Rnd 67: Ch 5, (sc in next ch lp, ch 5) 4 times, (cl, ch 3, cl) in next ch lp, *ch 5, (sc in next ch lp, ch 5) 11 times, (cl, ch 3, cl) in next ch lp; repeat from * around to last 6 ch lps, (ch 5, sc in next ch lp) 6 times, join (360 ch-5 lps, 30 ch-3 lps).

Rnds 68-72: (Ch 5, sc in next ch lp) around, join as before in joining dc on last rnd (390 ch lps).

Rnd 73: Ch 5, sc in next ch lp, ch 5, (cl, ch 3, cl) in next ch lp, *ch 5, (sc in next ch lp, ch 5) 12 times, (cl, ch 3, cl) in next ch lp; repeat from * around to last 10 ch lps, (ch 5, sc in next ch lp) 10 times, join (390 ch-5 lps, 30 ch-3 lps).

Rnds 74-76: (Ch 5, sc in next ch lp) around, join as before in joining dc on last rnd.

Rnds 77-78: Repeat rnds 20 and 21. Fasten off at end of last rnd. ❧

LYRIC TABLECLOTH

Continued from page 117

JOINING DIAGRAM

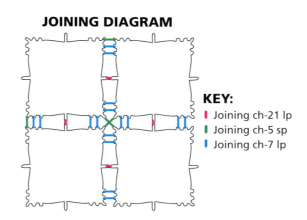

KEY:
- Joining ch-21 lp
- Joining ch-5 sp
- Joining ch-7 lp

HEIRLOOM CROCHET TREASURES

FAN DUCHESS

ESSENTIALS

SIZE: Large Doily is 11½" across; small Doilies are 8½" across.

MATERIALS FOR ALL THREE: Size 20 crochet cotton — 250 yds. cream and 150 yds. burgundy; No. 11 steel crochet hook or size needed to obtain gauge.

GAUGE: 12 tr sts = 1"; 3 tr rows = ⅞".

NOTE: For **double crochet back post (dc bp)**, yo, insert hook from back to front around post of st, yo, draw lp through, complete as dc.

INSTRUCTIONS

LARGE DOILY

Rnd 1: With burgundy, ch 12, sl st in first ch to form ring, ch 6, (dc in ring, ch 3) 9 times, join with sl st in 3rd ch of ch-6 (10 dc, 10 ch-3 sps).

Rnd 2: Sl st in first ch-3 sp, (sc, ch 2, 3 dc, ch 2, sc) in same sp; repeat between ( ) in each ch-3 sp around, join with sl st in first sc (10 petals).

Rnd 3: Ch 5, *dc bp around next dc on rnd 1, ch 2; repeat from * around, join with sl st in 3rd ch of

Continued on next page

FAN DUCHESS

Continued from page 125

ch-5 (10 dc bp).

Rnd 4: Sl st in first ch-2 sp, (sc, ch 2, 5 dc, ch 2, sc) in same sp; repeat between ( ) in each ch-2 sp around, join (10 petals). Fasten off.

Row 5: Working in rows, join cream with sl st in 3rd dc of any petal of rnd 4, ch 4, 2 tr in same st, *ch 1, dtr in next space between petals, ch 1, 3 tr in 3rd dc of next petal; repeat from * 6 times leaving remaining petals unworked, turn (24 tr, 7 dtr).

NOTE: For treble front post (tr fp), yo 2 times, insert hook from front to back around post of st, yo, draw lp through, complete as tr.

Row 6: Sl st in first 2 sts, ch 4, 4 tr in same st, *ch 1, tr fp around next dtr, ch 1, 5 tr in center st of next 3-tr group; repeat from * across, turn (40 tr, 7 tr fp).

Row 7: Sl st in first 2 sts, ch 4, 5 tr in next st, tr in next st, *ch 1, skip next st, tr fp around next tr fp, ch 1, skip next st, tr in next st, 5 tr in next st, tr in next st; repeat from * across, turn (56 tr, 7 tr fp).

Row 8: Sl st in first 2 sts, ch 4, tr in next st, 5 tr in next st, tr in each of next 2 sts, *ch 1, skip next st, tr fp around next tr fp, ch 1, skip next st, tr in each of next 2 sts, 5 tr in next st, tr in each of next 2 sts; repeat from * across, turn (72 tr, 7 tr fp).

Row 9: Sl st in first 2 sts, ch 4, tr in each of next 2 sts, 5 tr in next st, tr in each of next 3 sts, *ch 1, skip next st, tr fp around next tr fp, ch 1, skip next st, tr in each of next 3 sts, 5 tr in next st, tr in each of next 3 sts; repeat from * across, turn (88 tr, 7 tr fp).

Row 10: Sl st in first 2 sts, ch 4, tr in each of next 3 sts, 5 tr in next st, tr in next 4 sts, *ch 1, skip next st, tr fp around next tr fp, ch 1, skip next st, tr in next 4 sts, 5 tr in next st, tr in next 4 sts; repeat from * across, turn (104 tr, 7 tr fp).

Row 11: Sl st in next 2 sts, ch 4, tr in next 4 sts, 5 tr in next st, tr in next 5 sts, *ch 1, skip next st, tr fp around next tr fp, ch 1, skip next st, tr in next 5 sts, 5 tr in next st, tr in next 5 sts; repeat from * across, turn (120 tr, 7 tr fp).

Row 12: Sl st in next 2 sts, ch 4, tr in next 5 sts, 5 tr in next st, tr in next 6 sts, *ch 1, skip next st, tr fp around next tr fp, ch 1, skip next st, tr in next 6 sts, 5 tr in next st, tr in next 6 sts; repeat from * across, turn (136 tr, 7 tr fp).

Row 13: Sl st in next 2 sts, ch 4, tr in next 6 sts, 5 tr in next st, tr in next 7 sts, *ch 1, skip next st, tr fp around next tr fp, ch 1, skip next st, tr in next 7 sts, 5 tr in next st, tr in next 7 sts; repeat from * across, turn (152 tr, 7 tr fp).

Row 14: Sl st in next 2 sts, ch 4, tr in next 7 sts, 5 tr in next st, tr in next 8 sts, *ch 1, skip next st, tr fp around next tr fp, ch 1, skip next st, tr in next 8 sts, 5 tr in next st, tr in next 8 sts; repeat from * across, turn (168 tr, 7 fp).

Row 15: Sl st in first 2 sts, ch 4, tr in next 8 sts, 5 tr in next st, tr in next 9 sts, *ch 1, skip next st, tr fp around next tr fp, ch 1, skip next st, tr in next 9 sts, 5 tr in next st, tr in next 9 sts; repeat from * across, turn (184 tr, 7 tr fp).

Row 16: Ch 5, skip next st, tr in next st, (ch 1, skip next st, tr in next st) 3 times, ch 1, skip next 2 sts, (tr, ch 3, tr) in next st, ch 1, skip next 2 sts, tr in next st, (ch 1, skip next st, tr in next st) 4 times, *tr in next tr fp, tr in next st, (ch 1, skip next st, tr in next st) 4 times, ch 1, skip next 2 sts, (tr, ch 3, tr) in next st, ch 1, skip next 2 sts, tr in next st, (ch 1, skip next st, tr in next st) 4 times; repeat from * across, turn (103 tr).

Row 17: Ch 4, tr in next 10 ch-1 sps or sts, (2 tr, ch 2, 2 tr) in next ch-3 sp, tr in next 11 sts or ch-1 sps, *skip next st, tr in next 11 sts or ch-1 sps, (2 tr, ch 2, 2 tr) in next ch-3 sp, tr in next 11 sts or ch-1 sps; repeat from * across with tr in 4th ch of ch-5, turn (208 tr).

Row 18: Ch 6, skip next st, tr in next st, (ch 2, skip next 2 sts, tr in next st) 3 times, ch 2, skip next st, (tr, ch 2, tr) in next ch-2 sp, ch 2, skip next st, tr in next st, (ch 2, skip next 2 sts, tr in next st) 3 times, *ch 2, skip next st, sc in each of next 2 sts, ch 2, skip next st, tr in next st, (ch 2, skip next 2 sts, tr in next st) 3 times, ch 2, skip next st, (tr, ch 2, tr) in next ch-2 sp, ch 2, skip next st, tr in next st, (ch 2, skip next 2 sts, tr in next st) 3 times; repeat from * across to last 2 sts, ch 2, skip next st, tr in last st, turn (82 tr, 14 sc).

Row 19: Ch 4, tr in next next ch-2 sp, tr in next st, (2 tr in next ch-2 sp, tr in next st) 4 times, (2 tr, ch 2, 2 tr) in next ch-2 sp, tr in next st, (2 tr in next ch-2 sp, tr in next st) 4 times, *sc in each of next 2 sc, tr in next st, (2 tr in next ch-2 sp, tr in next st) 4 times, (2 tr, ch 2, 2 tr) in next ch-2 sp, tr in next st, (2 tr in next ch-2 sp, tr in next st) 4 times; repeat from * across to last ch-2 sp, tr in last ch-2 sp, tr in 4th ch of ch-6. Fasten off.

Handle

Row 1: Working in ends of rows and remaining petals of rnd 4, join cream with sl st in top of row 6, ch 4, dtr in top of next row, ch 4, dtr in same st as next 3-dc group on rnd 5, ch 4, (dtr in next space between petals, ch 4) 3 times, dtr in same st as next 3-dc group of rnd 5, ch 4, dtr in top of row 5, ch 4, sl st in top of row 6, sl st over first tr in row 7, turn (8 ch-4 sps).

Row 2: 5 tr in each ch-4 sp across, sl st in end of row 7, turn (40 tr).

Row 3: Ch 1, sc in each st across, **do not** turn. Fasten off.

For **trim,** working around outer edge of doily, in sts and ends of rows, join burgundy with sc in any st, sc in next st; for **picot, ch 4, sl st in front lp of last dc made;** *sc in each of next 2 sts or 2 sc in end of next row, picot; repeat from * around, join with sl st in first sc. Fasten off.

S M A L L   D O I L Y (make 2)

Rnd 1: With burgundy, ch 9, sl st in first ch to form ring, ch 6, (dc in ring, ch 3) 7 times, join with sl st in 3rd ch of ch-6 (8 dc, 8 ch-3 sps).

Rnds 2-4: Repeat same rnds of Large Doily.

Row 5: Working in rows, join cream with sl st in 3rd dc of any petal on rnd 4, ch 4, 2 tr in same sp, *ch 1, dtr in next space between petals, ch 1, 3 tr in 3rd dc of next petal; repeat from * 4 times, turn (18 tr, 5 dtr).

Rows 6-11: Repeat same rows of Large Doily, ending with 90 tr and 5 tr fp.

Row 12: Ch 5, (tr in next st, ch 1, skip next st) 3 times, (tr, ch 3, tr) in next st, (ch 1, skip next st, tr in next st) 3 times, ch 1, tr in next st, *tr in next tr fp, tr in next st, ch 1, (tr in next st, ch 1, skip next st) 3 times, (tr, ch 3, tr) in next st, (ch 1, skip next st, tr in next st) 3 times,

ch 1, tr in next st; repeat from * across, turn (65 tr).

Row 13: Ch 4, tr in next 8 ch sps or sts, (2 tr, ch 2, 2 tr) in next ch-3 sp, tr in next 9 sts or ch sps, *skip next st, tr in next 9 sts or ch sps, (2 tr, ch 2, 2 tr) in next ch-3 sp, tr in next 9 sts or ch-1 sps; repeat from * across, turn (132 tr).

Row 14: Ch 6, skip next st, (tr in next st, ch 2, skip next 2 sts) 3 times, (tr, ch 2, tr) in next ch-2 sp, (ch 2, skip next 2 sts, tr in next st) 3 times, *ch 2, skip next st, sc in each of next 2 sts, ch 2, skip next st, (tr in next st, ch 2, skip next 2 sts) 3 times, (tr, ch 2, tr) in next ch-2 sp, (ch 2, skip next 2 sts, tr in next st) 3 times, repeat from * across to last 2 sts, ch 2, skip next st, tr in last st, turn (50 tr, 10 sc).

Row 15: Ch 4, (2 tr in next ch-2 sp, tr in next st) 4 times, (2 tr, ch 2, 2 tr) in next ch-2 sp, tr in next st, (2 tr in next ch-2 sp, tr in next st) 3 times, skip next ch-2 sp, *sc in each of next 2 sc, skip next ch-2 sp, tr in next st, (2 tr in next ch-2 sp, tr in next st) 3 times, (2 tr, ch 2, 2 tr) in next ch-2 sp, tr in next st, (2 tr in next ch-2 sp, tr in next st) 3 times; repeat from * across to last ch-2 sp, 2 tr in last ch-2 sp, tr in 4th ch of ch-6, turn (150 tr, 10 sc). Fasten off.

Handle

Rows 1-3: Repeat same rows of Large Doily Handle. For **trim,** work same as Large Doily trim. ⚜

PINEAPPLE CENTERPIECE

Instructions on page 120

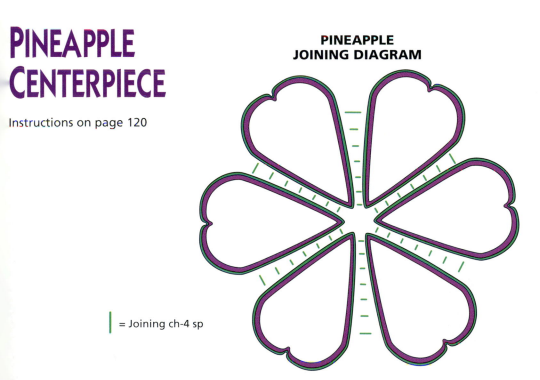

PINEAPPLE JOINING DIAGRAM

| = Joining ch-4 sp

H E I R L O O M   C R O C H E T   T R E A S U R E S

AUTUMN FLOWERS

E S S E N T I A L S

SIZE: 14" x 34".

MATERIALS: Size 20 crochet cotton — 970 yds. ecru; tapestry needle; No. 12 steel crochet hook or size needed to obtain gauge.

GAUGE: Rnds 1-2 = 1¼". Each Motif is 4" square when blocked.

NOTE: Runner may ruffle until blocked.

I N S T R U C T I O N S

MOTIF NO. 1

Rnd 1: Ch 15, sl st in first ch to form ring, ch 3, 31 dc in ring, join with sl st in top of ch-3 (32 dc).

Rnd 2: Ch 4, tr in each of next 3 sts, ch 5, (tr in next 4 sts, ch 5) around, join with sl st in top of ch-4 (32 tr, 8 ch lps).

Rnd 3: Ch 4, tr in same tr, 2 tr in each of next 3

128

tr, ch 5, (2 tr in each of next 4 tr, ch 5) around, join (64 tr, 8 ch lps).

Rnd 4: Sl st in next tr, ch 4, tr in next 5 tr, ch 9, skip next tr, skip next ch lp, *skip next tr, tr in next 6 tr, ch 9, skip next tr, skip next ch lp; repeat from * around, join (48 tr, 8 ch-9 lps).

Rnd 5: Ch 4, tr in next 5 tr, *ch 7, (tr, ch 3, tr) in 5th ch of next ch-9 lp, ch 7, tr in next 6 tr, ch 7, (sc, ch 5, sc) in 5th ch of next ch-9 lp, ch 7*, [tr in next 6 tr; repeat between **]; repeat between [ ] around, join.

NOTES: For **beginning 4-treble cluster (beg 4-tr cl),** ch 4, *yo 2 times, insert hook in next st, yo, draw lp through, (yo, draw through 2 lps on hook) 2 times; repeat from * 2 more times, yo, draw through all 4 lps on hook, ch 1.

For **4-treble cluster (4-tr cl),** *yo 2 times, insert hook in next st, yo, draw lp through, (yo, draw through 2 lps on hook) 2 times; repeat from * 3 more times, yo, draw through all 5 lps on hook, ch 1.

Ch-1 of tr cl's is not used or counted as a st.

Rnd 6: Sl st in next tr, beg 4-tr cl, *ch 7, skip next tr, skip next ch-7 sp, 2 tr in next tr, ch 3, tr in next ch-3 sp, ch 3, 2 tr in next tr, ch 7, skip next ch-7 sp, skip next tr, 4-tr cl, ch 7, skip next tr, sc in next ch-7 sp, ch 7, skip next ch-5 lp, sc in next ch-7 sp, ch 7*, [skip next tr, 4-tr cl; repeat between **]; repeat between [ ] around, join with sl st in top of beg cl.

NOTES: For **picot,** ch 5, sl st in top of last st made.

For **V-stitch (V-st),** (tr, ch 7, tr) in next st or sp.

Rnd 7: Ch 1, (sc, ch 5, sc) in top of same cl, ch 7, tr in next tr, picot, tr in next tr, ch 3, V-st in next tr, ch 3, tr in next tr, picot, tr in next tr, ch 7, (sc, ch 5, sc) in top of next cl, ch 7, skip next ch-7 sp, V-st in 4th ch of next ch-7 sp, ch 7, skip next ch-7 sp, [(sc, ch 5, sc) in top of next cl, ch 7, tr in next tr, picot, tr in next tr, ch 3, V-st in next tr, ch 3, tr in next tr, picot, tr in next tr, ch 7, (sc, ch 5, sc) in top of next cl, ch 7, skip next ch-7 sp, V-st in 4th ch of next ch-7 sp, ch 7, skip next ch-7 sp]; repeat between [ ] around, join with sl st in first sc, fasten off.

MOTIFS NO. 2-24

Rnds 1-6: Repeat same rnds of Motif No. 1.

NOTES: For **joining V-stitch (joining V-st),** tr in next st or sp, ch 3, sl st in ch sp of corresponding V-st on other Motif, ch 3, tr in same st or sp on this Motif.

For **joining picot,** ch 2, sl st in corresponding picot on other Motif, ch 2, sl st in top of last st made.

Rnd 7: Repeat same rnd of Motif No. 1, using joining V-sts and joining picots when joining Motifs according to Joining Diagram on page 131, making three rows of eight Motifs each.

BORDER

Rnd 1: For **first corner,** join with sl st in 4th ch of ch-7 sp on any corner V-st before any long edge, ch 8, dc in same ch; [ch 5, sc in last tr on same V-st, ch 5, *sc in next picot, ch 9, skip next ch-7 sp, tr in next ch-5 lp, ch 9, sc in first tr on next V-st, ch 5, sc in 4th ch of ch-7 sp on same V-st, ch 5, sc in last tr on same V-st, ch 9, skip next ch-7 sp, tr in next ch-5 lp, ch 9, sc in next picot*, (ch 9, sc in next joining, ch 9; repeat between **); repeat between ( ) across to next corner V-st, ch 5, sc in first tr on same corner V-st, ch 5]; ◊for **corner,** (dc, ch 5, dc) in 4th ch of ch-7 sp on same V-st; repeat between [ ]; repeat from ◊ around, join with sl st in 3rd ch of ch-8 (124 ch-9 sps, 64 ch-5 sps, 4 corners).

Rnd 2: Sl st in ch sp of first corner, ch 4, (2 tr, ch 5, 3 tr) in same sp, *ch 9, skip next ch-5 sp, (sc in next ch-5 or in next ch-9 sp, ch 9) around to last ch-5 sp before next corner, skip same ch-5 sp*, [(3 tr, ch 5, 3 tr) in ch sp of next corner; repeat between **]; repeat between [ ] around, join with sl st in top of ch-4 (180 ch-9 sps, 24 tr, 4 ch-5 sps).

Rnd 3: Ch 4, tr in each of next 2 tr, ◊[(3 tr, ch 5, 3 tr) in next ch-5 sp, tr in each of next 3 tr, ch 5, sc in next ch-9 sp, (ch 11, sc in next ch-9 sp) 3 times, ch 3, (5 tr, ch 5, 5 tr) in next ch-9 sp, ch 3, sc in next ch-9 sp, *(ch 11, sc in next ch-9 sp) 6 times, ch 3, (5 tr, ch 5, 5 tr) in next ch-9 sp, ch 3, sc in next ch-9 sp*]; repeat between ** 6 times, (ch 11, sc in next ch-9 sp) 3 times, ch 5, tr in each of next 3 tr; repeat between [ ]; repeat between ** one more time, (ch 11, sc in next ch-9 sp) 3 times, ch 5◊, tr in each of next 3 tr; repeat between ◊◊, join (268 tr, 132 ch-11 lps, 44 ch-3 sps, 34 ch-5 sps).

NOTE: For **5-treble cluster (5-tr cl),** yo 2 times, insert hook in next ch sp, *yo, draw lp through, (yo, draw through 2 lps on hook) 2 times*, ◊yo 2 times, insert hook in same sp; repeat between **; repeat from ◊ 3 more times, yo, draw through all 6 lps on hook, ch 1.

Rnd 4: Ch 4, tr next 2 tr tog, •◊picot, ch 5, tr next 3 tr tog, picot, ch 5, 5-tr cl in next ch-5 sp, picot, ch 5, tr next 3 tr tog, picot, ch 5, tr next 3 tr tog, picot, ch 11, skip next ch-5 sp, sc in next ch-11 sp, picot, ch 11, *5-tr cl in next ch-11 sp, picot, ch 11, sc in next ch-11 sp, picot, ch 5, skip next ch-3 sp, tr next 5 tr tog, picot, ch 5, 5-tr cl in next ch-5 sp, picot, ch 5, tr next 5 tr tog, picot, ch 5, skip next ch-3 sp, sc in next ch-11 sp, picot, ch 11, 5-tr cl in next ch-11 sp, picot, ch 11*, [(sc in next ch-11 sp, picot) 2 times; repeat between **]◊; repeat between [ ] 6 times, sc in next ch-11 sp, picot, ch 9, skip next ch-5 sp, tr next 3 tr tog; repeat between ◊◊; repeat between [ ], sc in next ch-11 sp, picot, ch 9, skip next ch-5 sp•, tr next 3 tr tog; repeat between ••, join, fasten off. ⚜

HEIRLOOM CROCHET TREASURES

HEIRLOOM BEDSPREAD

ESSENTIALS

SIZE: 102" x 118".

MATERIALS: Size 10 bedspread cotton — 14,800 yds. ecru; No. 4 steel crochet hook or size needed to obtain gauge.

GAUGE: 2 shells = 1"; 4 shell rows = 1½"; 4 mesh rows = 1⅜".

NOTES: Instructions are written for a Queen-size bedspread.

INSTRUCTIONS

For larger or smaller spread, work starting ch in multiples of 4, plus 5 at the end. Follow instructions as written, beginning and ending with shell rows.

For **beginning shell (beg shell),** (2 dc, ch 1, 2 dc) in 5th ch from hook.

For **shell,** (2 dc, ch 1, 2 dc) in next ch or ch-2 sp of next shell.

For **beginning mesh (beg mesh),** ch 4, dc in first

shell or in next dc.

For **mesh,** ch 1, dc in next dc, dc in next sp between shells, or dc in 3rd ch of ch-4.

BEDSPREAD

Row 1: Ch 817, beg shell, skip next 3 chs, shell in next ch) across, turn (204 shells).

Rows 2-4: Ch 3, shell in ch sp of each shell across with dc in top of turning ch, turn.

Row 5: Beg mesh, (mesh in next sp between shells, mesh in next shell) across, mesh in ch-3, turn (409 mesh).

Rows 6-8: Beg mesh, mesh in each dc across, with mesh in 3rd ch of ch-4, turn.

Row 9: Ch 3, skip first ch-1 sp, shell in next dc, (skip next dc, shell in next dc) across to last ch-1 sp, dc in ch-3, turn.

Rows 10-329: Repeat rows 2-9 consecutively.

Rows 330-332: Repeat rows 2-4.

Rnd 333: Working around outer edge, sl st in next 2 dc, sl st in first ch-1 sp, ch 3, 7 dc in same sp, skip next shell; for **large shell (lg shell),** 8 dc in next shell; (skip next shell, lg shell in next shell) across, lg shell in top of ch-3; working in ends of rows, *skip first row, (lg shell in next row, skip next row) across*, lg shell in end ch; working in opposite side of starting ch on row 1, (skip next 5 chs, lg shell in next ch) across; working in opposite ends of rows, repeat between **, join with sl st in top of ch-3, fasten off. ⚜

AUTUMN FLOWERS

Instructions on page 128

JOINING DIAGRAM

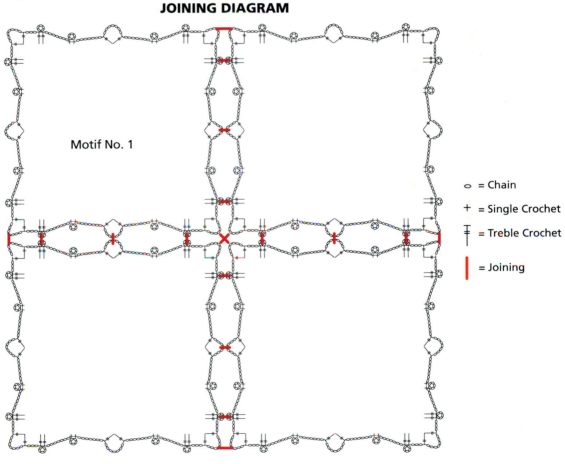

Motif No. 1

o = Chain

+ = Single Crochet

T = Treble Crochet

| = Joining

GIFTS TO TREASURE

Commemorate special events with
distinctive offerings made by hand and with
the heart. No one can resist the magical attraction found
in these wonderful designs that blend
enduring artistry with romantic appeal. Express your love
in a memorable way with handiwork
of incomparable quality, created especially
for that certain someone.

HEIRLOOM CROCHET TREASURES

RIBBONS & ROSES

ESSENTIALS

PICTURE FRAME

SIZE: Fits 8" x 10" photograph.

MATERIALS: Size 10 bedspread cotton — 135 yds. white; 1½yds. satin ¼" ribbon; twelve artificial rosebuds with leaves; 8" x 10" picture frame back; 8" x 10" piece white felt; fabric stiffener; craft glue; No. 7 steel crochet hook or size needed to obtain gauge.

GAUGE: 7 dc sts = 1".

INSTRUCTIONS

FRAME

Rnd 1: Ch 244, sl st in first ch to form ring, ch 3, 2 dc in same ch, *dc in next 55 chs, 3 dc in next ch, dc in next 65 chs*, 3 dc in next ch; repeat between **, join with sl st in top of ch-3 (252 dc).

Rnd 2: Sl st in next st, ch 4, (dc, ch 1, dc) in same st, *(ch 1, skip next st, dc in next st) around to next 3-dc corner, ch 1, skip next st*, [(dc, ch 1, dc, ch 1, dc) in next st; repeat between **]; repeat between [ ], join with sl st in 3rd ch of ch-4 (130 ch-1 sps).

Rnd 3: Sl st in first ch sp, (ch 3, sl st in next ch sp) around; to **join,** ch 1, hdc in first sl st.

Rnds 4-5: (Ch 4, sl st in next ch sp) around; to **join,** ch 1, dc in bottom of first ch.

Rnd 6: For **picot, ch 6, sl st in 4th ch from hook;** ch 2, (sl st in next ch-4 sp, picot, ch 2) around, join with sl st in joining dc of last rnd, fasten off.

FINISHING

1: Apply fabric stiffener to Frame according to manufacturer's instructions. Shape to fit around frame back. When almost dry, ruffle outer edge.

2: Glue felt to front of frame back. Place crocheted Frame over frame back. Glue together around sides and bottom leaving top open for inserting photo.

3: Weave ribbon through ch-1 sps of rnd 2, tie in bow at center top. Glue 3 rosebuds to each corner of crocheted Frame.

GARTER

SIZE: 2¼" wide.
MATERIALS: Size 10 bedspread cotton — 70 yds. white; 1½ yds. satin ¼" ribbon; 10" piece ¼" wide elastic; safety pin; white sewing thread; sewing and tapestry needles; No. 7 steel crochet hook.

GARTER

Rnd 1: Ch 120, sl st in first ch to form ring, ch 3, dc in each ch around, join with sl st in top of ch-3 (120 dc).

Rnd 2: Ch 5, skip next 2 sts, (dc in next st, ch 2, skip next 2 sts) around, join with sl st in 3rd ch of ch-5 (40 ch-2 sps).

Rnd 3: Sl st in first ch sp, (ch 4, sl st in next ch sp) around; to **join,** ch 1, dc in first sl st.

Rnd 4: (Ch 4, sl st in next ch sp) around, join as before in top of joining dc of last rnd.

Rnd 5: Picot (see Rnd 6 of Frame), ch 2, (sl st in next ch sp, picot, ch 2) around, join with sl st in top of joining dc on last rnd, fasten off.

Rnd 6: Working in starting ch on opposite side of rnd 1, join with sl st in any st, repeat rnd 2.

Rnds 7-9: Repeat rnds 3-5.

For **casing,** repeat rnd 1, fasten off. Sew to wrong side of rnd 1 leaving opening for elastic. Pull elastic through casing with safety pin, remove pin. Overlapping ends 1", using sewing needle and thread, sew together, trim. Sew opening closed.

Cut ribbon in half, weave through ch-1 sps of rnds 2 and 6, tie each in bow.

LARGE BASKET

SIZE: 5½" tall not including handle.
MATERIALS: Size 10 bedspread cotton — 200 yds. white; 1½ yds. satin ¼" ribbon and 14" satin ⅜" ribbon; six artifi-cial rosebuds with leaves; 1½" tall x 3½" across round piece of foam; fabric stiffener; craft glue; tapestry needle; No. 7 steel crochet hook or size needed to obtain gauge.
GAUGE: Rnds 1-2 = 1¾" across.

BASKET

Rnd 1: Ch 5, sl st in first ch to form ring, ch 4, 19 tr in ring, join with sl st in top of ch-4 (20 tr).

Rnd 2: Ch 4, tr in same st, 2 tr in each st around, join (40).

Rnd 3: Ch 4, 2 tr in next st, (tr in next st, 2 tr in next st) around, join (60).

Rnd 4: Ch 4, tr in next st, 2 tr in next st, (tr in each of next 2 sts, 2 tr in next st) around, join (80).

Rnd 5: Working this rnd in **back lps** only, ch 4, tr in each st around, join.

Rnd 6: Ch 5, skip next st, (tr in next st, ch 1, skip next st) around, join with sl st in 4th ch of ch-5 (40 tr, 40 ch-1 sps).

Rnd 7: Ch 4, tr in each ch sp and in each st around, join with sl st in top of ch-4.

Rnd 8: Ch 4, skip next st, (sl st in next st, ch 4, skip next st) around, join with sl st in bottom of first ch-4 (40 ch-4 sps).

NOTES: For **beginning shell (beg shell),** (ch 3, 2 dc, ch 2, 3 dc) in same sp.

For **shell,** (3 dc, ch 2, 3 dc) in next ch sp.

Rnd 9: Sl st in first ch sp, beg shell, *ch 2, sl st in next ch sp, (ch 4, sl st in next ch sp) 2 times, ch 2*, [shell in next ch sp; repeat between **]; repeat between [ ] around, join with sl st in top of ch-3 (20 ch-4 sps, 20 ch-2 sps, 10 shells).

Rnd 10: Sl st in next 2 sts, sl st in first ch-2 sp, beg shell, *ch 2, skip next ch-2 sp; for **V st, (dc, ch 1, dc)** in next ch-4 sp; ch 1, V st in next ch-4 sp, ch 2, skip next ch-2 sp*, [shell in ch-2 sp of next shell; repeat between **]; repeat between [ ] around, join (20 V sts, 20 ch-2 sps, 10 shells).

Rnds 11-14: Sl st in next 2 sts, sl st in first ch-2 sp, beg shell, *ch 2, skip next ch-2 sp, V st in ch-1 sp of next V st, ch 1, skip next ch-1 sp, V st in ch-1 sp of next V st, ch 2, skip next ch-2 sp*, [shell in next shell; repeat between **]; repeat between [ ] around, join.

Rnds 15-17: Sl st in next 2 sts, sl st in first ch-2 sp, beg shell, *ch 3, V st in next V st, ch 2, V st in next V st, ch 3*, [shell in next shell; repeat between **]; repeat between [ ] around, join.

Rnd 18: (Ch 4, sl st in next ch sp) around; to **join,** ch 1, dc in bottom of first ch-4 (60 ch-4 sps).

Rnds 19-20: (Ch 4, sl st in next ch sp) around, join as before in joining dc of last rnd.

Rnd 21: (Ch 5, sl st in next ch sp) around; to **join,** ch 2, dc in joining dc of last rnd.

Rnd 22: Picot, ch 2, (sl st in next ch sp, picot, ch 2) around, join with sl st in joining dc of last rnd, fasten

Continued on page 150

ELEGANT ENSEMBLE

CRIB COVER

SIZE: 32" x 51½" without ruffle.

MATERIALS: Size 10 bedspread cotton — 3,200 yds. white; 1 yd. yellow ¼" satin picot ribbon and matching sewing thread; sewing and tapestry needles; No. 1 steel crochet hook or size needed to obtain gauge.

GAUGE: 6 dc sts = 1"; 3 dc rows = 1".

NOTE: For **puff st,** yo, insert hook in next st, yo, draw up ¼"-long lp, (yo, insert hook in same st, yo, draw up ¼"-long lp) 3 times, yo, draw through all 9 lps on hook.

COVER

Row 1: Ch 193, dc in 4th ch from hook, dc in each ch across, turn (191 dc).

Row 2: Ch 3, dc in next 4 sts, (puff st, dc in next 5 sts) across, turn (160 dc, 31 puff sts).

Row 3: Ch 3, dc in each st across, turn (191).

Row 4: Ch 3, dc in next st, (puff st, dc in next 5 sts) across to last 3 sts, puff st, dc in each of last 2 sts, turn (159 dc, 32 puff sts).

Row 5: Repeat row 3.

Rows 6-155: Repeat rows 2-5 consecutively, ending with row 3. At end of last row, **do not** turn.

Rnd 156: Working around outer edge, ch 1, 2 sc in end of each row and sc in each st around with 3 sc in each corner, join with sl st in first sc.

Rnd 157: For **ruffle,** (ch 5, sc in next st) around; to **join,** ch 2, dc in bottom of first ch-5.

Rnds 158-162: (Ch 6, sc in next ch lp) around; to **join,** ch 3, dc in joining dc of last rnd.

Rnds 163-164: (Ch 7, sc in next ch lp) around; to **join,** ch 4, dc in joining dc of last rnd.

Rnd 165: Ch 1, 3 sc over joining dc just made, 7 sc in each ch-7 lp around with 4 sc in joining ch-4 sp of last rnd, join with sl st in first sc. Fasten off.

Cut ribbon into four 9" pieces. Tie in bows and sew to each corner.

PILLOW

SIZE: 10" x 15" without ruffle.

MATERIALS: Size 10 bedspread cotton — 500 yds. white; 9" yellow ¼" satin picot ribbon; ½ yd.

bleached muslin; five ½" shank buttons; white sewing thread; polyester fiberfill; sewing and tapestry needles; No. 1 steel crochet hook or size needed to obtain gauge.

GAUGE: 6 dc sts = 1"; 3 dc rows = 1".

NOTE: For **puff st,** see Crib Cover NOTE

FRONT

Row 1: Ch 85, dc in 4th ch from hook, dc in each ch across, turn (83 dc).

Rows 2-33: Repeat rows 2-5 of Crib Cover consecutively. At end of last row, **do not** turn.

Rnd 34: Repeat rnd 156 of Crib Cover.

Rnd 35: For **ruffle,** working this rnd in **front lps** only, (ch 4, sc in next st) around; to **join,** ch 1, dc in bottom of first ch-4.

Rnds 36-38: (Ch 4, sc in next ch lp) around, join as before in joining dc of last rnd.

Rnd 39: (Ch 5, sc in next ch lp) around; to **join,** ch 2, dc in joining dc of last rnd.

Rnd 40: Ch 1, 3 sc over dc just made, 6 sc in each ch-5 lp around with 3 sc in joining ch-2 sp of last rnd, join with sl st in first sc. Fasten off.

BACK

Row 1: Repeat same row of Pillow Front.

Rows 2-33: Ch 3, dc in each st across, turn. At end of last row, **do not** turn.

Rnd 34: Repeat rnd 156 of Crib Cover. Fasten off.

For **pillow form,** using Front as pattern, from muslin, cut two pieces ⅝" larger on all sides. Sew wrong sides together leaving opening for stuffing. Turn right sides out, stuff, sew opening closed.

Holding Front and Back wrong sides together, working in **back lps** of rnd 34, sew 3 sides (2 long, 1 short) together. Insert pillow form. Sew buttons to wrong side of Front using corresponding spaces between sts on Back as buttonholes.

BIB

SIZE: Fits 0-9 months.

MATERIALS: Size 10 bedspread cotton — 300 yds. white; 9" yellow ¼" satin picot ribbon and matching sewing thread; sewing and tapestry needles; No. 1 steel crochet hook or size needed to obtain gauge.

GAUGE: 6 dc sts = 1"; 3 dc rows = 1".

Continued on page 142

CLASSIC PINEAPPLES

E S S E N T I A L S

SIZE: 12½" across after blocking.
MATERIALS: Size 20 crochet cotton — 400 yds. pink; No. 9 steel crochet hook or size needed to obtain gauge.
GAUGE: Rnd 1 = ½" across.

I N S T R U C T I O N S

D O I L Y

Rnd 1: Ch 7, sl st in first ch to form ring, ch 1, 16 sc in ring, join with sl st in first sc (16 sc).

Rnd 2: Ch 1, sc in same st, ch 3, skip next st, (sc in next st, ch 3, skip next st) around, join (8 ch sps).

NOTES: For **beginning 5-tr cluster (beg 5-tr cl),** ch 4, *yo 2 times, insert hook in same sp, yo, draw lp through, (yo, draw through 2 lps on hook) 2 times; repeat from * 3 more times, yo, draw through all 5 lps on hook, ch 1.

For **5-tr cluster (5-tr cl),** yo 2 times, insert hook in next sp, *yo, draw lp through, (yo, draw through 2 lps on hook) 2 times*, [yo 2 times, insert hook in same sp; repeat between **]; repeat between [ ] 3 times, yo, draw through all 6 lps on hook, ch 1.

Ch-1 of tr cl is not used or counted as a st.

Rnd 3: Sl st in first ch sp, beg 5-tr cl, ch 6, (5-tr cl in next ch sp, ch 6) around, join with sl st in top of beg cl (8 ch sps).

Rnd 4: Sl st in first ch sp, ch 1, 9 sc in each ch sp around, join with sl st in first sc (72 sc).

Rnd 5: Ch 1, sc in first 9 sc, *ch 15, drop lp from hook, insert hook in first sc of last 9-sc group made, draw dropped lp through, sl st in ch-15 lp just made, ch 1, (10 sc, ch 5, 10 sc) in same lp*, [sc in next 9 sc on rnd 4; repeat between **]; repeat between [ ] around, join with sl st in first sc (232 sc, 8 ch-15 lps, 8 ch-5 lps).

Rnd 6: Sl st in next 10 sc on first ch-15 lp, sl st in first ch-5 lp, ch 7, (tr, ch 3, tr, ch 3, tr) in same lp, ch 7, *(tr, ch 3, tr, ch 3, tr, ch 3, tr) in next ch-5 lp, ch 7; repeat from * around, join with sl st in 4th ch of first ch-7 (32 tr, 24 ch-3 sps, 8 ch-7 sps).

Rnd 7: Ch 4, *4 tr in next ch-3 sp, tr in next tr, 5 tr in next ch-3 sp, tr in next tr, 4 tr in next ch-3 sp, tr in next tr, ch 5, skip next ch-7 sp*, [tr in next tr; repeat between **]; repeat between [ ] around, join with sl st in top of ch-4 (136 tr, 8 ch-5 sps).

Rnd 8: Ch 1, sc in same st, (ch 3, skip next tr, sc in next tr) 8 times, ch 7, skip next ch-5 sp, [sc in next tr, (ch 3, skip next tr, sc in next tr) 8 times, ch 7, skip next ch-5 sp]; repeat between [ ] around, join with sl st in first sc (64 ch-3 lps, 8 ch-7 sps).

Rnd 9: Sl st in first ch-3 lp, ch 1, sc in same lp, (ch 4, sc in next ch-3 lp) 7 times, ch 3, sc in next ch-7 sp, ch 3, [sc in next ch-3 lp, (ch 4, sc in next ch-3 lp) 7 times, ch 3, sc in next ch-7 sp, ch 3]; repeat between [ ] around, join (56 ch-4 lps, 16 ch-3 sps).

Rnd 10: Sl st in first ch-4 lp, ch 1, sc in same lp, (ch 4, sc in next ch-4 lp) 6 times, ch 3, skip next ch-3 sp, (tr, ch 3, tr) in next sc, ch 3, skip next ch-3 sp, [sc in next ch-4 lp, (ch 4, sc in next ch-4 lp) 6 times, ch 3, skip next ch-3 sp, (tr, ch 3, tr) in next sc, ch 3, skip next ch-3 sp]; repeat between [ ] around, join (48 ch-4 lps, 24 ch-3 sps, 16 tr).

Rnd 11: Sl st in first ch-4 lp, ch 1, sc in same lp, *(ch 4, sc in next ch-4 lp) 5 times, ch 3, skip next ch-3 sp, 7 tr in next ch-3 sp, ch 3, skip next ch-3 sp*, [sc in next ch-4 lp; repeat between **]; repeat between [ ] around, join (56 tr, 40 ch-4 lps, 16 ch-3 sps).

NOTE: For **3-tr cluster (3-tr cl),** yo 2 times, insert hook in next st, *yo, draw lp through, (yo, draw through 2 lps on hook) 2 times*, [yo 2 times, insert hook in same st; repeat between **]; repeat between [ ], yo, draw through all 4 ps on hook, ch 1.

Rnd 12: Sl st in first ch-4 lp, ch 1, sc in same lp, *(ch 4, sc in next ch-4 lp) 4 times, ch 5, skip next ch-3 sp, tr next 3 tr tog, ch 5, 3-tr cl in next tr, ch 5, tr next 3 tr tog, ch 5, skip next ch-3 sp*, [sc in next ch-4 lp; repeat between **]; repeat between [ ] around, join.

Rnd 13: Sl st in first ch-4 lp, ch 1, sc in same lp, *(ch 4, sc in next ch-4 lp) 3 times, ch 5, 3-tr cl in top of next tr, ch 9, sc in top of next 3-tr cl, ch 9, 3-tr cl in top of next tr, ch 5, skip next ch-5 sp*, [sc in next ch-4 lp; repeat between **]; repeat between [ ] around, join.

Rnd 14: Sl st in first ch-4 lp, ch 1, sc in same lp, *(ch 4, sc in next ch-4 lp) 2 times, ch 5, 3-tr cl in top of next 3-tr cl, ch 9, (sc in next ch-9 sp, ch 9) 2 times, 3-tr cl in top of next 3-tr cl, ch 5, skip next ch-5 sp*, [sc in next ch-4 lp; repeat between **]; repeat between [ ] around, join.

Continued on page 143

HEIRLOOM CROCHET TREASURES

HEIRLOOM BABY DRESS

ESSENTIALS

SIZE: Instructions given fit up to 18" chest. Changes for chests up to 19" and 20" are made by changing hook sizes to achieve gauges given below.

MATERIALS: Size 10 crochet cotton — 1,450 yds. white; pink and green embroidery floss; 2 yds. pink ¼" satin picot ribbon; three ⅜" buttons; white sewing thread; sewing and tapestry needles; steel crochet hook listed in gauge or size needed to obtain gauge.

GAUGE: For **18" chest,** No. 10 hook, 8 dc sts = 1"; 4 dc rows = 1". For **19" chest,** No. 9 hook, 15 dc sts = 2"; 7 dc rows = 2". For **20" chest,** No. 7 hook, 7 dc sts = 1"; 7 dc rows = 2".

NOTE: For **shell,** (2 dc, ch 2, 2 dc) in next ch.

INSTRUCTIONS

DRESS

Row 1: Starting at neck, ch 146, dc in 4th ch from hook, dc in next 19 chs, *shell in next ch, dc in next 31 chs, shell in next ch*, dc in next 36 chs; repeat between **, dc in last 21 chs, turn (140 dc, 4 shells).

Rows 2-11: Ch 3, dc in each dc across with shell in ch sp of each shell, turn, ending with 300 dc and 4 shells in last row.

Rnd 12: Working in rnds, ch 3, dc in next 42 dc, *2 dc in next ch sp; for **armhole,** skip next 75 dc; 2 dc in next ch sp*, dc in next 80 dc; repeat between **, dc in last 43 dc, join with sl st in top of ch-3, **turn** (174 dc).

Rnd 13: Ch 3, dc in next st, (ch 1, skip next st, dc in next st) across, join, **turn** (88 dc, 86 ch sps).

Rnd 14: Ch 3, dc in each dc and in each ch sp around, join, **turn** (174 dc).

Rnd 15: For **skirt,** ch 3, dc in same st, 2 dc in each st around, join, **turn** (348).

Rnds 16-47: Ch 3, dc in each st around, join, **turn.** At end of last row, **do not** turn.

Rnd 48: Ch 1, sc in each st around, join with sl st in first sc.

NOTES: For **beginning V-stitch (beg V-st),** ch 4, dc in same st.

For **V-stitch (V-st),** (dc, ch 1, dc) in next st.

For **picot,** ch 3, sl st in 3rd ch from hook.

Rnd 49: Beg V-st, V-st in each st around, join with

sl st in 3rd ch of beg V-st.

Rnd 50: Sl st in first ch sp, ch 4, (tr, ch 2, 2 tr) in same sp, tr in next space between V-sts, *(2 tr, ch 2, 2 tr) in ch sp of next V-st, tr in next space between V-sts; repeat from * around, join with sl st in top of ch-4.

Rnd 51: Ch 1, sc in each tr around with (sc, picot, sc) in each ch sp, join with sl st in first sc, fasten off.

Neck Trim

Row 1: Working in starting ch on opposite side of row 1, join with sc in first st, sc in each st across, turn.

Row 2: Working this row in **front lps** only, ch 3, dc in next st, (ch 1, skip next st, dc in next st) across, turn (73 dc, 71 ch sps).

Row 3: Ch 1, sc in each of first 2 dc, picot, (sc in each of next 2 dc, picot) across to last dc, sc in last dc, fasten off.

Neck Ruffle

Row 1: Working in **back lps** of row 1 on Neck Trim, join with sl st in first st, beg V-st, V-st in each st across, turn.

Row 2: Sl st in first ch sp, ch 4, (tr, ch 2, 2 tr) in same sp, *tr in next space between V-sts, (2 tr, ch 2, 2 tr) in ch sp of next V-st; repeat from * across, turn.

Row 3: Ch 1, sc in each tr across with (sc, picot, sc) in each ch sp, fasten off.

Sleeve Ruffle

Rnd 1: Working around armhole, join with sc in any underarm st, sc in each st around, join with sl st in first sc (75 sc).

Rnds 2-4: Repeat rnds 49-51 of Dress.

FINISHING

1: With embroidery floss, using pink and French Knot, and green and Lazy Daisy Stitch, embroider five sets of rosebuds and leaves 1" apart across front of bodice according to Embroidery Diagram on page 142 and one set over bottom left corner of skirt.

2: Starting at center back, weave 14" of ribbon through dc of row 2 on Neck Trim to center front.

Continued on page 142

HEIRLOOM BABY DRESS

Continued from page 140

Repeat on opposite side. Turn ends under at center back and tack in place with sewing needle and thread. Tie opposite ends in bow at center front. Weave 30" of ribbon through dc of rnd 13 on Dress. Tie in bow at center front. Tie 8" of ribbon in bow and tack below rosebuds on bottom of skirt.

3: Sew buttons evenly spaced across left back using corresponding spaces between sts on right back as buttonholes. ⚜

EMBROIDERY DIAGRAM

French Knot   Lazy Daisy

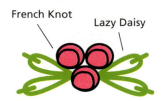

ELEGANT ENSEMBLE

Continued from page 136

NOTE: For **puff st,** see Crib Cover NOTE on page 136.

BIB

Row 1: Ch 55, dc in 4th ch from hook, dc in each ch across, turn (53 dc).

Rows 2-24: Repeat rows 2-5 of Crib Cover consecutively, ending with row 4.

Row 25: For **first side,** ch 3, dc next 2 sts tog, dc in next 14 sts, dc next 2 sts tog, turn, leaving remaining sts unworked (17).

Row 26: Ch 3, dc in next st, puff st, (dc in next 5 sts, puff st) across to last 2 sts, dc in each of last 2 sts, turn (14 dc, 3 puff sts).

Row 27: Ch 3, dc next 2 sts tog, (dc in next st, dc next 2 sts tog) across to last 2 sts, dc in each of last 2 sts, turn (12).

Row 28: Ch 3, dc in each of next 3 sts, (puff st, dc in each of next 3 sts) across, turn (10 dc, 2 puff sts).

Row 29: Ch 3, (dc next 2 sts tog) across to last st, dc in last st, turn (7).

Row 30: Ch 3, dc in each of next 3 sts, puff st, dc last 2 sts tog, turn (6).

Rows 31-32: Ch 3, (dc next 2 sts tog) across to last st, dc in last st, turn (4, 3).

Row 33: Ch 3, dc last 2 sts tog (2). Fasten off.

Row 25: For **second side,** skip next 15 sts on row 24, join with sl st in next st, ch 3, dc next 2 sts tog, dc in each st across with dc last 2 sts tog, turn (17).

Rows 26-33: Repeat same rows of first side. At end of last row, turn, **do not** fasten off.

Rnd 34: Repeat rnd 156 of Crib Cover.

Row 35: Working in rows; for **ruffle,** (ch 3, sc in next st) across to opposite side, ending with ch 1, hdc in last st, turn.

Rows 36-38: (Ch 3, sc in next ch-3 sp) across with (ch 1, hdc) in last ch-3 sp, turn.

Row 39: Ch 1, 4 sc in each ch sp across. Fasten off.

For **tie,** join with sl st in top corner, ch 80, hdc in 3rd ch from hook, hdc in each ch across, sl st in same sp as first sl st. Fasten off. Repeat on opposite corner.

Tie ribbon in bow and sew to one bottom corner.

DIAPER PIN PILLOW

SIZE: 5" x 6" without ruffle.

MATERIALS: Size 10 bedspread cotton — 100 yds. white; 9" yellow ¼" satin picot ribbon; ¼ yd. bleached muslin; white sewing thread; polyester fiberfill; sewing and tapestry needles; No. 1 steel crochet hook or size needed to obtain gauge.

GAUGE: 6 dc sts = 1"; 3 dc rows = 1".

NOTE: For **puff st,** see Crib Cover NOTE on page 136.

FRONT

Row 1: Ch 37, dc in 4th ch from hook, dc in each ch

across, turn (35 dc).

Rows 2-15: Repeat rows 2-5 of Crib Cover consecutively, ending with row 3. At end of last row, **do not** turn.

Rnd 16: Repeat rnd 156 of Crib Cover. Fasten off.

Rnd 17: Working around outer edge, in **front lps** only, (ch 3, sc in next st) around; to **join,** ch 1, hdc in bottom of first ch-3.

Rnds 18-19: (Ch 3, sc in next ch-3 sp) around, join as before in joining hdc of last rnd.

Rnd 20: Ch 1, 2 sc over hdc just made, 3 sc in each ch-3 sp around with sc in joining ch-1 sp of last rnd, join with sl st in first sc. Fasten off.

BACK

Row 1: Repeat same row of Diaper Pin Pillow Front.

Rows 2-15: Ch 3, dc in each st across, turn.

Rnd 16: Repeat rnd 156 of Crib Cover. Fasten off.

For **pillow form,** work same as for Pillow on page 136.

With wrong sides together, working in **back lps** of rnd 16, sew Front and Back together, inserting pillow form or stuffing before closing.

Tie ribbon in bow and sew to one corner of Pillow Front.

BOTTLE COVER

SIZE: Fits standard 8-oz. baby bottle.

MATERIALS: Size 10 bedspread cotton — 100 yds. white; 14" yellow ¼" satin picot ribbon; tapestry needle; No. 1 steel crochet hook or size needed to obtain gauge.

GAUGE: 6 dc sts = 1"; 3 dc rows = 1".

NOTE: For **puff st,** see Crib Cover NOTE on page 136.

COVER

Rnd 1: Starting at bottom, ch 4, sl st in first ch to form ring, ch 3, 11 dc in ring, join with sl st in top of ch-3 (12 dc).

Rnd 2: Ch 3, dc in same st, 2 dc in each st around, join (24).

Rnd 3: Ch 3, 2 dc in next st, (dc in next st, 2 dc in next st) around, join (36).

Rnd 4: Working this rnd in **back lps** only, ch 3, dc in each st around, join.

Rnd 5: Working in **both lps,** ch 3, dc in next 4 sts, puff st, (dc in next 5 sts, puff st) around, join (30 dc, 6 puff sts).

Rnd 6: Ch 3, dc in each st around, join (36).

Rnd 7: Ch 3, dc in next st, puff st, (dc in next 5 sts, puff st) around to last 3 sts, dc in each of last 3 sts, join.

Rnd 8: Repeat rnd 6.

Rnds 9-21: Repeat rnds 5-8 consecutively, ending with rnd 5.

Rnd 22: Repeat rnd 4. Fasten off.

Ruffle

Rnd 1: With top facing you, working in **front lps** of rnd 21, join with sl st in any st, (ch 3, sc in next st) around; to **join,** ch 1, hdc in bottom of first ch-3.

Rnds 2-3: (Ch 3, sc in next ch-3 sp) around, join as before in joining hdc of last rnd.

Rnd 4: Ch 1, 3 sc over hdc just made, 4 sc in each ch-3 sp around with sc in joining ch-1 sp of last rnd. Fasten off.

Weave ribbon through every 2 sts on rnd 22. Place Cover over bottle, tie ribbon in bow. ⚜

CLASSIC PINEAPPLES

Continued from page 139

Rnd 15: Sl st in first ch-4 lp, ch 1, sc in same lp, ch 4, sc in next ch-4 lp, ch 5, 3-tr cl in top of next 3-tr cl, *ch 11, sc in next ch-9 sp, ch 9, 5 tr in 5th ch of next ch-9 sp, ch 9, sc in next ch-9 sp, ch 11, 3-tr cl in top of next 3-tr cl*, [ch 5, skip next ch-5 sp, sc in next ch-4 lp, ch 4, sc in next ch-4 lp, ch 5, 3-tr cl in top of next 3-tr cl; for **horizontal cluster (horizontal cl), turn,** 3-tr cl in top of 3-tr cl on opposite side of pineapple motif (see Cluster Diagram on page 149), sl st back into top of 3-tr cl made before turning, **turn;** repeat between **]; repeat between [ ] around to last ch-5 sp; **do not** turn, horizontal cl in top of first 3-tr cl made, turn, ch 5, skip last ch-5 sp, join, fasten off.

Rnd 16: Join with sl st in first tr of any 5-tr group, ch 4, tr next 4 tr tog, *ch 9, (tr in center ch of next ch-9 or ch-11 sp, ch 9) 2 times, tr over center of next horizontal cl, ch 9, (tr in center ch of next ch-9 or ch-11 sp, ch 9) 2 times*, [tr next 5 tr tog; repeat between **]; repeat between [ ] around, join with sl st in top of ch-4 (48 ch sps).

Rnd 17: Sl st in first 5 chs of ch-9 sp, ch 13, (tr in 5th ch of next ch-9 sp, ch 9) around, join with sl st in 4th ch of ch-13.

Rnd 18: Sl st in first ch sp, ch 1, 11 sc in same sp, *ch 15, drop lp from hook, insert hook in first sc of 11-sc group just made, draw dropped lp through, sl st in ch-15 lp just made, ch 1, (10 sc, ch 5, 10 sc) over same lp*, [11 sc in next ch-9 sp; repeat between **]; repeat between [ ] around, join with sl st in first sc, fasten off. ⚜

HEIRLOOM CROCHET TREASURES

HEIRLOOM CROCHET TREASURES

ANTIQUE BIB & BOOTIES

ESSENTIALS

SIZE: Bib instructions given fit up to 18" chest; changes for chest up to 20" are in [ ]. Bootie instructions given fit up to 3" sole; changes for a sole up to 4" are in [ ].

GAUGE: 11 sc sts = 1"; 12 sc rows = 1".

MATERIALS FOR SET: Size 20 crochet cotton — 250 [300] yds. ecru; 2¼ yds. satin ¼" ribbon; 1¼ yds. ruffled ¾" lace ribbon with matching sewing thread and tapestry needles; No. 9 steel crochet hook or size needed to obtain gauge.

INSTRUCTIONS

BIB
Front

Row 1: Ch 8 [10], sc in 2nd ch from hook, sc in each of next 2 [3] chs, 3 sc in next ch, sc in each of last 3 [4] chs, turn (9 sc) [11 sc].

Row 2: Ch 1, sc in first 4 [5] sts, 3 sc in next st, sc in last 4 [5] sts, turn (11) [13].

Row 3: Ch 1, sc in first 5 [6] sts, 3 sc in next st, sc in last 5 [6] sts, turn (13) [15].

Row 4: Ch 1, sc in first 6 [7] sts, 3 sc in next st, sc in last 6 [7] sts, turn (15) [17].

Rows 5-62 [5-79]: Working in established pattern, ch 1, sc in each st across with 3 sc in center st, turn, ending with (131) [167] sts in last row.

Row 63 [80]: For **first shoulder,** ch 1, sc in first 10 sts leaving remaining sts unworked, turn (10).

Rows 64-121 [81-153]: Ch 1, sc in each st across, turn. Leaving 3" for sewing, fasten off at end of last row.

To form **first armhole,** skip next 20 [35] sts on row 62 [79], sew last row made to next 10 sts on same row.

Row 63 [80]: For **second shoulder,** skip next 81 [102] sts, join with sc in next st, sc in last 9 sts, turn (10).

Rows 64-121 [81-153]: Repeat same rows of first shoulder.

To form **second armhole,** skip next 20 [35] unworked sts on row 62 [79], sew last row made to next 10 sts on same row.

Sleeve Edging

Rnd 1: Working around armhole opening, in sts and in end of rows, join with sc in first unworked sc on row 62 [79], ch 2, skip next 2 sc, (sc in next sc, ch 2, skip next 2 sc) around, join with sl st in first sc.

Rnd 2: Sl st into first ch-2 sp, ch 1, 2 sc in same sp, 2 sc in each ch-2 sp around, join, fasten off.

Finishing

1: Cut ribbon into 4 pieces each 18" long. Weave one piece through rnd 1 of each Sleeve Edging. Tie in bow at top of shoulder.

2: Fold back remaining unworked sts on row 62 [79] between sleeves, tack in place. Tie 9" of ribbon in bow and sew to fold.

3: Easing to fit, sew lace around outer edge of Bib.

BOOTIE (make 2)

Row 1: Ch 46 [56], sc in 2nd ch from hook, sc in each ch across, turn (45 sc) [55 sc].

Rows 2-29 [2-41]: Working these rows in **back lps** only, ch 1, sc in each st across, turn.

Rnd 30 [42]: Ch 3, dc in each st around, join with sl st in top of ch-3 (45) [55].

Rnds 31-35 [43-47]: Ch 3, dc in each st around, join.

Rnd 36 [48]: Draw up ¼" loop in each st around; to **close,** yo, draw through all 45 [55] lps, fasten off. Sew back seam.

Edging

Working around **ankle opening,** join with sc in end of any row, work 12 [14] ch-5 sps evenly spaced around opening, join with sl st in first sc, fasten off.

Easing to fit, sew lace around ankle opening. Weave one 18" piece of ribbon through each ch-5 sp on edging, tie in bow. ⚜

HEIRLOOM CROCHET TREASURES

VINTAGE LACE

ESSENTIALS

SIZE: 14" x 21".
GAUGE: 9 sc sts = 1"; rnds 1-4 = 1".
MATERIALS: Size 10 bedspread cotton — 225 yds. green; No. 9 steel crochet hook or size needed to obtain gauge.
NOTE: Doily should ruffle slightly to achieve effect shown in photo.

INSTRUCTIONS

DOILY

Rnd 1: Ch 62, 4 sc in 2nd ch from hook, sc in next 59 chs, 4 sc in end ch; working on opposite side of ch, sc in last 59 chs, join with sl st in first sc, **turn** (126 sc).

Rnd 2: Ch 1, sc in first 61 sts, 3 sc in each of next 2 sts, sc in next 61 sts, 3 sc in each of last 2 sts, join, **turn** (134).

Rnd 3: Ch 5, dc in next st, (ch 2, dc in next st) 6 times, (ch 2, skip next 2 sts, dc in next st) 20 times, (ch 2, dc in next st) 7 times, ch 2, skip next 2 sts, (dc in next st, ch 2, skip next 2 sts) 19 times, join with sl st in 3rd ch of ch-5, **do not** turn (54 dc, 54 ch sps).

Rnd 4: Ch 1, sc in same st, *(2 sc in next ch sp, sc in next st) 2 times, ch 4, skip next ch sp*, [sc in next st; repeat between **]; repeat between [ ] around, join with sl st in first sc (126 sc, 18 ch sps).

Rnd 5: Sl st in next 3 sts, ch 1, sc in same st, ◊ch 5, skip next 3 sts, tr in next ch sp, (ch 3, tr) 5 times in same sp, *ch 5, skip next 3 sts, sc in next st, ch 5, skip next 3 sts, tr in next ch sp*, (ch 3, tr) 3 times in same sp; repeat between **, [(ch 3, tr) 2 times in same sp; repeat between ** one more time]; repeat between [ ] 5 times, (ch 3, tr) 3 times in same sp◊, ch 5, skip next 3 sts, sc in next st; repeat between ◊◊; to **join,** tr in first sc (64 tr, 46 ch-3 sps, 36 ch-5 sps, 18 sc).

Rnd 6: Ch 8, [skip next sc, (tr in next tr, ch 4) 6 times, skip next sc, (tr in next tr, ch 4) 4 times, skip next sc, *(tr in next tr, ch 4) 3 times, skip next sc*; repeat between ** 5 times], (tr in next tr, ch 4) 4 times; repeat between [ ], (tr in next tr, ch 4) 3 times, join with sl st in 4th ch of ch-8 (64 tr, 64 ch sps).

Rnd 7: Ch 9, tr in next tr, ch 5, tr in next tr, ch 5, (tr, ch 5, tr, ch 5) in each of next 2 tr, (tr in next tr, ch 5) 30 times, (tr, ch 5, tr, ch 5) in each of next 2 tr, (tr in next tr, ch 5) around, join with sl st in 4th ch of ch-9 (68 tr, 68 ch-5 sps).

Rnd 8: Ch 4, 2 tr in same st, ch 5, sc in next tr, ch 5, (3 tr in next tr, ch 5, sc in next tr, ch 5) around, join with sl st in top of ch-4 (102 tr, 68 ch-5 sps, 34 sc).

Rnd 9: Ch 4, tr in same st, tr in next tr, 2 tr in next tr, *(ch 7, skip next 2 ch sps, 2 tr in next tr, tr in next tr, 2 tr in next tr) 5 times*, (ch 5, skip next 2 ch sps, 2 tr in next tr, tr in next tr, 2 tr in next tr) 12 times; repeat between **, ch 5, skip next 2 ch sps, (2 tr in next tr, tr in next tr, 2 tr in next ch sp, ch 5, skip next 2 ch sps) across, join (170 tr, 24 ch-5 sps, 10 ch-7 sps).

Rnd 10: Ch 1, sc in first 5 sts, *(7 sc in next ch sp, sc in next 5 sts) 5 times*, (5 sc in next ch sp, sc in next 5 sts) 12 times; repeat between **, 5 sc in next ch sp, (sc in next 5 sts, 5 sc in next ch sp) around, join with sl st in first sc (360 sc).

NOTE: For **V-stitch (V-st),** (sc, ch 4, sc) in next st or ch.

Rnd 11: Ch 1, (sc, ch 4, sc) in same st, (ch 9, skip next 3 sts, V-st) 16 times, (ch 9, skip next 5 sts, V-st, ch 9, skip next 3 sts, V-st) 12 times, (ch 9, skip next 3 sts, V-st) 15 times, (ch 9, skip next 5 sts, V-st, ch 9, skip next 3 sts, V-st) 11 times; to **join,** ch 5, skip last 5 sts, tr in first sc.

NOTE: For **picot,** sl st in 4th ch from hook or in top of cl.

Rnds 12-15: Ch 1, (sc, ch 4, sc) in top of joining tr, *ch 9, (sc, ch 4, sc) in 5th ch of next ch-9 lp; repeat from * around; to **join,** ch 5, tr in first sc.

Rnd 16: Ch 1, sc over joining tr, *ch 4, (tr, ch 6, picot, ch 2, tr, ch 7, tr, ch 6, picot, ch 2, tr) in 5th ch of next ch-9 lp, ch 4*, [sc in 5th ch of next ch-9 lp; repeat between **]; repeat between [ ] around, join with sl st in first sc, fasten off (156 tr, 39 sc).

NOTES: For **beginning cluster (beg cl),** ch 4, *yo 2 times, insert in same sp, yo, draw lp through, (yo, draw through 2 lps on hook) 2 times; repeat from *, yo, draw through all 3 lps on hook.

For **cluster (cl),** *yo 2 times, insert hook in sp, yo, draw lp through, (yo, draw through 2 lps on hook) 2 times; repeat from * 2 times in same sp,

Continued on page 151

H E I R L O O M   C R O C H E T   T R E A S U R E S

PACIFIC MIST

ESSENTIALS

SIZE: 11" across.
GAUGE: Rnds 1-3 = 2¼".
MATERIALS: Size 20 crochet cotton — 150 yds. lt. blue and 75 yds. blue; No. 11 steel crochet hook or size needed to obtain gauge.

INSTRUCTIONS

DOILY
  Rnd 1: With lt. blue, ch 8, sl st in first ch to form ring, ch 5, (tr in ring, ch 1) 15 times, join with sl st in 4th ch of ch-5 (16 tr, 16 ch-1 sps).
  Rnd 2: Ch 5, tr in same st, ch 2, *(tr, ch 1, tr) in next tr, ch 2; repeat from * around, join (32 tr, 16

ch-1 sps, 16 ch-2 sps).

Rnd 3: Ch 4, tr in same st, ch 2, (2 tr in next tr, ch 2) around, join with sl st in top of ch-4 (64 tr, 32 ch-2 sps).

Rnds 4-5: Ch 4, tr in next tr, ch 3, tr in each of next 2 tr, ch 2, (tr in each of next 2 tr, ch 3, tr in each of next 2 tr, ch 2) around, join.

NOTE: For **cluster (cl),** yo 2 times, insert hook in next ch sp, yo, draw through sp, (yo, draw through 2 lps on hook) 2 times, *yo 2 times, insert hook in same sp, yo, draw through sp, (yo, draw through 2 lps on hook) 2 times; repeat from *, yo, draw through all 4 lps on hook.

Rnd 6: Ch 4, tr in next tr, ch 2, cl in next ch-3 sp, ch 2, *(tr in each of next 2 tr, ch 2) 2 times, cl in next ch-3 sp, ch 2; repeat from * around to last 2 tr, tr in each of next 2 tr, ch 3, join (64 tr, 16 cls).

Rnd 7: Ch 4, tr in next tr, ch 5, sc in next cl, ch 5, tr in each of next 2 tr, ch 2, *tr in each of next 2 tr, ch 5, sc in next cl, ch 5, tr in each of next 2 tr, ch 2; repeat from * around, join (64 tr, 16 sc).

NOTE: For **picot,** ch 4, sl st in top of st just made.

Rnd 8: Ch 4, tr in next tr, *ch 7, sc in next sc, picot, ch 7, tr in each of next 2 tr, ch 2*, [tr in each of next 2 tr; repeat between **]; repeat between [ ] around, join.

Rnd 9: Ch 4, tr in next tr, *ch 7, skip next picot, tr in each of next 2 tr, ch 5*, [tr in each of next 2 tr; repeat between **]; repeat between [ ] around, join (64 tr, 32 ch lps).

Rnd 10: Ch 4, tr in next tr, *ch 3, sc in next ch-7 lp, picot, ch 3, tr in each of next 2 tr, ch 9*, [tr in each of next 2 tr; repeat between **]; repeat between [ ] around, join (64 tr, 32 ch-3 sps, 16 ch-9 lps).

Rnd 11: Ch 4, tr in next tr, *picot, skip next 2 ch-3 sps, tr in each of next 2 tr, ch 13*, [tr in each of next 2 tr; repeat between **]; repeat between [ ] around, join, fasten off (64 tr, 16 ch-13 lps).

Rnd 12: Join blue with sc in first ch-13 lp, 16 sc in same lp, ch 7, (17 sc in next ch-13 lp, ch 7) around, join with sl st in first sc (272 sc, 16 ch-7 lps).

Rnd 13: Sl st in next sc, ch 1, *sc in next 13 sc, skip next 2 sc, ch 4, (tr, ch 2, tr, ch 2, tr, ch 2, tr) in 4th ch of next ch-7 lp, ch 4, skip next 2 sc; repeat from * around, join (208 sc, 64 tr).

NOTE: For **V-stitch (V-st),** (tr, ch 3, tr) in next tr.

Rnd 14: Sl st in next 2 sts, ch 1, *sc in next 7 sc, ch 4, skip next 3 sc, V-st, ch 3, tr in next tr, ch 3, tr in next ch-2 sp, ch 3, tr in next tr, ch 3, V-st, ch 4, skip next 3 sc; repeat from * around, join (112 sc, 48 tr, 32 V-sts).

Rnd 15: Sl st in next 3 sts, *ch 4, skip next 3 sc, V-st, ch 3, (tr in next tr, ch 3) 2 times, V-st, ch 3, (tr in next tr, ch 3) 2 times, V-st, skip next 3 sc*, [tr in next sc; repeat between [ ] around, join with sl st in top of ch-4, fasten off.⚜

CLASSIC PINEAPPLES

Instructions on page 139

CLUSTER DIAGRAM

 = Wrong side

 = Right side

RIBBONS & ROSES

Continued from page 135

off.

HANDLE

Row 1: Ch 158, dc in 8th ch from hook, (ch 2, skip next 2 chs, dc in next ch) across, **do not** turn (52 dc, 51 ch-2 sps).

Rnd 2: Working in rnds, on opposite side of starting ch and in sts, (ch 4, sl st in next st) around; to **join,** ch 1, dc in bottom of first ch-4.

Rnd 3: Picot, ch 2, (sl st in next ch sp, picot, ch 2) around, join with sl st in joining dc of last rnd, fasten off.

FINISHING

1: Apply fabric stiffener to Basket and Handle according to manufacturer's instructions. Shape bottom of Basket over foam, turning upper edges outward as shown in photo on page 134. Lay Handle flat. Curve before completely dry.

2: Weave ⅜" ribbon through ch-1 sps of rnd 6 on basket. Fold ends under, glue to secure.

3: Cut ¼" ribbon in half. Starting at ends (fold ribbon ends under and glue to secure), weave each piece through Handle to middle. Tie in bow at top of Handle. Trim any excess ribbon.

4: Glue ends of Handles to inside of Basket. Glue 3 rosebuds to each side of Handle above Basket.

SMALL BASKET

SIZE: 2¼" tall not including handle.

MATERIALS: Size 10 bedspread cotton — 50 yds. white; ¾ yd. satin ¼" ribbon; two artificial rosebuds with leaves; 3-liter bottle lid; fabric stiffener; craft glue; tapestry needle; No. 7 steel crochet hook or size needed to obtain gauge.

GAUGE: Rnds 1-2 = 1⅛" across.

BASKET

Rnd 1: Ch 5, sl st in first ch to form ring, ch 3, 19 dc in ring, join with sl st in top of ch-3 (20 dc).

Rnd 2: Ch 3, dc in same st, 2 dc in each st around, join (40).

Rnd 3: Working this rnd in **back lps** only, ch 3, dc in each st around, join.

Rnd 4: Ch 4, skip next st, (dc in next st, ch 1, skip next st) around, join with sl st in 3rd ch of ch-4.

Rnd 5: Ch 3, dc in each ch sp and in each st around, join.

Rnd 6: Ch 4, skip next st, (sl st in next st, ch 4, skip next st) around, join with sl st in bottom of first ch-4

(20 ch-4 sps).

Rnd 7: Sl st in first ch sp, beg shell (see page 135), *ch 2, sl st in next ch sp, (ch 4, sl st in next ch sp) 3 times, ch 2*, [shell in next ch sp; repeat between **]; repeat between [ ] around, join (12 ch-4 sps, 8 ch-2 sps, 4 shells).

Rnds 8-10: Sl st in next 2 sts, sl st in first ch-2 sp of same shell, beg shell *ch 2, skip next ch-2 sp, V st (see page 135) in next ch-4 sp, (ch 1, V st in next ch-4 sp) 2 times, ch 2, skip next ch-2 sp*, [shell in ch-2 sp of next shell; repeat between **]; repeat between [ ] around, join (12 V sts, 4 shells).

Rnds 11-12: Repeat rnds 18 and 19 of Large Basket on page 135.

Rnd 13: Repeat rnd 22 of Large Basket.

HANDLE

Row 1: Ch 71, dc in 8th ch from hook, (ch 2, skip next 2 chs, dc in next ch) across, **do not** turn (23 dc, 22 ch-2 sps).

Row 2: Working in rnds, on opposite side of starting ch, picot, ch 2, (sl st in next st, picot, ch 2) around, join with sl st in bottom ch of first picot, fasten off.

FINISHING

1: Repeat same step of Large Basket Finishing, using bottle lid to shape bottom of Basket.

2: Weave 6" piece ribbon through ch-1 sps of rnd 4. Secure ends. Cut remaining ribbon in half. Repeat step 3 of Large Basket, gluing one rosebud to each side of Handle above Basket.

RING PILLOW

SIZE: 8" x 8½".

MATERIALS: Size 10 bedspread cotton — 200 yds. white; 1 yd. satin ¼" ribbon; three artificial rosebuds with leaves; craft glue; polyester fiberfill; tapestry needle; No. 7 steel crochet hook or size needed to obtain gauge.

GAUGE: 7 dc sts = 1"; 3 dc rows = 1".

BACK

Row 1: Ch 4, 4 dc in 4th ch from hook, turn (5 dc).

Row 2: Ch 3, dc in same st, (dc in next st, 2 dc in next st) across, turn (8).

Row 3: Ch 3, dc in next st, (2 dc in next st, dc in each of next 2 sts) across, turn (10).

Row 4: Ch 3, dc in same st, (dc in each of next 3 sts, 2 dc in next st) 2 times, dc in last st, turn (13).

Row 5: Ch 3, dc in same st, (dc in next 4 sts, 2 dc in

next st) 2 times, dc in each of last 2 sts, turn (16).

Row 6: Ch 3, dc in same st, (dc in next 5 sts, 2 dc in next st) 2 times, dc in each of last 3 sts, turn (19).

Row 7: Ch 3, dc in same st, (dc in next 6 sts, 2 dc in next st) 2 times, dc in last 4 sts, turn (22).

Row 8: Ch 3, dc in same st, (dc in next 7 sts, 2 dc in next st) 2 times, dc in last 5 sts, turn (25).

Row 9: Ch 3, dc in same st, (dc in next 8 sts, 2 dc in next st) 2 times, dc in last 6 sts, turn (28).

Row 10: Ch 3, dc in same st, (dc in next 9 sts, 2 dc in next st) 2 times, dc in last 7 sts, turn (31).

Row 11: Ch 3, dc in same st, (dc in next 10 sts, 2 dc in next st) 2 times, dc in last 8 sts, turn (34).

Row 12: Ch 3, dc in same st, (dc in next 11 sts, 2 dc in next st) 2 times, dc in last 9 sts, turn (37).

Row 13: Ch 3, dc in same st, (dc in next 12 sts, 2 dc in next st) 2 times, dc in last 10 sts, turn (40).

Row 14: Ch 3, dc in same st, (dc in next 13 sts, 2 dc in next st) 2 times, dc in last 11 sts, turn (43).

Rows 15-17: Ch 3, dc in each st across, turn.

Row 18: For **first side,** ch 3, dc in next 20 sts leaving remaining sts unworked, turn (21).

NOTE: (Ch 2, dc in next st) counts as dc first 2 sts tog.

Rows 19-21: Ch 2, dc in next st, dc in each st across with dc last 2 sts tog, turn, ending with 15 sts in last row.

Row 22: Ch 1, sc in first st, hdc in each of next 3 sts, dc in each of next 3 sts, tr in next st, dc in each of next

3 sts, hdc in each of next 3 sts, sc in last st, fasten off.

Row 18: For **second side,** skip next st on row 17, join with sl st in next st, ch 3, dc in each st across, turn (21).

Rows 19-22: Repeat same rows of first side. At end of last row, **do not** fasten off.

Rnd 23: Working around outer edge, in ends of rows and in sts, ch 3, 2 dc in each dc row and in each st around with 3 dc on opposite side of starting ch and (dc next 2 sts tog) at center top, join with sl st in top of ch-3.

Rnd 24: Ch 5, skip next st, (dc in next st, ch 2, skip next st) around, join with sl st in 3rd ch of ch-5.

Rnd 25: Sl st in first ch sp, (ch 4, sl st in next ch sp) around; to **join,** ch 1, dc in bottom of first ch-4.

Rnd 26: Picot (see page 135), ch 2, (sl st in next ch sp, picot, ch 2) around, join with sl st in joining dc of last rnd, fasten off.

FRONT

Rows 1-22: Repeat same rows of Back.

Rnd 23: Repeat same rnd of Back.

To **join,** holding wrong sides together, using tapestry needle and white bedspread cotton, sew Front and Back together, stuffing before closing.

Weave ribbon through ch-2 sps of rnd 24 on Back, tie in bow at center bottom. Glue rosebuds to center top of Front between first and second sides.✤

VINTAGE LACE

Continued from page 146

yo, draw through all 4 lps on hook.

Rnd 17: Join with sl st in first ch-7 sp, beg cl, ch 4, picot, (ch 5, cl, ch 4, picot) 2 times in same sp, [*ch 7, cl in next ch-7 sp, ch 4, picot, (ch 5, cl, ch 4, picot) 2 times in same sp]; repeat from * 10 times, (ch 5, cl, ch 4, picot) 3 times in each of next 9 ch-7 sps; repeat between [ ] 10 times; (ch 5, cl, ch 4, picot) 3 times in each of last 8 ch-7 sps, ch 5, join with sl st in top of first beg cl (117 cls).

Rnd 18: Sl st in first ch sp, beg cl, *picot, ch 9, picot, ch 5, cl in next ch sp, picot, ch 7, sc in next ch sp, ch 7*, [cl in next ch sp; repeat between **]; repeat between [ ] around, join, fasten off.✤

PERFUME SET

SIZE: Tray is 8¾" long; bottles are 5" tall.

MATERIALS FOR ONE SET: Size 10 bedspread cotton — 400 yds. lt. blue, small amount each dk. blue and metallic gold; three small round balloons; plastic wrap; craft glue or hot glue gun; fabric stiffener; tapestry needle; No. 7 steel crochet hook or size needed to obtain gauge.

GAUGE: 8 dc sts = 1"; 2 dc rows = ½".

NOTES: Items may ruffle until stiffened.
Use lt. blue unless otherwise stated.

INSTRUCTIONS

TRAY

Rnd 1: Ch 27, 4 dc in 4th ch from hook, dc in each ch across with 5 dc in end ch; working on opposite side of starting ch, dc in each ch across, join with sl st in top of ch-3 (54 dc).

Rnd 2: (Ch 4, skip next st, sl st in next st) 2 times, *(ch 4, skip next 2 sts, sl st in next st) 7 times*, (ch 4, skip next st, sl st in next st) 3 times; repeat between **, ch 4, skip last st, join with sl st in joining sl st on last rnd (20 ch sps).

Rnd 3: Sl st in first ch sp, (ch 5, sl st in next ch sp) around; to **join**, ch 2, dc in first sl st.

NOTE: Joining (ch 1, dc) counts as ch-4 sp.

Rnd 4: [*Ch 2, 7 dc in next ch sp, ch 2, sl st in next ch sp*, ch 4, sl st in next ch sp; repeat between ** one more time, (ch 4, sl st in next ch sp) 2 times; repeat between **], ch 4, sl st in next ch sp; repeat between [ ]; to **join,** ch 1, dc in top of joining dc of last rnd (42 dc, 12 ch-2 sps, 8 ch-4 sps).

Rnd 5: Ch 4, sl st in next ch-2 sp, [*ch 2, dc in next dc, (ch 1, dc in next dc) 6 times, ch 2, sl st in next ch-2 sp*, (ch 4, sl st in next ch-4 or ch-2 sp) 2 times; repeat between **, ch 4, (sl st in next ch-4 sp, ch 4) 2 times, sl st in next ch-2 sp; repeat between ** one more time], (ch 4, sl st in next ch-4 or ch-2 sp) 2 times; repeat between [ ], join as before.

Rnd 6: Ch 4, sl st in next ch-4 sp, ch 4, [sl st in next ch-2 sp, *ch 2, sl st in next ch-1 sp, (ch 3, sl st in next ch-1 sp) 5 times, ch 2, sl st in next ch-2 sp*, ch 4, (sl st in next ch-4 sp, ch 4) 2 times, sl st in next ch-2 sp; repeat between **, ch 4, (sl st in next ch-4 sp, ch 4) 3 times, sl st in next ch-2 sp; repeat between ** one more time], ch 4, (sl st in next ch-4 sp, ch 4) 2 times; repeat between [ ], join.

Rnd 7: Ch 4, (sl st in next ch-4 sp, ch 4) 2 times, [*sl st in next ch-2 sp, ch 2, sl st in next ch-3 lp, (ch 3, sl st in next ch-3 lp) 4 times, ch 2, sl st in next ch-2 sp*, ch 4, (sl st in next ch-4 sp, ch 4) 3 times; repeat between **, ch 4, (sl st in next ch-4 sp, ch 4) 4 times; repeat between ** one more time], ch 4, (sl st in next ch-4 sp, ch 4) 3 times; repeat between [ ], join.

Rnd 8: Ch 4, (sl st in next ch-4 sp, ch 4) 3 times, [*sl st in next ch-2 sp, ch 2, sl st in next ch-3 lp, (ch 3, sl st in next ch-3 lp) 3 times, ch 2, sl st in next ch-2 sp*, ch 4, (sl st in next ch-4 sp, ch 4) 4 times; repeat between **, ch 4, (sl st in next ch-4 sp, ch 4) 5 times; repeat between ** one more time], ch 4, (sl st in next ch-4 sp, ch 4) 4 times; repeat between [ ], join (32 ch-4 sps, 18 ch-3 sps, 12 ch-2 sps).

Rnd 9: Ch 4, (sl st in next ch-4 sp, ch 4) 4 times, [*sl st in next ch-2 sp, ch 2, sl st in next ch-3 lp, (ch 3, sl st in next ch-3 lp) 2 times, ch 2, sl st in next ch-2 sp*, ch 4, (sl st in next ch-4 sp, ch 4) 5 times; repeat between **, ch 4, (sl st in next ch-4 sp, ch 4) 6 times; repeat between ** one more time], ch 4, (sl st in next ch-4 sp, ch 4) 5 times; repeat between [ ], join.

Rnd 10: Ch 4, (sl st in next ch-4 sp, ch 4) 5 times, [*sl st in next ch-2 sp, ch 2, sl st in next ch-3 lp, ch 3, sl st in next ch-3 lp, ch 2, sl st in next ch-2 sp*, ch 4, (sl st in next ch-4 sp, ch 4) 6 times; repeat between **, ch 4, (sl st in next ch-4 sp, ch 4) 7 times; repeat between ** one more time], ch 4, (sl st in next ch-4 sp, ch 4) 6 times; repeat between [ ], join.

Rnd 11: Ch 4, (sl st in next ch-4 sp, ch 4) 6 times, [*sl st in next ch-2 sp, ch 2, (dc, ch 1, dc) in next ch-3 lp, ch 2, sl st in next ch-2 sp*, ch 4, (sl st in next ch-4 sp, ch 4) 7 times; repeat between **, ch 4, (sl st in next ch-4 sp, ch 4) 8 times; repeat between ** one more time], ch 4, (sl st in next ch-4 sp, ch 4) 7 times; repeat between [ ], join (50 ch-4 sps, 12 ch-2 sps, 6 ch-1 sps).

Rnd 12: (Ch 4, sl st in next ch-4 or ch-1 sp) around skipping each ch-2 sp, join (56 ch-4 sps).

Rnd 13: (Ch 4, sl st in next ch sp) around, join.

Continued on page 154

PERFUME
SET

Continued from page 152

Rnd 14: Ch 3, 2 dc over joining dc, 3 dc in each ch sp around, join with sl st in top of ch-3 (168 dc).

Rnd 15: For **rim,** ch 3, dc in each st around, join.

Rnd 16: Sl st in each st around, join with sl st in first sl st, fasten off.

Apply fabric stiffener to Tray according to manufacturer's instructions. Shape and let dry, shaping rim as Tray dries.

BOTTLE NO. 1

Rnd 1: Ch 5, sl st in first ch to form ring, ch 3, 19 dc in ring, join with sl st in top of ch-3 (20 dc).

Rnd 2: Ch 3, dc in same st, 2 dc in each st around, join (40).

Rnd 3: Working this rnd in **back lps,** ch 3, dc in each st around, join.

NOTES: For **beginning popcorn (beg pc),** ch 3, 2 dc in same st, drop lp from hook, insert hook in top of ch-3, draw dropped lp through st and lp on hook, ch 1.

For **popcorn (pc),** 3 dc in next st, drop lp from hook, insert hook in first st of 3-dc group, draw dropped lp through st and lp on hook, ch 1.

It may be necessary to push popcorn stitches to right side of work.

Rnd 4: Beg pc, sc in next st, (pc, sc in next st) around, join with sl st in top of beg pc (20 pc, 20 sc).

Rnd 5: (Ch 4, skip next sc, sl st in top of next pc) around; to **join,** ch 2, hdc in joining sl st of last rnd (20 ch sps).

NOTE: Joining counts as ch sp.

Rnd 6: (Ch 4, sl st in next ch sp) around, join as before in top of joining hdc of last rnd.

Rnd 7: (Ch 4, sl st in next ch sp) around; to **join,** ch 1, dc in joining hdc of last rnd.

Rnd 8: Ch 3, 6 dc over joining dc just made, ch 2, sl st in next ch sp, (ch 4, sl st in next ch sp) 3 times, ch 2, [7 dc in next ch sp, ch 2, sl st in next ch sp, (ch 4, sl st in next ch sp) 3 times, ch 2]; repeat between [ ] around, join with sl st in top of ch-3.

Rnd 9: Ch 4, dc in next dc, (ch 1, dc in next dc) 5 times, *ch 2, skip next ch-2 sp, sl st in next ch-4 sp, (ch 4, sl st in next ch-4 sp) 2 times, ch 2, skip next ch-2 sp*, [dc in next dc, (ch 1, dc in next dc) 6 times; repeat between **]; repeat between [ ] around, join with sl st in 3rd ch of ch-4.

Rnd 10: Sl st in first ch-1 sp, *(ch 3, sl st in next ch-1 sp) 5 times, ch 2, skip next ch-2 sp, sl st in next ch-4 sp, ch 4, sl st in next ch-4 sp, ch 2, skip next ch-2 sp*, [sl st in next ch-1 sp; repeat between **]; repeat between [ ] around, join with sl st in first sl st.

Rnd 11: Sl st in first 2 chs of first ch-3 lp, (ch 3, sl st in next ch-3 lp) 4 times, ch 2, skip next ch-2 sp; for **V-stitch (V-st), (dc, ch 2, dc)** in next ch-4 sp; ch 2, skip next ch-2 sp, [sl st in next ch-3 lp, (ch 3, sl st in next ch-3 lp) 4 times, ch 2, skip next ch-2 sp, V-st in next ch-4 sp, ch 2, skip next ch-2 sp]; repeat between [ ] around, join with sl st in 2nd sl st.

Rnd 12: (Ch 3, sl st in next ch-3 lp) 3 times, ch 2, skip next ch-2 sp, V-st in ch-2 sp of next V-st, ch 2, skip next ch-2 sp, [sl st in next ch-3 lp, (ch 3, sl st in next ch-3 lp) 3 times, ch 2, skip next ch-2 sp, V-st in ch-2 sp of next V-st, ch 2, skip next ch-2 sp]; repeat between [ ] around, join with sl st in first ch of first ch-3.

Rnd 13: Sl st in first 2 chs of first ch-3 lp, *(ch 3, sl st in next ch-3 lp) 2 times, ch 2, skip next ch-2 sp, V-st in next V-st, ch 2, skip next ch-2 sp*, [sl st in next ch-3 lp; repeat between **]; repeat between [ ] around, join with sl st in 2nd sl st.

Rnd 14: Ch 3, sl st in next ch-3 lp, ch 2, skip next ch-2 sp, V-st in next V-st, ch 2, skip next ch-2 sp, [sl st in next ch-3 lp, ch 3, sl st in next ch-3 lp, ch 2, skip next ch-2 sp, V-st in next V-st, ch 2, skip next ch-2 sp]; repeat between [ ] around, join with sl st in joining sl st of last rnd.

Rnd 15: Sl st in first ch-3 lp, (ch 4, sl st in next V-st or next ch-3 lp) around; to **join,** ch 2, hdc in first sl st (8 ch-4 sps).

Rnds 16-17: (Ch 4, sl st in next ch sp) around, join as before in top of joining hdc of last rnd.

Rnd 18: (Beg pc, sc) over joining hdc just made, (pc, sc) in each ch sp around, join with sl st in top of beg pc (8 pc, 8 sc).

Rnd 19: Ch 3, dc in each sc and in top of each pc around, join with sl st in top of ch-3 (16 dc).

Rnd 20: Ch 3, (dc next 2 sts tog, dc in next st) around, join (11 dc).

Rnds 21-22: Ch 3, dc in each st around, join. Fasten off at end of last rnd.

Cap

Rnd 1: With gold, ch 2, 6 sc in 2nd ch from hook, join with sl st in first sc (6 sc).

Rnd 2: Ch 1, 2 sc in each st around, join (12).

NOTE: Work in **back lps** unless otherwise stated.

Rnd 3: Ch 2, hdc in each st around, join with sl st in top of ch-2.

Rnd 4: Ch 3, dc in same st, 2 dc in each st around, join with sl st in top of ch-3 (24).

Rnd 5: Ch 3, dc in each st around, join.

Rnd 6: Working this rnd in **both lps,** ch 3, dc in each st around, fasten off.

Pump

Rnd 1: With dk. blue, ch 5, sl st in first ch to form ring, ch 3, 17 dc in ring, join with sl st in top of ch-3 (18 dc).

Rnd 2: Ch 3, 2 dc in next st, (dc in next st, 2 dc in next st) around, join (27).

Rnds 3-5: Ch 3, dc in each st around, join.

Rnd 6: Ch 3, dc next 2 sts tog, (dc in next st, dc next 2 sts tog) around, join (18).

Rnd 7: Ch 2, dc in next st, (dc next 2 sts tog) around, join, fasten off.

Rnd 8: Join gold with sl st in any st, ch 2, hdc in each st around, join with sl st in top of ch-2, fasten off.

Finishing

1: Apply fabric stiffener to all pieces according to manufacturer's instructions.

2: Insert balloon into bottom of Bottle, inflate. Pop balloon when Bottle is almost dry, flatten rnds 1 and 2 so Bottle will stand. Allow to dry completely.

3: Stuff Cap and Pump with plastic wrap. When dry, remove plastic wrap.

4: Glue rnd 8 of Pump over rnds 3 and 4 on side of Cap. Glue Cap over top of Bottle.

BOTTLE NO. 2

Rnds 1-18: Repeat same rnds of Bottle No. 1.

Rnd 19: Ch 1, sc in each sc and in top of each pc around, join with sl st in first sc, fasten off.

Top

Rnd 1: Ch 5, sl st in first ch to form ring, ch 3, 13 dc in ring, join with sl st in top of ch-3 (14 dc).

Rnd 2: Ch 3, 2 dc in next st, (dc in next st, 2 dc in next st) around, join (21).

Rnd 3: (Ch 4, skip next 2 sts, sl st in next st) around to last 2 sts; to **join,** ch 2, skip last 2 sts, hdc in top of ch-3 on last rnd (7 ch sps).

Rnds 4-5: (Ch 4, sl st in next ch sp) around, join as before in top of joining hdc of last rnd (7 ch sps).

Rnd 6: (Ch 3, sl st in next ch sp) around, join.

Rnd 7: Ch 3, dc over joining hdc, 2 dc in each ch sp around, join with sl st in top of ch-3 (14).

Rnd 8: Ch 3, (dc next 2 sts tog) 2 times, (dc in next st, dc next 2 sts tog) around, join with sl st in top of ch-3 (9).

Rnd 9: Ch 3, dc in each st around, join, fasten off.

Finishing

1: Apply fabric stiffener to Bottle and Top according to manufacturer's instructions.

2: Repeat same step of Bottle No. 1 Finishing.

3: Stuff Top with plastic wrap. When dry, remove plastic wrap. Place Top on Bottle.

BOTTLE NO. 3

Rnds 1-7: Repeat same rnds of Bottle No. 1.

Rnd 8: Ch 1, 7 sc over joining dc just made, *ch 2, sl st in next ch sp, (ch 4, sl st in next ch sp) 3 times, ch 2*, [7 sc in next ch sp; repeat between **]; repeat between [ ] around, join with sl st in first sc.

Rnd 9: Ch 1, sc in same sc, *(ch 1, sc in next sc) 6 times, ch 2, skip next ch-2 sp, sl st in next ch-4 sp, (ch 4, sl st in next ch-4 sp) 2 times, ch 2, skip next ch-2 sp*, [sc in next sc; repeat between **]; repeat between [ ] around, join.

Rnds 10-17: Repeat same rnds of Bottle No. 1.

Rnd 18: Ch 1, 2 sc over joining hdc, 2 sc in each ch sp around, join, fasten off.

Top

Rnds 1-5: With lt. blue, repeat same rnds of Bottle No. 2 Top.

Rnd 6: Repeat rnd 7 of Bottle No. 2 Top.

Rnd 7: Ch 2, dc in next st, (dc next 2 sts tog) around, join (7).

Rnds 8-9: Ch 3, dc in same st, 2 dc in each st around, join with sl st in top of ch-3 (14, 28).

Rnd 10: Ch 4, skip next st, (sl st in next st, ch 4, skip next st) around, join with sl st in first ch of first ch-4, fasten off.

Finishing

Work same as Bottle No. 2 Finishing. ⚜

GENERAL INSTRUCTIONS

THREAD & HOOKS

When purchasing thread, be sure to check the label for the size specification. By using the size stated in the pattern, you will be assured of achieving the proper gauge. Size 10 cotton is commonly referred to as bedspread cotton, and may not bear a size marking on the label. Sizes other then 10 should be clearly labeled.

The hook size suggested in the pattern is a guide to determine the size you will need. Always work a swatch of the type stitches stated in the gauge section of the pattern with the suggested hook. If you find your gauge is smaller or larger than what is specified, choose a different hook.

GAUGE

Gauge is measured by counting the number of stitches, chains, rows or rounds per inch. Each of the patterns featured in this book will have a gauge listed. In some, gauge for motifs or flowers is given as an overall measurement. Gauge must be attained in order for the project to come out the size stated and to prevent ruffling and puckering.

Before beginning your project, work up a small swatch with the stated thread to check your gauge. Lay the piece flat and measure the stitches or chains per inch. If you have more

per inch than specified in the pattern, your gauge is too tight and you need a larger hook. Fewer stitches or chains per inch indicates a gauge that is too loose. In this case, choose the next smaller hook size.

Generally if the stitch gauge is achieved, the row or round gauge will also be correct. However, due to differing crochet techniques and hook styles you may need to adjust your gauge slightly by pulling the loops down a little tighter on your hook, or by pulling your loops up slightly to extend them.

PATTERN REPEAT SYMBOLS

Written crochet instructions typically include symbols such as parentheses, asterisks and brackets. In some patterns, a fourth or fifth symbol usually diamonds ◊ or bullets •, may be added. These symbols are used as signposts to set off a portion of instructions that will be worked more than once or in a single space or stitch.

Parentheses ( ) enclose instructions which are to be worked the number of times indicated after the parentheses. For example, "(2 dc in next st, skip next st) 5 times" means to follow the instructions within the parentheses a total of five times. Parentheses may also be used to enclose a group of stitches which should be worked in one space or stitch. For example, "(2 dc, ch 2, 2 dc) in next st" means to work all the stitches within the parentheses in the next stitch.

Asterisks * may be used alone or in pairs, many times in combination with parentheses. used in pairs, a set of instructions enclosed within asterisks will be followed by instructions for repeating. These repeat instructions may appear later in the pattern or immediately after the last asterisk. For example, "*Dc in next sts, (2 dc, ch 2, 2 dc) in corner sp*, dc in next sts; repeat between ** 2 more times," means to work through the instructions up to the word "repeat," then repeat only the instructions that are enclosed within the asterisks twice.

If used alone, an asterisk marks the beginning of instructions which are to be repeated. For example, "Ch 2, dc in same st, ch 2, *dc in next st, (ch 2, skip next 2 sts, dc in next st) 5 times; repeat from * across" means to work from the beginning, then repeat only the instruction after the *, working all the way across the row. Instructions for repeating may also specify a number of times to repeat, followed by further instructions. In this instance, work through the instructions one time, then repeat the number of times stated, then follow the remainder of the instructions.

Brackets [ ] and diamonds ◊ are used in the same manner as asterisks. Follow the specific instructions given when repeating.

FINISHING

Patterns that require assembly will suggest a tapestry needle in the materials. This should be a #18 or #22 blunt-tipped tapestry needle. Sharp-pointed needles are not appropriate, as they can cut the thread and weaken the stitches.

Hiding loose ends is never a fun task, but if done correctly, may mean the difference between an item that looks great for years, or one that soon shows signs of wear. Always leave about 6" when beginning or ending. Thread the loose end into your tapestry needle and carefully weave it through the back of several stitches. Then, to assure a secure hold, weave in the opposite direction, going through different strands. Gently pull the end, and clip, allowing the end to pull up under the stitches. A small amount of fabric glue may be placed on the end for extra hold.

If your project needs blocking, gentle steaming followed by spray starching works well. Lay your project flat on a surface large enough to spread it out completely. Smooth out wrinkles by hand as much as possible. Set your steam iron to the permanent press setting, then hold slightly above the stitches, allowing the steam to penetrate the thread. Do not rest the iron on the item. Gently pull and smooth the stitches into shape, spray lightly with starch, and allow to dry completely.

STIFFENING

There are many liquid products on the market made specifically for stiffening doilies and other soft items. For best results, carefully read the manufacturer's instruc-

tions on the product you select before beginning.

Forms for shaping can be many things. Styrofoam® shapes and plastic margarine tubs work well for items such as bowls and baskets. Glass or plastic drinking glasses are used for vase-type items. If you cannot find an item with the dimensions given in the pattern to use as a form, any similarly sized item can be shaped by adding layers of plastic wrap. Place the dry crochet piece over the form to check the fit, remembering that it will stretch when wet.

For shaping flat pieces, corrugated cardboard, Styrofoam® or a cutting board designed for sewing may be used. Be sure to cover all surfaces of forms or blocking board with clear plastic wrap, securing with cellophane tape.

If you have not used fabric stiffener before, you may wish to practice on a small swatch before stiffening the actual item. For proper saturation when using conventional stiffeners, work liquid thoroughly into the crochet piece and let stand for about 15 minutes. Then, squeeze out excess stiffener and blot with paper towels. Continue to blot while shaping to remove as much stiffener as possible. Stretch over form, shape and pin with rust-proof pins; allow to dry, then unpin.

STITCH GUIDE

BASIC STITCHES

Front Loop (A)/Back Loop (B)
(front lp/back lp)

Chain
(ch)

Yo, draw hook through lp.

Slip Stitch
(sl st)

Insert hook in st, yo, draw through st and lp on hook.

Single Crochet
(sc)

Insert hook in st (A), yo, draw lp through, yo, draw through both lps on hook (B).

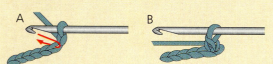

Half Double Crochet
(hdc)

Yo, insert hook in st (A), yo, draw lp through (B), yo, draw through all 3 lps on hook (C).

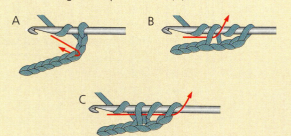

Double Crochet
(dc)

Yo, insert hook in st (A), yo, draw lp through (B), (yo, draw through 2 lps on hook) 2 times (C and D).

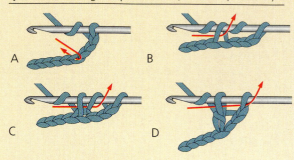

Treble Crochet
(tr)

Yo 2 times, insert hook in st (A), yo, draw lp through (B), (yo, draw through 2 lps on hook) 3 times (C, D and E).

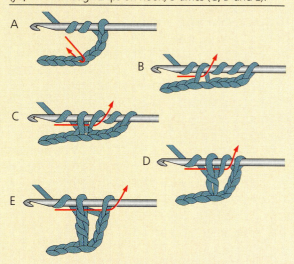

Standard Stitch Abbreviations

ch(s)	chain(s)
dc	double crochet
dtr	double treble crochet
hdc	half double crochet
lp(s)	loop(s)
rnd(s)	round(s)
sc	single crochet
sl st	slip stitch
sp(s)	space(s)
st(s)	stitch(es)
tog	together
tr	treble crochet
tr tr	triple treble crochet
yo	yarn over

HEIRLOOM CROCHET TREASURES

Double Treble Crochet (dtr)

Yo 3 times, insert hook in st (A), yo, draw lp through (B), (yo, draw through 2 lps on hook) 4 times (C, D, E and F).

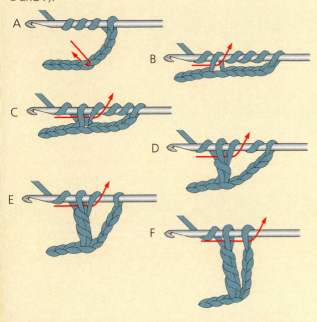

SPECIAL STITCHES

Front Post/Back Post Stitches (fp/bp)

Yo, insert hook from front to back (A) or back to front (B) around post of st on indicated row; complete as stated in pattern.

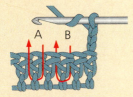

Reverse Single Crochet (reverse sc)

Working from left to right, insert hook in next st to the right (A), yo, draw through st, complete as sc (B).

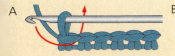

CHANGING COLORS

Single Crochet Color Change (sc color change)

Drop first color; yo with 2nd color, draw through last 2 lps of st.

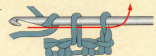

Double Crochet Color Change (dc color change)

Drop first color; yo with 2nd color, draw through last 2 lps of st.

DECREASING

Single Crochet next 2 stitches together (sc next 2 sts tog)

Draw up lp in each of next 2 sts, yo, draw through all 3 lps on hook.

Half Double Crochet next 2 stitches together (hdc next 2 sts tog)

(Yo, insert hook in next st, yo, draw lp through) 2 times, yo, draw through all 5 lps on hook.

Double Crochet next 2 stitches together (dc next 2 sts tog)

(Yo, insert hook in next st, yo, draw lp through, yo, draw through 2 lps on hook) 2 times, yo, draw through all 3 lps on hook.

INDEX